---

## What they never tell their patients . . .
## What they never tell each other . . .

**ON RESIDENCY—**

"As I opened the bladder, I simply fell asleep. So as I was
standing there operating on the patient, everyone thought,
well, he is being very careful. They didn't know I was unconscious."

**ON PSYCHIATRISTS—**

"I would not send my dog to three-fourths of them."

**ON NEGLIGENCE—**

"The baby wasn't getting enough oxygen. But we were too
busy to notice. The baby was born dead, but if the right
things had been done, he would have been fine."

---

ALSO BY JOHN PEKKANEN

The American Connection

Victims

The Best Doctors in the U. S.

Donor

My Father, My Son
(with Admiral Elmo Zumwalt, Jr.,
and Elmo Zumwalt III)

# M·D·

## Doctors talk about themselves

## JOHN PEKKANEN

A DELL BOOK

Published by
Dell Publishing
a division of
Bantam Doubleday Dell Publishing Group, Inc.
666 Fifth Avenue
New York, New York 10103

For information address: Delacorte Press, New York, New York.

The trademark Dell ® is registered in the U.S. Patent
and Trademark Office.

ISBN: 0-440-20444-5

Reprinted by arrangement with Delacorte Press

Printed in the United States of America
Published simultaneously in Canada
January 1990

10 9 8 7 6 5 4 3 2 1

OPM

*Again, and always, for Lynn*

# Contents

# Acknowledgments

I first want to thank all the physicians I interviewed for trusting me and for giving so generously of their time and thoughts. Even though I often intruded into painful and private areas of their lives, they remained universally courteous and accommodating. I hope they find this book an honest portrayal of their work and feel that their trust has been rewarded.

There are many other people I also want to thank. My literary agent, John Boswell, was and always has been a consistent source of support, enthusiasm, and friendship, and his suggestions helped shape the direction of the book. I also want to thank John's assistant, Patty Brown, for her thoughts and encouragement and for being such a pleasant and cheerful person with whom to deal.

Carole Baron and Jackie Farber at Delacorte Press were most supportive and played an important role in moving this book forward. Jane Rosenman, my editor at Delacorte, helped improve the manuscript by offering many thoughts and suggestions. The nicest compliment a writer can pay an editor is to say he or she improved the manuscript; Jane's attentiveness to detail and interest in the subject of this book did just that.

A doctor I knew once said a good surgeon is a gift of God. I have been blessed to know two of them, Dr. Dwight Harken of Boston and Dr. Malcolm Ellison of New London, Connecticut. I have not seen either of these fine men for many years, but if it were not for their dedication, skill, and caring, I would not be alive to write this book. They are examples of the best that medicine can be and, in their own way, served as inspirations for my chosen career of medical writing.

I also want to thank my three children, Robert, Sarah and Ben, for their indulgence and their love. They are wonderful people, and I am proud of them. I also want to thank my mother, Lucille Pekkanen, for her ongoing love and for giving me the wings to fly.

There are other people I want to thank for reasons that may be obscure to them but not to me: Bill Bruns, Cynthia Byers, Elaine Freeman, Betty Miller Johns, Rita K. Pickett, Coleman White, and Richard Woodley.

Finally, I wish to thank my wife, Lynn, who is an enduring source of support for me and a wonderful person to spend my life with. She assisted me with this book in every way possible. She helped transcribe interview tapes, read every entry in the book, and offered her thoughts and criticisms. Many of her ideas were incorporated into this book. I've always trusted Lynn's instincts, and I think every one of them was right.

*I swear by Apollo the physician, by Aesculapius, Hygeia, and Panacea, and I take to witness all the gods, all the goddesses, to keep according to my ability and my judgment the following oath.*

*To consider dear to me as my parents him who taught me this art; to live in common with him and if necessary to share my goods with him; to look upon his children as my own brothers, to teach them this art if they so desire without fee or written promise; to impart to my sons and the sons of the master who taught me and to the disciples who have enrolled themselves and have agreed to the rules of the profession, but to these alone, the precepts and the instruction. I will prescribe regimen for the good of my patients according to my ability and my judgment and never do harm to anyone. To please no one will I prescribe a deadly drug, nor give advice which may cause his death. Nor will I give woman a pessary to procure abortion. But I will preserve the purity of my life and my art. I will not cut for stone, even for patients in whom the disease is manifest; I will leave this operation to be performed by specialists in this art. In every house where I come I will enter only for the good of my patients, keeping myself from all intentional ill-doing and all seduction, and especially from the pleasures of love with women or with men, be they free or slaves. All that may come to my knowledge in the exercise of my profession or in daily commerce with men, which ought not to be spread abroad, I will keep secret and will never reveal. If I keep this oath faithfully, may I enjoy my life and practice my art, respected by all men and in all times; but if I swerve from it or violate it, may the reverse be my lot.*

Oath of Hippocrates of Kos,
Fifth century B.C.

# Introduction

The doctor was broad-shouldered and had a powerful chest and neck. His hands seemed almost too large for the delicate surgery that he routinely performs. His gaze was steady; his voice resonated with quiet assurance. I asked him about patients he remembered. He began matter-of-factly.

"I was on the medical service when this man came to the hospital. He ran a department store in upstate New York and had gone into kidney failure and developed an infection, so he already had serious problems when I first saw him.

"It was a long stay and we did everything we could, but he kept dwindling, not responding to any of our treatments. Through the whole thing I got to know him and his family very well—his wife, children, even his brother. Some patients you get drawn to. You can't help yourself. This was a wonderful family. His wife was one of the kindest people I have ever met. And he was a strong guy, very stoic through all this suffering.

"I worked as hard as I knew how for him. I tried everything, talked to everyone, but we couldn't do anything to reverse his illness, and he died. I felt awful, just awful. There was nothing else I knew how to do or anyone knew how to do, but I still asked myself, Where did we go wrong? Wasn't there something we could have done? I don't handle death well at all.

"About six weeks later, a letter and small package addressed to my wife arrived. It was a picture frame, and attached to it was a note from this man's wife that said, 'I just wanted to thank you for the many hours you gave up your husband to be with mine.' We still have that note and frame."

There was a slight pause in the doctor's voice, and he

looked away for a moment. "Some patients you just don't forget," he said.

The emotion was real, almost palpable. It was one of my earliest exposures to the inner feelings of doctors. Theirs has long been a private world, shrouded in mystique and fiercely protected by the image of control and competence that most doctors seek to project. But it is a world that has now been made less secure by malpractice suits, by regulation, and by intense competition, and less rewarding because of the suspicion and skepticism of patients and the public at large. But the private world of doctors is ultimately replete with human emotion, with feelings of doubt, guilt, fear, anxiety, grief, and anger that reflect a lifetime of meeting human suffering head-on.

It is also a world divided between art and science, between technology and intuition. It's a world in which doctors find themselves both damned and deified, accused of arrogance, incompetence, and greed and looked to as saviors, helpers, and consolers. As one doctor said, "We're held anywhere from beneath contempt to above reproach." We are seldom neutral about doctors, and we are always fascinated by them.

For this book I sought to penetrate that world, to go beyond the image, beyond the characters portrayed on television shows, beyond the stories of the newest medical miracle or the latest medical catastrophe, and look inside the human beings. How do doctors see their work? What drives them? How are they different from one another? What hurts them? What stresses them? What is happening to their profession and to themselves?

My preparation for this book included my own medical history, which has exposed me to many doctors, good and bad, and fifteen years of medical reporting and writing. I have witnessed firsthand organ-transplant operations, trauma surgery, eye surgery, and coronary bypass surgery. Besides allowing me into the inner sanctum of the operating room, doctors have permitted me to don a white lab coat and sit in on diagnostic conferences and go on rounds.

I interviewed physicians from different regions of the country, of different specialities, different economic status, different ages and races, and different points of view. Although medicine continues to be dominated by men, women are entering the profession in increasing numbers; nearly a third of those I interviewed were women. Some of the doctors were in training; others were retired department chairmen from major medical institutions. I interviewed medical school deans, country doctors who routinely make house calls, and superspecialists to whom patients are referred from around the world.

I talked with doctors in the medical mainstream and some outside it. I interviewed researchers and clinicians, academics and private practice doctors. I interviewed a wide range of specialists, including surgeons, internists, radiologists, anesthesiologists, pediatricians, and psychiatrists.

I interviewed doctors in their offices, laboratories, and homes, in hospital waiting rooms and cafeterias, and even once while fishing along a quiet riverbank. In all, I interviewed more than seventy doctors, many of them several times, all in person. I'd known some of them beforehand; others I met for the first time. All the interviews are anonymous, and I promised the doctors complete confidentiality. I think confidentiality does more to unearth the truth than to hide it.

Doctors do live in a closed society, although I have always found them surprisingly candid when they trust the person they are talking with. But the bluntness with which they spoke to me was a revelation. Despite the hundreds of hours I had spent interviewing doctors for other books and articles, nothing quite prepared me for their descriptions of how difficult and grueling the practice of medicine can be or for the anger many of them feel because of the rapid and radical changes in the field. Medicine is clearly a profession in crisis.

The doctors were unsparing in their opinions about their colleagues, lawyers, their own failures, their training, and their patients. I appreciated their candor and confess that I came away from the vast majority of these interviews liking and sometimes admiring them.

I thought that virtually every doctor I interviewed was open and truthful. There would have been little for them to gain by lying. Since I fully explained to them what I intended to do beforehand, a doctor who didn't wish to be open could simply refuse to talk. Only a very few did. Some were self-serving, and I think the reader can make his or her own judgments about them. Others revealed things about themselves that they may not have even thought they revealed. A few were reluctant to discuss some areas, but they were rare. The vast majority spoke frankly about their lives and work, revealing levels of intimacy that they seldom, if ever, shared elsewhere. Some wept as they recalled incidents, and more than one doctor who unburdened himself said the interview had been like "a psychotherapy session."

Surgeons, who pride themselves on being men and women of action, were generally the most outspoken, the most willing to make hard judgments. Although many of their medical colleagues consider them nonreflective people, I found most of the surgeons I spoke with not only thoughtful but willing to reveal their private agonies. In this regard they were similar to the psychiatrists, who were remarkably open about themselves.

As befits their reputation, internists were the most thoughtful and analytical, and neurologists, who enjoy the reputation within medicine of being the brightest doctors, were the most precise.

A number of the doctors asked me to explain the purpose of the book. I told them it had many. I said that I wanted to explore how they perform a vital job under difficult circumstances, how they view patients, how the profession is being buffeted by all the changes, and how doctors are reacting to them. But the real purpose, I said, was to expose doctors for the human beings they are.

*"The absolute asceticism of the residency recreates, for the young physician, the sacrificial ethic of monastic medicine. That ethic is severe: immediate response to the needs of the patient, to the call of the emergency room, to the demands of reports; unmitigated responsibility for correct decisions made promptly and communicated clearly; flagellating denial of sleep, self-indulgence, and frivolity, even to the point of depression and deterioration of personal life, of friendship and love."*

"Watching the Doctor"
*New England Journal of Medicine*
June 23, 1983

*"Medical training is a hazing rite. It's who can stand the most and stay the longest."*

A professor of surgery
January 1988

*"How I admire the interns. How I fear losing my compassion while becoming one of them."*

"A Piece of My Mind"
*Journal of the American Medical Association*
December 18, 1987

# I

# Making Doctors

The second-year resident had just finished another hundred-hour workweek. Although his eyes were rimmed in red, he shrugged off his fatigue. "There's a lot of macho in medical training," he said. "You don't give in to exhaustion, because you don't want to look bad in front of the other residents. So you force yourself to keep going no matter what."

Becoming a doctor is an arduous journey of intellect, stamina, and perseverance. It begins in medical school, where the first two years are devoted to assimilating a bewildering number of facts about biochemistry, anatomy, pharmacology, and other sciences, too many facts for any doctor to ever remember or need. Although the 128 medical schools in the United States take different approaches, they nonetheless offer the same basic educational diet, and they graduate about sixteen thousand new doctors a year.

In their third and fourth years, medical students begin clinical clerkships by rotating through different medical specialties. Three months of obstetrics may be followed by three months of cardiac surgery. For the first time the students are confronted with real, live patients. They learn to take a medical history and perform a physical examination. In many medical schools today, students perform medical examinations on one another—a practice some doctors find appalling but others find enlightened.

Even today, many states legally require a minimum of training beyond medical school in order to qualify for a medical license. Some states—including California, Iowa, Illinois, and Florida as well as the District of Columbia—only require a year of post–medical school training. West Virginia requires none. As a practical matter, however, medical school graduates who want to practice medicine undergo extensive residency training.

Residency is the most pivotal phase of medical training because that is where doctors learn to be doctors. Residency programs differ depending on the specialty. For an internist, an internship (the first year of residency training) and two additional years of residency prepare him or her to practice medicine, unless he or she wants to go into cardiology, endocrinology, gastroenterology, or any of the other internal medicine subspecialties. That can take another two or three years. Psychiatrists also undergo four years of post–medical school training, and those who want to become psychoanalysts are required to undergo their own psychoanalysis. For a general surgeon, five years are required, but to go into a surgical specialty, such as plastic, cardiac, or neurosurgery, two or more additional years are usually required.

I was surprised to find that many physicians spoke bitterly of their residency training, even after the passage of many years. They felt that they were overburdened with responsibility, woefully underpaid, and asked to work impossibly long hours.

As one doctor explained, "A lot of medical training is to throw you in the water so you'll learn to swim. You have books, you have demonstrations, and then you are on your own." Because of growing demands on medical school faculties to support themselves by seeing their own patients, senior doctors now have even less time to teach than before. "The most astonishing thing is that this terrible teaching system actually produces fine physicians," one doctor concluded.

But is this training method the best way to make doctors? Some physicians contend that by giving medical residents too much to handle, they learn to function under stress. "Only when you're pushed to your limits do you understand what your limits are," said one physician.

A fourth-year medical resident sees it differently: "Let's be real about this. Residents are overworked because we're a cheap source of labor for the hospital."

After satisfactorily completing their residency training, doctors are eligible to take examinations to become board certified. These exams are a combination of oral and written tests and are administered by the boards of the different medical specialities to test a physician's clinical knowledge. A doctor has three chances to pass it; about 60 percent of all U. S. physicians are board certified. Although teaching hospitals seldom if ever grant privileges to noncertified doctors, doctors can still be licensed to practice medicine even if they're not board certified. There are still many hospitals—a diminishing number, fortunately—that grant them privileges.

To be board certified in a surgical or medical subspecialty, doctors must pass not only their general boards but their subspecialty boards as well. For surgeons this process, from the beginning of medical school to the beginning of practice, can take in excess of eleven years.

I'm a second-year resident in obstetrics at a big hospital in Florida. We're getting more and more patients who can't afford doctors, patients who've come from Haiti and Cuba, so we're overloaded.

We have a new labor and delivery suite that was built for six thousand deliveries a year, but we're doing sixteen thousand a year. We have women on stretchers lining the halls. We've kept the same number of residents, despite the fact that we're delivering more than twice as many babies as the facilities and the program were designed for.

I'm working 110 to 120 hours a week, and I'm on call

every other night or every third night. I start doing C-sections early in the morning, and I'll do six or seven during the day and continue with them all night long. As fast as I do one, there's another patient waiting. Yet our C-section rate at this hospital is about 15 percent, which is the lowest by far of any hospital in the community. It's just that we have so many patients. We're running at the edge, and I'm afraid some patients have suffered for it.

We had one woman who was fully dilated and had been pushing for three hours. There had also been severe decelerations in the fetal heartbeat, which is a clear signal that the baby isn't getting enough oxygen. We were so busy that no one was able to take notice of this. It wasn't that it was completely missed; it's just that it didn't fully register because we were so overwhelmed with what we had to do. The baby was born dead, but if the right things had been done, he would have done fine.

Because there aren't enough residents, you never call in sick even when you are because you feel like you'd be letting down the other residents. We've had two residents faint in the hospital. One collapsed in the emergency room; we put two liters of fluid into him, got him up, and put him back to work. Another resident, a guy in his twenties, had chest pains and was admitted to the hospital. It appeared at first that he had had a heart attack, but it turned out that he suffered from exhaustion and dehydration.

Despite the fact it's a university hospital, we're really not taught by the attendings. They're not around much because they're too busy with other things, so I'm really learning obstetrics from more senior residents, which means I'm getting my medical training from people who have been at it a year or two longer than I have.

*"I start doing C-sections early in the morning, and I'll do six or seven during the day and continue with them all night long."*

What worries us most is AIDS. We're scared to death about it and talk about it all the time. We have a very high rate of AIDS-infected pregnant women. Six percent of the Haitian mothers are infected with the AIDS virus, and when you deliver a baby, coming in contact with blood is unavoidable. I've delivered more than fifty babies from these mothers. I wear goggles, double gloves, and a plastic apron when I deliver.

Sometimes we know the mother is infected. But we don't have enough money to test all the women, so most of the patients I deliver I have no idea whether or not they are infected.

I did one C-section on a patient who we knew had AIDS, and another resident was assisting me. I had a needle in the tissue, and when he reached down to retract the skin, he caught the needle tip in his hand. It punctured his skin. He's been tested for the AIDS virus for a few months, and he's shown no signs of infection yet. Besides being frightened, he's very angry about the fact that we're risking our lives to take care of these patients.

The last block of my senior year in medical school, I was shipped out to a satellite mental health center. By that time, I had decided I wanted to go into psychiatry.

I had very little supervision at this place, and they put me in charge of a guy who said he had this intense feeling of wanting to kill someone. He didn't have anyone in mind. He said he would kill anybody he could get his hands on, including me. He had these beady little eyes, and he'd stare at me. He scared the hell out of me. I sat right by the door every time he was in the place because I wanted to be able to get out and run. I was there for three months, never knowing what this guy was going to do. He came to see me twelve times, and the only thing I could think to do was to ask him why he was feeling this way. I had no idea what to do for this guy. I didn't realize at the time that he needed hospitalization and medication.

I was so unnerved by this experience, I told myself I was not going to live this way and I just wanted out of psychiatry.

🖋 I was in training in the psychiatric unit of a hospital when the police brought in this guy who'd been standing in the flight line at the airport. I don't mean in the terminal; he was out on the flight line with all the planes taxiing toward the runway for takeoff. When they found him, he had his arms stretched out, making like the wings of an airplane.

I asked him what he was doing out there. He said he was on his way to London.

🖋 I did a year of training in general medicine at a university-affiliated, inner-city hospital, and it was the worst year of my life. The place was a snake pit.

I was a resident, and each resident had two or three interns who worked for them. The interns would admit two to four patients a night on average—and these were sick-unto-death patients. They couldn't get into this hospital unless they were going to die within twenty-four hours, so they took a lot of time and attention. And there was too little support to care for them properly.

The patients were there either because they abused drugs, or had an illness like diabetes that they wouldn't take care of, or were alcoholic, or had gotten beaten on the head while they were robbing a store. Almost all of them had self-inflicted illness. It's very hard to get real sympathetic with people who make themselves sick.

We were also burdened by an onerous patient record-keeping requirement at this hospital. The chief of medicine had devised this data base to fill out for each patient. It would take an hour and a half at the best of times. Then you had to write up a problem list, and you couldn't write an

order unless it was keyed to something on the problem list.
So the patient could be in shock, but you couldn't put the
patient's feet up or put in an IV line unless you first wrote
down that the patient was in shock. This system was intended to aid in diagnosis, but it was unwieldy. And the
doctor who devised it pursued it like a maniac all the time I
was there. His record-keeping system appeared to be more
important to him than the patients. It was an impossible
situation.

Constantly learning by mistakes rather than being
guided is no way to be trained as a doctor, but that's how I
was trained here. It was inhuman, demoralizing. There was
no emotional support. Patients were dying all the time. I
was getting so distanced from them, and I'd do a head count
in the morning to see who was still alive. There was more
work than anyone could possibly have done. I was overwhelmed by it. I couldn't do it even though I was spending
120 hours a week at the hospital. Sometimes at four in the
morning I was so exhausted, I just didn't give a shit anymore and I'd go to bed. I just didn't care. It was a matter of
self-preservation.

One time I was at the bedside of a patient who had
come in from a nursing home. He was sort of rotting away
in front of us, a disgusting sight. The intern told me he'd
found out this patient was hypothyroid, which could explain
why he was so gorked out. We tried to decide whether it was
worth wasting some thyroid medication on this patient, deciding in effect whether this patient's life was worth a few
pennies a day. We were discussing this at the foot of the bed!
In front of the patient!

It makes my skin crawl to think I ever did something
like this. I had sunk to depths I never thought I could sink
to and that I hope never to sink to again. I was breaking my
own value system, which was that I would never talk in
front of patients in a way that would demean them. Not that
this patient could fully understand or remember, but that
isn't the point.

What I saw was my failure as a physician and as a human being. I'm a resilient person and it takes a lot to knock me down, but I couldn't take this anymore. I had reached the point where this experience had made me into someone I did not like. After my year there, I was so burned out and soured, I quit medicine for six months.

I was a first-year resident on a thirty-six-hour shift, and I'd been up thirty-two hours. I was exhausted. At about two thirty in the morning I went to the on-call room to sleep, when the nurse phoned me and said, "You'd better come back downstairs. There is a guy here who says his back hurts him."

I went to the emergency room, and the guy was lying down, and I asked what was the matter. He said, "My back hurts."

"How long has it been bothering you?" I asked him.

"Five days," he said.

"Then what are you doing here at two thirty in the morning?" I asked him.

He said, "Tomorrow is the Super Bowl, and if you don't fix my back, I'm not going to be able to watch it."

That's the only time I ever threatened a patient with bodily harm. I said, "You've got thirty seconds to get off that stretcher and get out of here, or I will personally break your arm."

He said, "You can't do that."

"Watch me," I said.

It makes good copy to talk about physicians who abuse the system, and there are some who do. But I have also seen every conceivable kind of abuse of physicians by the urban population. Take anybody who has done six months in a big-city emergency room, and see if there is anything in the world that shocks them. There isn't.

*✐* During the first year of medical school, when we began dissecting a human body, the first depressions in the class showed up. One kid hung himself in his garage; another had a psychotic break. We had our share of people fainting in the dissecting room or running out to vomit and not coming back for a day or two. Most people get through it without any major emotional problems, but I am convinced it is a more difficult and dramatic period for medical students than is generally acknowledged.

It's also the time the gallows humor begins, which is a way of protecting yourself from really examining what you are doing—cutting up the body of another human being. Pranks have been going on in medical schools as long as there have been medical students. Putting skeletons on subways or sticking a cadaver's arm out of a car window at a toll booth I'm sure have been done many times. When I was there, someone removed the glans of the penis from one of the cadavers and stuck it on a metal probe. It looked like a well-preserved Greek olive, and he kept teasing this woman medical student during lunch by offering it to her. She's now a nationally respected writer on sex and sexuality.

*✐* The first thing we dissected in human anatomy was the hand. We started in the early fall, and by Thanksgiving we had worked up to the shoulder, exposing the muscles and tendons. I wasn't aware at the time that cutting open a human being was bothering me, but it must have. I went home for Thanksgiving and I had always loved taking the drumstick, but when I saw it with all the tendons in it, I couldn't eat it, and to this day I can't eat the drumstick.

*✐* You're trained as a surgeon not just by book knowledge but by your role models. They teach you how to operate, how to react to pressure situations, how to deal with patients.

My most memorable teacher is a guy we called Wild

Willie. A wonderful surgeon, skilled, very courageous. He's a legend.

One night a car sped up to the emergency room and dropped a guy off at our doorstep and sped away. This guy had been shot eight times, had thirteen holes, and was bleeding everywhere. He was dead, literally.

We poured fluids into him, and they came out as fast as we were putting them in. We got him to the operating room and tried to ventilate him, but his lungs collapsed, and we were doing everything we could to keep him alive, and in walked Wild Willie. He took one look at this guy and said, "Cut him."

We opened him from the neck to the pubis. He had holes everywhere; his lung, liver, intestine, kidney, vena cava, and femoral artery were all perforated. We operated on him for thirteen and a half hours, gave him more than forty units of blood. A month and a half later, the guy walked out of the hospital. I learned more from that single case than I did in a year of residency.

I learned a lot medically because Wild Willie is so skilled and knowledgeable, but I also learned about courage. Some surgeons would have backed off from doing anything. They'd just close him up and shake their head, but Wild Willie refused to quit.

Medical training is constantly a process of proving yourself, but I think the rules are different. Women are judged inferior until they prove themselves equal, and men are judged equal until they prove themselves inferior.

I came through medical training as more women were coming into medicine, but I was still the only woman in surgical training. Many of the nurses didn't like to have me around, and the OR nurses wouldn't even respond to me in the operating room. If I asked for instruments, they wouldn't give them. They talked to the male doctors, but it was as if I wasn't there. It was very isolating.

I had demanded to use the doctors' locker room because that's where all the doctors discuss the cases. It's a good place to learn. At first I was relegated to the nurses' locker room, but I finally got to go into the doctors' locker room when I told them, either let me in or discuss the cases outside.

One old guy, a very abrasive surgeon, threw me out one time. He yelled, "This is the doctors' locker room. You have to leave."

I said, "I am a doctor."

He yelled back, "I don't care! When I'm here, you have to leave anyway."

What was I supposed to do, punch him out? I said, "I think you're wrong," and I left.

*"Women are judged inferior until they prove themselves equal, and men are judged equal until they prove themselves inferior."*

Much more bothersome was the fact that when I finished surgical training, the doctors who had been nice to me —the ones who liked my work and trusted me—told me they couldn't give me a job because they were afraid I couldn't get any male patients. One of the doctors liked me so much, he'd wanted me to marry his son. He told me to my face that he was afraid I wouldn't bring any money into his practice. He suggested I work at a women's clinic or go into breast surgery.

My first day in medical school, they gave me a little book written by a man named Francis Peabody entitled *The Care of the Patient*. And I thought, oh God, here come the violins again. I read through it, and I didn't understand what it was all about except the last line of the book, which is often quoted in the hallowed halls of Harvard Medical

School. It says, "The secret of the care of the patient is caring for the patient."

You can teach people to cut and sew and make diagnoses, but treating people with respect and understanding, being emotionally supportive and gentle while being honest, is both the essence of caring and the essence of being a good doctor. It's not something that's really taught in medical training, and I'm not sure how much of it can be taught. If you didn't learn good human values from your parents, I think it's a bit late in the game to try to learn it when you're being trained to be a superspecialist.

When things go wrong in the operating room, some surgeons scream and throw instruments, turn into absolute beasts. I sometimes think they go into surgery so they can act out and do whatever the hell they want in the OR, where nobody can say anything to them.

I was trained by a brilliant and well-known neurosurgeon who had an explosive temper. I had been an intern for only a month or so the first time I scrubbed with him. He was doing brain surgery, and the chief resident was assisting. The chief resident apparently did something this neurosurgeon didn't like, and he stepped back from the operating table and punched him. Really gave him a smack. I couldn't believe what I was seeing. But he must have thought punching this guy was a good idea, because he hauled off and punched him again with his other hand. I thought to myself, what is going on here? This is brain surgery. Am I crazy?

Four years later, when I was chief resident, I worked with this same neurosurgeon during another brain operation. I can't even remember what he got mad about, but he stepped back from the table. And there was a metal bucket that we threw the sponges into. He kicked that bucket like a place-kicker. The sound of his foot hitting it still reverberates in my ears. It flew through the air and hit the OR walls as he was screaming, *"I am sick of training one ten-thumbed son of a bitch after another!"*

I tried to get even with him. He always hated to see anything out of place, like a little dirt somewhere. So one night before he made rounds, I walked around and stuck little bits of tape everywhere just to make him crazy.

But the time I really got him was when he admitted one of his friends to our service. He did that sometimes. I couldn't stand his friends—they were arrogant, pompous people who treated us like servants. This one time he admitted a friend with back pain. Right after he admitted this guy, he had to go out of town. The next morning I went into this patient's room. The first thing he said to me was, "There are people outside the window looking at me."

I immediately called the psychiatric service and had him shipped over there for an evaluation. Of course, I didn't mention there were men on scaffolds cleaning the windows that morning.

I can remember crying when I was a young resident because one of the attendings had me send a street person with a broken arm back onto the street without operating on him. If it had been anyone else, he would have had an operation. I thought that was awful. He had broken both bones in his forearm.

If you don't operate on these patients, they will usually end up with a crooked arm. If you do operate, the results are about 95 percent good. But after you operate, the patient has to come back for follow-up, and people who live on the street usually don't do that, and the attending thought he wouldn't come back, so he didn't want to operate. I guess in some way he was right, but it was very upsetting.

One thing medical training does is smash your ideals and take away your niceness as a person. The hours that you work, the years of deprivation, being treated like a piece of dirt by everyone, being put under all this stress and pressure and nobody cares, and nobody thinks of you as a human being. You become an automaton doing things for the big guys.

I know a lot of really good people who came out of their training being not as good or as caring as when they went in. All the years of deprivation make some of them reach a point where they come into their own and think they deserve all they get. I've seen that happen to people, and when it does, there's no charity anymore.

The surgical specialties are the ones I admire most in terms of quality control and catching irresponsible physicians early. There is a case-review, postmortem process, whether the case was a success or not, and everybody checks on everybody else. And if you mess up, you have to face the chairman of surgery, and he will make you wish you were in another universe. But there is a purpose to the brutality. You learn you don't fuck around with peoples' lives!

But my speciality, psychiatry, is the worst, absolutely the worst! When I trained, no one knew what the hell I was doing with the patients. I talked about cases with my supervisors, but I could have been an utter sociopath and made everything up. There still isn't good supervision in psychiatry, but there is no excuse for it now with video cameras and one-way mirrors. There should and can be closer supervision.

When I trained there were people in training who were frankly disturbed, and they were not properly dealt with in the training program. I think most of them still aren't, and psychiatry unfortunately seems to attract more than its share of people with unresolved emotional problems.

When I was a member of the junior faculty in one program—a very prestigious program, I might add—we had one guy who began dressing more and more strangely, acting less and less professional, and becoming more eccentric in his interactions with patients. It was pretty obvious early on that he exhibited signs of disturbance. We kind of talked about him, not that it was a secret. But there was a feeling that, well, once he's in our program, we will nurture him through and tolerate what the teachers called his "differences."

He became more and more outrageous until he came in one day and sat in the waiting room of the clinic with his entire body painted, wearing nothing but a bathing suit, playing a guitar. It sounds like I'm making that up, but it's true. Only then was it finally said, "Well, maybe he shouldn't be allowed to finish his psychiatric training program. Maybe he has some bad problems."

He was finally kicked out of the program, but that was the kind of behavior it took to convince everyone he should be.

During my training we operated on a series of open-heart patients, and every one of them had to go back to the operating room at nine or ten at night to stop some small bleeding. The whole team was getting punchy because we had been up with these patients day and night for so long.

It was my job to make sure all the bleeding had been stopped before we closed after the surgery, so I felt terrible. By the time the fourth or fifth patient began to bleed, I told everyone in the OR that this time we would pack the wound and put the wires in the sternum to close the chest, but we would not close him. Then I said to turn out all the lights because the bleeding never started until dark.

Everybody got into the spirit of it, and I started going around the room, banging on a tin pot, chanting, "If you are going to bleed, bleed now." Other people started chanting with me. Then the attending walked in and saw this bizarre scene and said, "What in the hell is going on in here?"

I explained that this was our suture-closure ceremony, and if he would just wait another two minutes, we would turn on the lights and look into the patient's chest. He got into the spirit of it as well, and when we turned the lights on to examine the patient's chest, by God, we found five little bleeders. We cauterized them, and from that time on, that patient didn't bleed a drop.

So we began doing this suture-closure ceremony every time after surgery, and it became kind of a trademark, like putting a penny in your loafers for good luck. In my own practice I still conclude every surgical case this way. When a patient has a spinal and remains awake, I tell them, "You might not understand what is happening, and it's not that I'm superstitious, but I just don't want you to have bad luck." And because my residents go out into practice, I heard this ceremony is now being performed in Nashville, Cincinnati, Atlanta, and Jacksonville.

✍ A surgeon I knew was one of the smartest people I ever met. He knew loads of information, seemed to read all the medical literature. But he would stand in the operating room and turn his head one way and say, "Well, I think we ought to do this," and then he would turn the other way and say, "But on the other hand there are several articles that say we ought to do this." His surgery was just a long, fumbling, indecisive exercise.

*"We're in a very litigious society these days, and we have to document things very carefully . . ."*

As a teacher of surgeons, one of the most serious problems with our whole medical education system is that we've not had enough courage or foresight to redirect young people early on and say, "You're not fit for surgery. Let's get some counseling and see what you would be best at." Instead, we're letting them go through the system, and they become mediocre surgeons, or unhappy surgeons, or surgeons who scream and yell in the operating room because they're insecure.

We're in a very litigious society these days, and we have to document things very carefully because people will take you to court and say you are interfering with their education if you try to weed them out of a surgery training program. But I don't think that should dissuade us from our mission of training the best surgeons we can.

I had a surgical trainee. When I'd meet him at casual encounters in the cafeteria or at a party, he was very winning, very warm. And then I'd see him in the operating room, and he was a completely different person. He was tense and tight, and I finally realized he was frightened. And there are some doctors, some surgeons, who are absolutely frightened in the operating room. They become uncomfortable when a wound is incised and there is bleeding or when things have to be done quickly.

We persuaded this young man to consider another area of medicine away from the operating room, and he just blossomed and became very happy and successful. I know that if we had let him finish as a surgeon, he would have perforated an ulcer, gotten a divorce, done all the things that tear people up when they are not fit for what they are doing.

But when you talk to some of these young surgical trainees who you know are struggling, some of them just won't quit. They say, "I'm going to get through. I'm going to get better. I'm going to conquer my fear of the operating room." Some of them do get better, but some do not, and so often we find young people right at the end of their five years of general surgical training unable to do the job. And what happens is that we just let them get by and go off and practice somewhere.

✒    We had a young diabetic woman on the ward. Her toe had become infected from an ingrown toenail. Diabetics have a lot of worries about infections, but the medical stu-

dent with me was a wise-ass, and right in front of this patient he said we ought to amputate her leg right above the
knee.

I yanked him out into the hall and said, "You just
flunked the course."

A little later, he came up to me in tears and said, "You
know, I've never been flunked. This is the first time I have
ever failed anything." He told me he had rotated in another
institution where calling patients "gomers" and "dorks" and
"pains in the ass" was cool. He told me this and expected
me to rescind the failure.

I said I did not tolerate that kind of behavior and that
the failure would stand. I asked him, "What if it had been
your wife or your daughter? How would you feel about it?"

I've only flunked students for bad bedside manner,
never because of their level of intelligence. I have always
believed if a physician isn't lazy, he can practice good medicine as long as he is cautious and analyzes things properly.
But if you have a bad bedside manner, you are dead meat as
far as I'm concerned. I don't see how you can be a physician.

Many cases justify the public perception that there
are poor doctors or insensitive doctors, and in my opinion
doctors do misbehave too often. I think part of the reason is
the dilution of talent. There was a big rush during the recent
past to build medical schools. There were ninety medical
schools when I applied less than twenty years ago, and now
there are more than 120. There are schools I've never heard
of where students are taught things I've never heard of. I
think the training of many young doctors has suffered, and
the quality of a significant number of the students is poor.

After I did my training, I taught at one of the new
medical schools that was affiliated with a prestigious university. The people who hired me told me the medical school
was having "growing pains," but I didn't realize what those

growing pains were until I arrived. I was shocked at the quality of some of the students. I wondered how they had ever got out of high school, much less college.

And the students were not well led by the faculty. I sat in on some of the discipline committees for this medical school, and we let people through who in my opinion should not have been let through. There were some students who didn't even know the basics, things like using insulin for diabetes. They should never have been advanced to the next year, yet they were.

We had one third-year medical student who had had sexual intercourse with a psychiatric patient with whom he had had a therapeutic relationship. He was clearly taking advantage of and abusing the doctor-patient relationship. I'd been trained at Cornell, and if that had happened there, he'd have just packed his bags and left. He wouldn't have had a prayer of staying. But this school's faculty didn't even consider kicking the guy out. They only disciplined him, and he appealed the disciplinary action. The upshot of it all was that nothing was done, and this student remained in medical school.

I left after a year because I couldn't take it and I couldn't change it. My opinions were well known to the medical faculty, and I think they were happy to have me leave.

One of the women in my medical school class was very squeamish about dissecting cadavers. Before exams, we'd work on the cadavers at all times of day or night. One time, some guys in the class found out she was going to the lab at night to work on her cadaver, and they convinced the person who was going with her to back out at the last minute so she'd have to go alone.

A group of them got there before she did and moved her cadaver to another table, and one of the students lay down on her table and they put a sheet on him. When she came into the lab and walked to her table, he just rose up with the sheet draped over him, and bingo, she passed out on the spot. She didn't even scream.

✍   There used to be a kind of mystique about entering medical school. The scores on the Medical College Aptitude Tests were deeply guarded secrets. Students could never find out what they got on those tests.

The medical school interview was incredibly important, a very key part of your application. And the reason for this was that medical schools believe there is a lot of art to medicine, that it is not all science, and that personal qualities are an important part of being a doctor.

Unlike business schools and some other graduate schools, test scores were not the most important thing for medical school admission. I recognize there were abuses in this. The admissions committees could play favorites. I'm sure more alumni children got into medical school than would have under a more objective system. But by and large the system screened for applicants who appeared as if they would become humane physicians.

But with civil rights suits, medical schools were forced to reveal the test scores, and thus they were subject to accusations of discrimination from students who had been denied admission but had higher test scores than students who were admitted. This has forced medical schools to accept students more on the basis of test scores.

So now interviews have become less important, and you have a lot of test-taking automatons getting into medical school, or people who don't have to be shy about going into medicine for money because they're not being turned down for having an inappropriate personality.

✍   There are some surgeons you train who can't tie knots or put a suture where it ought to go, or hold the tissue properly when they're operating. But technical shortcomings are not the real problems with surgeons. I have actually seen some fairly mediocre technical surgeons who were so conscientious, so careful in what they did, and so devoted to their art and their patients that they really were very fine surgeons. They're much like a utility infielder who is good and reliable but not flashy or a big hitter. But they get the job done, and they get it done with integrity.

The major reason people fail in their training as surgeons or as doctors is a failing of their home training, a failing in the way they were raised, a failing of values. They don't want to work. They may be dishonest or thoughtless. Did they get up in the middle of the night when the nurse called them and actually go examine the patient, or did they just mumble something over the phone and go back to sleep? These are the values you have to have learned as a child, or didn't learn. You don't get in a position as a surgeon and suddenly learn integrity and conscientiousness.

A medical student interviewed a patient, and the patient asked him for some information about the diagnosis. The student very honestly answered, "I don't know."

After we were pulled out of the patient's room, the attending surgeon turned to this medical student and said, "You never tell the patient that you don't know! You are the one they are looking to for confidence, and if you don't know the answer, you make it up."

I was a third-year medical student, and even then I knew that was bullshit. But that is the mentality that pervades medical school and medicine. The mentality that says, *We know everything. We don't make mistakes.* So when something goes wrong, we blame the patient.

The students who get into medical school in the first place are academic achievers, people who have been near the top of their class. They've taken ridiculous, boring courses in college so they could get into medical school and had to work hard to get As or at least Bs in them. So by and large, medical students are independent, compulsive, competitive, often perfectionist people. These are the kind of people who find it difficult to admit feelings or mistakes anyway. Then to put these people in a system that says doctors are supposed to keep their doubts and mistakes to themselves and suddenly expect them to admit their own vulnerability, or the limits of their knowledge, or their mistakes and say, "I really blew it," is unrealistic.

So doctors end up not calling for help very much, even when they need it. And they don't talk about their mistakes, and their mistakes haunt them because there is no mechanism to fully air them in a professional way. It would be very helpful if we recognized up front that the profession by its very nature is subject to mistakes. We all make them. And we should have forums where we can deal with our mistakes at an emotional level. But we don't do that.

I was an intern on the urology service on call every other night. The resident got sick one time and had to be hospitalized, so I had to work his shift and mine because there was nobody else to cover. I worked seven days and six nights without ever leaving the hospital. I probably got eight hours of sleep that entire week.

We had nine major operations, and you have to understand that as a intern at that stage of training, to have the opportunity to do the operations was enough to keep my motor running flat out. But you didn't have to be a genius to see that by the end of the week I could barely put one foot in front of the other. The chief of the service chose to ignore that.

I had a patient I had operated on the day before. He was bleeding to death. The chief of service was doing another case, and I had to find another doctor to help me. I did find one. As we got ready to go into the operating room, I began to hallucinate and speak in what neurologists call "word salad." I vaguely remember putting the patient on the table and preparing to reopen his abdomen. As I opened the bladder, I fell asleep. So as I was standing there operating on the patient, everyone thought I was being very careful. They didn't know I was unconscious.

I woke up about five minutes later and found everyone watching me. I said, "I'm having a little trouble seeing where the bleeding is coming from. Can you help me?"

While I took a nap, the other doctor put in the stitches. I thanked him profusely for helping me. He had obviously saved the patient's life. When I got out of the OR, I knew I couldn't go on any longer. I went to the chief of service and said, "I've got trouble."

"What do you mean?" he asked me, as if he didn't know.

I said, "Come on. You know that I have worked seven days and six nights without sleep."

He looked at me and with real innocence in his voice he said, "Well, I had no idea this was going on."

I was too tired and angry to care, and I said, "Nonsense. You certainly did know what was going on."

Then I did something unthinkable. I said, "I'm not working anymore. You are the chief of the service, you are a licensed physician, and it's your responsibility, not mine. I'm leaving tomorrow morning, and you are going to take care of the patients because you didn't give a damn about it when I couldn't." And I walked away.

Unfortunately, that typifies the experiences many doctors go through in training, and it is one of the ways in which doctors' attitudes are changed for the worse. The people who go into medicine are by and large reasonably idealistic and motivated to help humanity. I had expected I was going to work hard at my profession and earn a good living. But making a lot of money wasn't primary to me and did not override my idea of hard work and service. Nor did it for most of the other people studying medicine.

But medical school is very regimented and very grueling. You start at the bottom of a very long ladder, and nobody has time for you or your concerns or to treat you well. It really buffets your ego.

When you become an intern or resident—a house officer—your ego really gets bruised. You are asked to work much longer than is tolerable. You are cannon fodder. You are asked to do all kinds of menial things because you are in a position where you can't say no. You are treated with contempt.

And you look around and see people with your ability in graduate school having lunch under the trees and people who went to law school out practicing and, by our standards, making an incredibly good living before we even graduated from medical school.

So doctors look around and say, "Hey, it's not fair. We are really getting the short end of the stick. We work twice as long and twice as hard as anybody, and we get paid nothing." And when I was a house officer, we did get paid next to nothing. We also got very little external thanks. And because of our work load, we neglected our families or curtailed our social lives to the point that we married the first person of the opposite sex who came along and smiled. This system is exploitative to a degree that is not justifiable.

Your attitudes are also shaped in the clinics and the emergency room. Many urban people use these facilities as their primary social service agency. It puts a strain on young doctors who are already overburdened by a system designed to exploit them. By the end of your training, you no longer romanticize the poor, and much of your original idealism and liberalism gets pretty well beaten out of you. I can tell you I was a hell of a lot less liberal when I finished than when I started.

After seven or eight years of medical training, they turn out someone who is competent, tough, experienced, and pretty cynical. So if you wonder why many doctors are concerned about making money and enjoying life, it's often because of what happened to them before they got there.

Medical diagnosis is not complicated in real life. Most every time the diagnosis is very straightforward. When there is a quandary about what is wrong with a patient, things have gotten so sophisticated and the tests so knee-jerk that you get a CAT scan or some other study and the diagnosis is obvious.

But in medical school all the emphasis is on diagnosis, the possibilities of what may be wrong with a patient. I think that's because it is so easily teachable. If you're in a hospital with something seriously wrong and no one knows what it is, then a doctor who's really up on differential diagnoses can make a big difference.

But for 95 percent of the patients I treat in my internal medicine practice, that isn't important. The important stuff is not emphasized in medical school. We don't learn how to do a really good physical examination or take a good medical history. We don't dwell on the subtleties of treatment, or the management of a chronically ill patient, or whether to recommend surgery for this patient or that patient, or whether to use this drug or that drug. That's where I have needed the most help in my practice, but it's something I've had to learn on my own.

An old guy came into the hospital late at night from a nursing home with a huge bedsore, the deepest I've ever seen. I don't think he'd moved in six months. The nursing home sent him to us because he had a fever. I ran some tests, and he had the highest values for certain things that I have ever seen or heard about in terms of dehydration. His sodium and chloride levels showed he was 30 percent dehydrated, which is not consistent with life.

He was eighty years old. It was clear he hadn't functioned in a long time. I was the resident on call that night, and I made a decision not to save him. I gave him some antibiotics and hung an IV so to someone passing by in the hall, it would look as if I were doing something to save his life. It's one of the tricks you learn working in a public hospital—how to look good superficially. You can even make the chart look better without lying, but if it is held up to scrutiny by a medical person, they'll see what you're up to.

The man died within twenty-four hours, and the director of medicine reviewed the case and knew what I had done. He was one of those guys who called everyone a murderer for everything. In the middle of the ICU, this doctor would yell, "You trying to murder this patient?"

That's just what he did to me. I had to say yes, I was playing God. I was not trying to save him. Absolutely. He had no family I knew of, his eyes were fixed and dilated; by all the criteria I knew about, he had no useful life left. The director asked, "How do you know he couldn't have recovered? I've had patients like that walk out of here."

I tried to defend myself, but he didn't permit much talk. In the end I think he kind of respected me for defending myself. But I probably would have criticized me, too. Not for playing God but for playing God without going through all the steps one should go through before playing God. Like trying hard to see if I could locate a family member or a close friend to determine what his wishes might have been and doing all I could to save him before deciding he could not be saved. I didn't do that.

I don't have any sense of guilt over what I did. I felt I was in an impossible situation, and I made a decision, and I learned from it. My criticism really goes to the issue of how it happens that we have a health care system that has an overabundance of doctors, yet an inadequately trained twenty-three-year-old ends up making life-and-death decisions like this in the middle of the night.

A lot of doctors have gotten all through medical school and training faking how to do deep tendon reflexes or faking hearing breath sounds. Some of the brightest medical students during the first two years proved inept in the second two years when they had to interact with people.

Watching some of these students come close to falling apart when they were confronted with a real human being instead of a textbook was a real revelation. We all had serious levels of stage fright, and we worked very hard to keep ourselves organized by trying to remember everything we had to do. But some students didn't even know how to introduce themselves or take a patient's history. One student had to examine a well-endowed middle-aged woman, and he began to sweat profusely and get red in the face. His hands were shaking like crazy, and finally the woman had to put his stethoscope on her chest. These people never learned how to examine a patient.

When you're a medical student, you pretend a lot that you're a doctor. If a patient calls you doctor, you don't correct them—at least, that's what my medical school class did. When I was on the obstetrical rotation, a psychotic man came into the ward apparently looking for his wife, who had just delivered a child. The first thing he asked was, "Who's the doctor?" The doctor assumed this guy wanted to know about the baby, so he stepped up very proudly and said, "I am." This guy pulled out a gun and shot him. Then he ran into the delivery room and began spraying bullets all around. A very grim scene. No one was killed, but the guy's wife was shot in the spine and paralyzed.

For weeks afterward, when somebody came up to us and asked, "Are you the doctor?" we'd all answer, "No! No! I'm just a medical student."

A seventeen-year-old girl came into the emergency room in full cardiac arrest. She appeared to be very healthy, and she had a look of innocence on her face. She had no history of epilepsy, but she had had some kind of seizure and then a cardiac arrest when she was out shopping with her boyfriend that afternoon.

I was a young resident at the time. I thought I could easily save her because all we had to do was countershock her with defibrillation pads and her heart would respond and she would come right back. We countershocked her, and she didn't respond. We did it again and again, and she still didn't respond. We also gave her everything we could from the crash cart to get her heart started, the whole nine yards, but nothing happened. We worked on her for more than an hour and couldn't bring her back. She just died. The autopsy came back later. Nothing—no drugs, no sign of what went wrong. One of those things you can't explain.

I felt incredible frustration at not having been able to do anything for her. She was a patient I had been so sure I could save, and when I couldn't, I just went off into a corner somewhere that afternoon and cried about it. She was the only patient I have ever cried over.

I thought about her death for a long time. I still think about it. But I also realized there was a danger in feeling so strongly about patients, of becoming too emotionally involved in them. I realized that I had to hold something back, or every case was going to be a problem for me. I knew I couldn't continue this way, and as I grew older and more experienced, I realized that there are some patients who, for reasons you can't understand, don't make it, even though you think they should. It's something I have learned to accept, although it has been difficult. I think we physicians have to divorce ourselves from the patient so we can do our job, because so much of our job is judgment and we need a clear head for that.

*"But I also realized there was a danger in feeling so strongly about patients, of becoming too emotionally involved in them."*

So now these groups come around and say we have to teach the medical students more sensitivity. What are they talking about? Don't teach the students sensitivity! For crying out loud, they have too much sensitivity for their patients as it is! Some of my students are barely able to function because they are so emotionally involved with patients. They can hardly do the things that are necessary because they sit there and hold hands, and they get upset about everything. I have to teach most of my students how to keep their distance from patients, not become more sensitive to them.

One medical student put his stethoscope on a patient's chest and reported he heard a murmur. The problem was, he'd forgotten to put the stethoscope's earpieces in his ears. We all fake things like this in medical school and in practice. Right now in medicine, it's going on all the time, all over the country. Doctors are faking their physical diagnoses, putting things on a patient's chart that have no connection to what they've actually done or observed.

Fudging at the margins is something you learn in medical training, and you usually get away with it. Unless of course you do something as obvious as forgetting to put in your earpieces. Only rarely does it happen that what you didn't do turns out to be the crux of the diagnosis.

One of the areas where just about every doctor fakes it is the eye examination, looking into the fundi. The fundi are the optic discs in the back of the eyes. Well, I guarantee every medical chart will say, "Fundi normal. Disc sharp." But most doctors don't see anything when they look into the eyes with a scope to examine the fundi. I have even seen doctors put down that a fundus is normal with a patient who had a false eye. That turned out to be only mildly embarrassing. No one is called down for that.

The best one I ever saw was a surgical resident who put down on a patient's chart, "Heart/lungs present." I mean, he did not even pretend he had listened to the heart and lungs.

Certain parts of the body are notoriously unreliable for physical findings. Feeling the thyroid gland, for example. That's hard to do unless you've been very well trained in it, and not many doctors have been.

The whole clinical examination process is designed to encourage fraud because it is so imprecise. Yet this kind of data gets accepted and ratified. There have been studies of cardiologists listening to murmurs, and they all hear something different. We know there are margins of error in lab tests, but all this is only given lip service. I can't imagine another profession where that kind of sloppiness would be tolerated. Yet it's on the basis of this information that diagnoses are made and treatments recommended.

Except for three or four doctors in the country, no one seems very concerned about this issue. The National Institutes of Health have not given out big grant money to study the reliability of physical diagnoses and patient charting. You get money for stamping out disease. So the problem goes on and on.

*"We can no longer stand idly by while plastic surgeons try to discredit thousands of qualified dermatologic surgeons."*

> Remarks of the immediate past president of the American Society for Dermatologic Surgery, in response to a report issued by the American Society of Plastic and Reconstructive Surgeons. As quoted in *Medical World News* November 9, 1987

*"If I screw up, I just kill someone. But if you screw up, they suffer for the rest of their lives."*

> A remark made by a surgeon to to a psychiatrist

# 2

# Colleagues

The medical profession is a closed society in many ways. It has its own language and code of behavior, and to outsiders it erects a formidable wall. But inside that wall is an increasingly dynamic and pluralistic world. Once dominated by white males, women and minorities now account for 50 percent or more of many medical school classes.

There is a surface collegiality among doctors. They socialize among themselves, and most doctors count at least one other doctor as a close friend. But I've always found doctors to be a highly critical group who tend to find flaws in just about everything. So it's not surprising that they turn their criticism on their colleagues, too. They regard them with disdain, bemusement, envy, and respect, and a very few with something approaching awe.

In the past few years the number of physicians has increased dramatically—three times faster than the general population—so competition has become keener. The Federal Trade Commission has also given the green light for physicians to advertise. Many doctors have mixed feelings about doctors who advertise. "There's a difference between putting a tasteful ad in the Yellow Pages and being a medical huckster on television," one said.

Doctors spoke of other causes of conflicts among peers. Establishing themselves in the eyes of their colleagues in order to get referrals has always been a complicated minuet of tact, availability, and ability. But with the increasing competition among doctors, it's becoming even more complicated. Bitterness toward colleagues can and does develop easily when doctors feel bypassed in the referral network.

I also found sharp divisions between good doctors and those who they think are not as good. Many doctors spoke of lesser colleagues with contempt, calling them "hackers." Academic doctors look down on private practice doctors, and many private practice doctors I spoke with accused academic doctors of living in ivory towers and not knowing the first thing about taking care of patients. It is akin to class warfare in some parts of the country.

Some male doctors don't like the idea of women doctors, and there are women doctors who believe that white male doctors are arrogant and unfeeling. "There's not the slightest doubt in my mind that women make far superior physicians because they are more caring," one woman doctor said. But I also found in a number of interviews that the harshest judges of women doctors were other women doctors. A woman surgeon who had applied to a university surgical staff had a reputation for sometimes crying during tense moments in surgery. After she stopped crying, she would complete the surgery. The male surgeons were willing to overlook this, but the women surgeons found her conduct intolerable and spoke against her. She was not accepted.

Many doctors I interviewed also expressed considerable anger toward doctors who display their wealth. "The Buick used to be the doctor's car," one physician said. "Even if he could afford a more expensive car, he didn't buy it. And even though he could afford a bigger house, he chose to live in a more modest one. But now we have some of these hotshot doctors riding around in Mercedes-Benzes and living in mansions with swimming pools and tennis courts, and it really makes us all look like we're money-hungry. It bothers the hell out of me."

Conflicts between doctors may also extend into entire

specialties. The plastic surgeons I spoke with are angry at dermatologists and ear, nose, and throat (ENT) specialists for moving in on their territory. They argue that the dermatologists and ENT surgeons aren't trained in plastic surgery and shouldn't be doing it. Dermatologists insist they are well trained to do many procedures—such as liposuction to surgically contour localized fat deposits—and that plastic surgeons just want to have the whole pie. They accuse the plastic surgeons of being elitist. Ditto for the ENT surgeons.

There are other skirmishes. Radiologists snipe at internists and other nonradiologists who own office X-ray machines. Money isn't the issue, one told me; it's simply that these other doctors aren't trained to know how to read X rays. Transplant surgeons spoke bitterly of nephrologists (kidney specialists). They charged that some private practice nephrologists don't refer kidney patients for transplants because they want to keep them on kidney dialysis so they can continue to earn money off of them.

There are long-standing antagonisms between internal medicine specialties and surgery. Many doctors I spoke with took swipes at psychiatrists, although no one took harder swipes at psychiatrists than other psychiatrists. And nobody seems to understand pathologists, whom other physicians sometimes characterize as doctors who love diseases and hate people.

As one doctor understated, "It's not like we're one big happy family."

I have never seen more intoxicated people than psychiatrists at their annual meetings. Just unbelievably drunk people wandering around. And to see the pocketbooks that get stuffed with rolls and shrimp at receptions—it's really shocking. It wouldn't quite fit your image of how you'd like a mentally healthy, well-put-together psychiatrist to act.

There are a significant number—I don't know what the percentage is—of psychiatrists who I think suffer family and

personal problems well into their forties, who have not yet
worked these problems out and attained any mastery over
them. I believe it's a higher percentage than you'd find in
the general population. They have problems with relationships and communications and intimate situations that I
think clearly impair their professional ability. Some have
extreme pathology—they're abusive to their spouses or children—and there are some who are substance abusers.

I practice psychiatry in a sophisticated area of the
country where there are a lot of psychiatrists, and I'll say
without exaggeration that I would not send my dog to three-
fourths of them. That's not to say they're all child or drug
abusers, but many have not worked through issues in their
personal lives, or they may be excessively rigid and unimagi-
native in their thinking and just adhere to one of the many
variations of the psychiatric priesthood, one of the cults of
psychiatry, without thinking the issues through.

*"I practice psychiatry in a sophisticated area
of the country where there are a lot of psychiatrists, and I'll say without exaggeration that I
would not send my dog to three-fourths of
them."*

I think only about a quarter of the psychiatrists I know,
no more than that, are truly capable of listening to a patient
in the context of that patient's growth, development, and
personal history, and then using what they know about the
behavioral sciences to help that patient the best way possible.

✒ In private surgical practice you depend on the medical doctors, the internists, for your bread and butter. You
have to play the game, go to the cocktail parties, appear at

hospital grand rounds, and attend various meetings to get known.

The way you keep on good terms with these doctors is by calling them when a patient has a postoperative medical problem. If a patient develops a lung problem, you call a pulmonary specialist. You call different specialists depending on the problem so they can bill for it. It's how the referral game is played.

I was well trained at an academic center to handle most postoperative problems myself. I have a lot of experience managing patients in the intensive care unit, and I know how to do it. I also know when I'm in over my head and need to get help.

Sometimes when I call one of these medical doctors they order something that, according to my training at least, is contraindicated. That's a problem, and the only way around it is to be as tactful with that doctor as possible. And sometimes I don't feel comfortable calling these specialists to do something I can do and often better than they can. But if you don't call these guys when your patient needs postoperative care and the pulmonary docs find out you're doing all the respiratory care yourself, it's insulting to them. They respond by sending their surgical patients elsewhere, because they know these other surgeons will refer back to them.

This referral business can also rob you of your own surgical judgment because there is an expectation from the referring physician that you will operate on the patients he sends you to operate on. One doctor who fancied himself a gastroenterologist wanted me to perform a type of ulcer operation on a patient that was not indicated. I suggested to this doctor that he consult with another gastroenterologist, which was a not-too-subtle way of saying he really didn't know what he was talking about. I did not do the surgery.

But unless there is some glaring, outrageous contraindication not to operate, it is pretty much expected that you will operate on every patient referred to you. And if not, it's a big deal explaining why not.

A woman was in the recovery room right after surgery, still sedated, lying on the table. The surgeon walked in and said, "You have pancreatic cancer, and you have three months to live." I found this behavior unbelievable. I hate it.

It's doctors playing God. You know, "I have gone to medical school, and I know all about life and death." Well, they're wrong to do that. If terminal patients have a good mental attitude, eat well, and have love and support, they can continue to function and do much better than anyone thinks they can.

I never teach the physicians I train to tell terminal cancer patients how long they have to live. I teach them to tell patients that some people with their illness live for only a few months, but others can survive for several years, and there is no way to predict how you will do. If a patient is desperate to know for insurance reasons or something, then I'll try to give him my best estimate, but I still don't give him a timetable.

In the case of the woman with pancreatic cancer, I treated her and offered her all the encouragement I could, and she lived for a full year with a reasonable quality of life. I've seen doctors get annoyed as hell when a patient lived for a year or two after the doctor had predicted they'd be dead in three months. These guys hate being proved wrong more than they enjoy seeing a patient live longer.

I was on the surgical rotation at a large hospital in New York City when this patient was transferred to us from a mental hospital. He had cancer of the lower esophagus, a very rare cancer site. He was in his seventies and was a catatonic-schizophrenic. He hadn't spoken a word to anyone in thirty years. And as far as we knew, he had no family. Given all that and the fact that his cancer was so far advanced, this man was not a candidate for a surgical attempt at a cure. Palliation treatment was clearly indicated.

The chief resident knew this, but he was one of those guys with an absolute surgical mentality. He loved to cut, and he knew he might never have an opportunity to do such a rare operation again. But he knew under the circumstances there wasn't a chance the attending surgeon, who was a kind of mushy guy who didn't like to operate, would give permission for the surgery.

But the chief resident wanted to operate so badly that he concocted this elaborate plan, and he swore me and the other residents to secrecy. I mean, your chief resident is your mentor. He is the guy you work with in the operating room at three in the morning. He is the guy who teaches you and gives you your grade. It's kind of a fraternity, and you want to win his respect. So even though I thought what he had in mind was outrageous, I kind of admired the genius of what he was doing and kept my mouth shut. So did the other residents.

What he did was to wheel this catatonic patient out of his room and put him in the patient lounge. Then he stuck a newspaper in his hands—*The Wall Street Journal,* I think— and propped it up so this guy looked as if he were reading it. Being a catatonic, this patient wouldn't move.

The chief resident knew that if the patient were in his room when he presented the case on rounds, the attending would want to talk to him. But if the patient were in the patient lounge, the attending would not go up and talk to him because there were eight or ten other patients around and he would be concerned about patient confidentiality. The chief resident also presented this case at the end of rounds, so there would not be enough time to move the patient back to his room for the attending to talk with him.

At the end of rounds we came by and looked into the lounge from the hall, and here was this catatonic patient sitting there like John Q. Citizen reading *The Wall Street Journal* as the chief resident presented his case to the attending, implying that surgery was the only thing that made sense medically. The attending had already seen the patient's X rays, and the presentation had been orchestrated so perfectly that he gave his permission for the chief resident to operate.

The operation was scheduled just as I was going off surgical rotation, so I don't know what eventually happened to the patient—or maybe I didn't want to know. I did catch up with my old chief resident when I attended a reunion awhile ago. He's now on the staff of the medical school and is a respected surgeon in the community.


✐   I've always thought of psychiatry as the Alaska of medicine. You go out into the backwoods of Alaska, and you're in areas where no one has ever been before. Psychiatry is like that. It is less developed than the other medical specialties by many years, so you're involved with a very underdeveloped area when you go into psychiatry.

You deal with therapies for which there is no consensus on what works and what doesn't for which patients. And judging good psychiatrists is like trying to judge good ministers, because there are different psychiatric religions. One may be more insight-oriented, another more behavior-oriented. You don't find divisions like this in other areas of medicine.

Also, psychiatry tends to attract unusual doctors. Many psychiatrists went to medical school and realized that they didn't like medicine. So practicing private psychiatry on well-to-do patients is about the only way they can still get paid for being a doctor without actually practicing medicine because it basically has nothing to do with medicine. If you went to medical school because your mother wanted you to and the last thing you want to do in life is give a rectal exam, you could become a psychiatrist.

✒ I had a patient come to me who had had a growth removed from his neck about two months before I first saw him. The doctor who removed it told this patient that the growth was malignant before he took it off. It turned out to be benign, and my patient swore to me that the doctor was furious because he had been wrong. Doctors get off on strange things, they really do.

✒ There are not many female surgeons in this city, or anywhere else for that matter, so when other doctors think of me, they think of breast surgery. Those are the only referrals I get from male doctors.

Today was typical. I saw twenty-three patients in my office, and all but one had a breast lump. So twenty-two times I had to repeat to an anxious patient all the options and possibilities involved if the lump turned out to be malignant. This is important, and I think a woman patient can be more open with a woman doctor than a male doctor. But you kind of get tired of hearing yourself say the same thing over and over all day long.

I think male doctors believe their male patients don't want to see a female surgeon, whether it's for a hernia or gall bladder or whatever. They have this perception that somehow their male patients will think a female surgeon is not as good as a male surgeon. But I think this is in the mind of the male doctors, not the patients, because I've never encountered any problem like that with the men I've treated.

I told all this to one of the more senior surgeons I know, and he said, "Oh, that will change. You'll see." But I'm not so sure it will change, and it has made me think twice about why I went into general surgery. The problem is, I really didn't like anything else that well.

*"They have this perception that somehow their male patients will think a female surgeon is not as good as a male surgeon."*

It's crossed my mind to go into another specialty. A lot will depend on what happens in the next five years. If my practice is still 90 percent breast surgery, I may switch.

And it's a shame because I have general surgical skills. It's what I am trained to do, and I know I can do those operations well. I didn't go into medicine for the money, and frankly I think women doctors in general are in medicine because they want to be, not because of the money or prestige. I went into medicine because I really enjoyed it. The same is true for surgery. Yet I'm disappointed, more disappointed than angry. I can't be too angry because the doctors at least send me some patients. It's just that I feel I'm wasting my skills.

A woman called me at home at midnight and said she'd just heard about me, and that I sounded like just the doctor she'd always been looking for. She said she'd been to dozens of doctors for her problem, but none of them were understanding. I asked her what her problem was.

"There are electric shocks emanating from my body," she said. "They're from a powerful, evil force, probably the CIA."

There's a neurosurgeon at my hospital I really don't like, so I explained to her that I was an internist and told her she really needed to see a neurosurgeon. Then I gave her his name and telephone number and told her to call him.

I'd had a nagging cough for a couple of weeks, and while attending an out-of-town conference I began to feel terrible, very weak and tired. It had been years since I'd had a physical exam, so when I returned home I called my internist. All the tests looked fine, but my wife became concerned because my cough grew worse, so I called my doctor back. This time he ordered a chest X ray, and it detected a mass in my chest.

He recommended a chest surgeon, and when I saw him,

I began to see the conflict between being a doctor and a patient at the same time. My surgeon asked me if I wanted to look at the chest X rays. I said, "Not really, but I will." I should have said no. I looked at them, and the surgeon was reading the film to me like I was a colleague instead of a patient.

I saw this thing about the size of a grapefruit in my chest, and I was trying to think of all the good things it could be—a cyst or some type of benign tumor. But at some point the surgeon mentioned the word cancer, and I felt a shudder. I never looked at my test results or X rays after that. I just didn't want to know.

A biopsy was done a couple of days later, and the pathology report said I had a type of cancer for which there is no treatment, and I knew death usually occurred within six months or so. My wife and I were both in tears.

The next day the doctors came in and said another pathologist had read the slides and determined that I had a form of lymphoma, a lymph cancer that is very treatable and often curable. That was the first lesson I learned as a patient: The value of a second opinion on your slides.

Although I felt some relief that I didn't have the worst type of cancer, I remembered all the people I had treated with cancer who had died, and I didn't think I would survive, no matter what kind of cancer I had. I think as a physician treating hospital patients, you see the sickest cancer patients, and the idea that people could survive this disease seemed foreign to me.

I then endured what every cancer patient endures—the interminable wait for test results as doctors try to determine the extent of the cancer's spread. These unbelievable, agonizing waits would determine what would happen to my life. I had not given the anxiety that patients feel during these waits much concern as a doctor, but another lesson I learned was that if a patient is waiting for test results, let them know as soon as possible.

I underwent extensive chemotherapy at a major medical center. It was a devastating experience. I vomited most of the time, lost all my hair, and rode an emotional roller coaster for months.

I had always been healthy and had never experienced weakness in my life, but now I did. Because I moved so slowly, I had to wait until other people walked through a door before I did. I remembered patients telling me they felt weak, but I had never experienced it, never appreciated just how weak chemotherapy can make you feel. I also began to see how helpless you feel as a patient, and how all the power is in the hands of the doctors, and how intimidating the doctor can be.

My doctor was a research fellow. He was an angry doom-and-gloom kind of guy. He didn't tell me I was going to die, but he was not the least bit encouraging or warm. I felt so defeated and so weakened in the face of this kind of attitude that it was hard for me to believe that I was a medical director of many doctors. I tried to be seen by an attending physician, but that proved very difficult. It became difficult for me just to ask this doctor a question. Once I called to ask him to write me a prescription for anti-nausea medicine to take before my chemotherapy later that same day. It was a perfectly legitimate request, and he gave me a hard time about interrupting him while he was on rounds. I had had no idea he was on rounds when I had called him. I needed caring, but I didn't get it.

I never confronted him over his attitude because I was a patient, and I was fearful because my life was in this guy's hands. The fact that I was also a doctor was immaterial. I didn't want him any angrier at me than he already was.

I am one of the lucky ones. I survived, and I'm now judged to be cured because there has been no reported case of recurrence with this kind of lymphoma. My strongest memory of my illness is the sense of helplessness and dependency I felt as a patient. I can say that I now feel much warmer, much closer to my patients and to people in general. I think going through a truly difficult illness sensitizes you toward patients in ways that nothing else can. It's a view of medicine that doctors seldom have.

This neurosurgeon is one of these big-shot kind of guys, and he was operating and having a lot of problems. Operating rooms usually don't have windows, but this one did, and as things got worse during the surgery, he got madder and madder. The nurse never seemed to have the right instrument when he asked for it. Finally he just exploded and said to the nurse, "Take these damned instruments and throw them out the window."

So the nurse picked up the instruments, went over to the window, and tossed them out. Of course the nurse was fired, but the surgeon got off without a hitch.

In the middle of an operation the surgeon—who is well known in my area—told the nurse to get him something. For whatever reason, she didn't do it. So he reached over with a hemostat and pinched her right on the boob and said, "Now I think you'll probably remember to do that when I ask, won't you?" Then he unclipped the hemostat and put it down and went on with the operation.

The chief of surgery, a very esteemed surgeon, skilled as hell, opens up this kid to resect a chest tumor, and he gets in there and goes after this tumor, and bang—he cuts right across the aorta. Cuts it right in half! This is a mistake you would think he could never make, but he makes it, and this kid is bleeding like a stuck pig.

The first thing the surgeon does is to stop the bleeding and call two of his associates. They come up to the OR, and he looks at them and says, "I can't fix this. You've got to bail me out." And he turns the operation over to them and just drops out entirely and sits down, looking really spent.

These two guys go to work and suture the aorta back together and get the tumor out and save the kid's life. But to me, the real hero was the chief. We've got this macho image of the surgeon. You gotta do it all, you gotta go all the way. But you have to have real character and confidence in yourself to know when you don't have it, to know when you have to ask for help.

The worst feeling in the world for a surgeon is when he hurts someone. When the chief hurt this kid, when he cut that aorta, it took so much out of him that he knew he couldn't and shouldn't go on. I consider that phenomenal judgment, because he knew that if he continued he would be putting the patient at risk. He knew that he no longer had the objectivity and the ability for his hands and mind to work. That kind of judgment is something you can't measure with boards or with any kind of test.

During my residency there was another resident who was a very arrogant, abrasive guy. The ICU nurses didn't like this guy. They hated him, in fact. Nurses feel demeaned, overworked, and undervalued as it is, so when a young know-it-all doctor made them feel even worse, it really set them off, and I can understand why.

When this resident was on call at night, you could see them laughing and saying, "We're gonna get this jerk tonight."

And they did. They never let him sleep. They'd call him every five minutes with something. You know, your patient has this, your patient has that. And when the nurses call, you've got to go.

Nurses can make your life miserable, especially when they are on a unit like the ICU. I always made sure I got along with the ICU nurses when I was a resident. I still do.

I work in a major medical center and get referrals from around the country for a couple of specialized procedures that I'm known for. But when I get a referral from a local neurosurgeon to operate on something outside my own specialty areas, it's usually a Medicaid patient or a fuck-up. They send the patient to me either because they're not going to get enough money from Medicaid, or else the case is so complex, they should never have operated in the first place.

Other neurosurgeons are reluctant to refer because it violates their own economic lifelines. If a doctor refers a patient to a general neurosurgeon, and the neurosurgeon refers that patient to me, then the next time the doctor will bypass the general neurosurgeon and refer directly to me. Knowing that, a lot of neurosurgeons convince themselves that they can handle a case even when they shouldn't because they're willing to put their own welfare before their patient's. When the patients end up in serious trouble, then I get them.

A surgeon at my hospital was having an affair with one of the scrub nurses. He was doing an arterial bypass procedure on a patient, and for some reason he wanted to get this nurse's attention. Apparently he couldn't get it very easily, and he became annoyed. So he took the clamp off the artery graft and blood gushed out right across the operating room. It splattered everywhere. Against the wall, everywhere. It was horrible, but that's what he did to catch her eye. The patient lost about three pints of blood.

One of our residents was caught in the special procedures room in the middle of the night screwing a nurse. He was married. They fired the nurse but nothing happened to the resident, except that his wife found out about it and didn't talk to him for a couple of weeks.

I know one surgeon, a very prominent guy, who actually reached over and cut a resident in the hand with a knife just because he didn't like what the resident was doing.

Another surgeon said something to a resident who either didn't hear him or didn't pay any attention to him, which is even worse. So this surgeon reached up and took the operating-room light and wheeled it down and smacked this resident on the head with it. It didn't knock him unconscious, but it got his attention.

🖋  This surgeon is one of those types who make a sport of teasing people. He seems to especially enjoy it in the operating room. Another surgeon he works with had been an officer in the German army in World War II. They go back a long time, and this guy knows where all of this German surgeon's sensitive spots are.

One time during surgery they sent out tissue to pathology. For some reason, the path report took much longer than usual, but they had to wait before they could continue. As they're waiting, this German surgeon, who has a very short fuse, begins to pace and mutter something about the incompetence of the lab. The other surgeon turns to him and in a voice loud enough for everyone to hear says, "Not like the old days when you could just line them up and shoot them, huh?"

I mean, this German surgeon just exploded.

Another time in the middle of an operation, a nurse working next to him liked the aftershave he was wearing.

"You smell good," she said. "What do you have on?"

"I have a hard-on, but I didn't know you could smell it."

🖋  A resident came up to me and said that another doctor's patient had suffered a clot on his brain and that they had to take him back to surgery. A mess—it happens sometimes in neurosurgery.

The resident told me about it with a certain amount of glee because it wasn't one of the patients he had worked with. When a colleague of mine has a problem with a patient, it reminds me of some of the psychology studies that came out of World War II. They hadn't understood why

soldiers felt a momentary euphoria when a buddy of theirs
was killed. It turned out that the euphoria was because it
wasn't them. We go through some of the same thing, in
neurosurgery especially, because we're always on the edge of
losing or harming patients. I don't wish my colleagues any
ill, but I almost have a sense of relief when something goes
wrong with one of their patients because it didn't happen to
me.

PHYSICIANS' WOES ARE PERVASIVE

> Headline, *Medical World News*
> April 13, 1987

HASSLES AND RED TAPE
DESTROY THE JOY OF THE JOB
FOR MANY PHYSICIANS

> Headline, *The Wall Street Journal*
> April 10, 1987

*"I discovered that the 'technification' of medicine has distanced us from our patients, unfairly raised their expectations, led us frequently to misdiagnose their illnesses and cruelly prolong their lives when they are insensate or terminally ill."*

> *High Tech and the Forgotten Patient*
> By Jonathan D. Trobe, M.D.
> *The Washington Post* "Outlook" section
> December 20, 1987

# 3

# What's Gone Wrong?

"I just got through talking to the Medicare reviewer at the hospital," the doctor explained as he hung up the telephone. "He told me that the eighty-year-old patient I admitted does not meet the Medicare criteria for hospitalization, and because Medicare won't pay, the hospital wants her out.

"I wrote 'back pain' as the reason for admitting her, but that isn't enough to satisfy Medicare. The problem is, she's also somewhat disoriented and barely able to walk, and she lives alone, so she can't take care of herself. So what am I supposed to do?"

Later that day, the doctor returned to the hospital and included disorientation and her walking difficulty, which are chronic conditions not likely to improve with hospitalization, as reasons for her admission, and she was allowed to stay. It is a small irritation but a constant one.

This incident illustrates a widespread frustration among physicians today, one that I heard expressed by physicians in all specialties in all parts of the country: the increasing sense that their ability to make decisions for patients is being taken away from them. The reasons range from legal and financial constraints to a runaway medical technology. But the focus of most doctors' complaints is the growing bureaucratization of medical care, which originates with federal and state governments and also comes from health insurance companies, health corporations, and hospitals. And it is coming fast and hard.

Doctors see this bureaucratization as a morass of rules and regulations that are suffocating them with paper work and robbing them of their autonomy. They feel buffeted by new rules for informed consent, by changing demands for patient admissions, by forms for quality assurance, and on and on. Virtually every doctor I interviewed feels that medicine is being inalterably changed for the worse and turning their profession into a job. Doctor after doctor complained that he or she feels like a mid-level manager, a functionary carrying out the orders of others, instead of a professional whose judgment and experience are paramount. They believe they and their patients are paying a heavy price and will continue to pay it.

Although many doctors I spoke with raged against these changes, they felt almost helpless to fight them. Doctors are not organized—less than half of U.S. physicians belong to the American Medical Association—so they feel there is no single voice making their case.

The number of disenchanted doctors is not certain, but it is undoubtedly great. Studies show that increasing numbers of doctors are retiring early, and medical schools are getting fewer applicants. The Physician Executive Management Center, an organization that guides doctors who want to change careers, reports that the number of doctors seeking their services has quadrupled in the past five years.

✍ I come from a medical family. Something like thirty-four people in our family have gone into medicine since the end of the last century, and most have become doctors. My father and grandfather were doctors, as was my aunt, who took care of most of the poor people in my hometown. For one hundred consecutive years there has been a doctor with our name there.

I had one child I could have led more strongly into

medicine and created another generation of physicians in our family, but I couldn't do it to him because of what is happening to medicine.

The children's hospital where I work used to be run by a doctor; now it's run by businessmen. We used to advertise our excellence by publishing in journals, by teaching, and by presenting our studies at medical meetings. Now we do marketing. And at the same time that the hospital is telling us we've got to make money to keep our departments going, we're also told to publish or perish to keep our academic appointments. I'm at a point where I can't staff my department as I should. And all this has happened in the past five years. The speed has been unbelievable.

*"We used to advertise our excellence by publishing in journals, by teaching, and by presenting our studies at medical meetings. Now we do marketing."*

We used to work for patients. It was our responsibility to do as well by them as we could. We were their advocates. No doubt we'd sometimes screw up or order too many tests, and some of us were probably lousy doctors, but the bottom line was that we were working for them. Now we're working for the company that owns the hospital.

Every kid who came in the front door got the same treatment. Money was never an issue. But now this open-door policy is being questioned because more than a third of our patients are nonpaying. We're not turning away children yet; it's more insidious than that. We used to hold ear, nose, and throat clinics here five days a week, and they were open to all the children. Minority children from the inner city got their care here. Now two days a week this clinic is held at a suburban hospital, where there are paying patients. And next year there will only be two a week here, and so the end result will be that many kids from the inner city won't be able to see the ENT doctor. We're headed toward two-tiered medicine—something that I thought would never happen, especially when it came to children.

The result is that the rewards of taking care of sick children, of figuring out what's wrong and then making them better, are going. It's still a privilege to practice, and I can still find joy in it, but it's becoming less and less joyful.

✒ Ten years ago I opened an internal medicine practice with a partner in a small New England city. We had to borrow a lot of money to start, and we lived on that until the practice built up. We had a very good professional relationship, and we practiced the kind of medicine we wanted to practice. We made house calls, covered at the local emergency room, got to know the people in the community. Then five years ago all the hassles with Medicare, Medicaid, and Blue Cross/Blue Shield really started and essentially put us out of business.

Medical insurance was designed to pay for big hospital fees, not primary-care doctors. The fee schedules developed for Medicare and Medicaid followed the private insurance policies, so the discrepancy between what you get to take out a gall bladder and what you get for an office visit is so out of sight that primary care is virtually not reimbursed.

Getting up in the middle of the night to take care of a patient isn't worth much under this reimbursement system. I was called to the hospital because a woman had taken an overdose of an asthma drug. She had the highest levels of this drug I have ever seen. She was on the brink of death. This drug makes you very agitated, so she was abusive, swearing at us—a terrible management problem for the nurses and me. It took me several hours to stabilize her, and we eventually transferred her to a tertiary hospital. She'd also left her three little children home alone, and this was at night. So we had to find some agency to go to her home to care for them.

I ended up getting about twenty-five dollars from Medicaid for spending that night in the hospital. And this wasn't some rare event. Things like this happened often, and I felt an ethical responsibility to take care of these patients, and I think most of the other doctors in the community did, too. But how many times can you do that and survive economically?

My partner saw the writing on the wall before I did, so he left the practice and took an administrative job with the Veterans Administration, where he earned $30,000 more a year for less work. I was floored when he left, but I couldn't blame him. That was the beginning of real problems for me.

I wanted to bring in another partner. I thought it would be good for me and my patients, and it was the way I wanted to practice medicine. I looked hard because it is difficult to attract doctors into a primary care practice in small cities nowadays. I finally found a family practitioner in solo practice. She was making about $20,000 a year and literally going under. I convinced her to come with me.

We got along well, but we encountered a number of problems in running the practice—mostly the ongoing struggle to collect our fees. She'd already been through all this, so after a year she left and took a salaried job at a local clinic.

So I was on my own again, and my overhead was still going up, and I really couldn't afford to be in practice alone. My income had dropped from the high sixties to the low sixties and was continuing to sink. I still drove my 1969 Valiant because I couldn't afford another car.

I advertised all over the place for another partner, but I couldn't find anybody. My former partners' patients didn't go away, so I had more work and nobody to share it with. I couldn't keep it up. And even though I was earning more money, the stress on me and my family was becoming unbearable.

I began to think I might become at risk for malpractice during these months because I was so stressed. I was doing things on the telephone that I would never have done on the phone before. After a year of looking, I still couldn't find another doctor to join the practice, so I looked for a job and found one with a university health service.

In the end, it wasn't the financial struggle that did me in. It was being alone and not wanting to be alone. But I was alone because the finances didn't attract anyone to join me in the practice.

I had mixed feelings closing my practice. My family had suffered because of the stress I was under, so we all were relieved that that was ending. But it was very hard for me to leave my patients, especially those in the nursing home. There were about sixty I visited regularly, and I'd known many of them for years. Leaving them was a wrench, and I literally had to beg other doctors in the area to take them.

At my office, every patient visit ended up with crying after I'd announced I was leaving. It was a horrible period. Patients were distraught with my office staff because there was nobody to take care of them. Many of them had been rejected by a local, for-profit health maintenance organization that had moved into town because the HMO only wanted healthy patients so it could make more money. Even some of my patients with well-controlled high blood pressure were turned down.

What happened to me isn't an isolated event. Another internist in town closed her practice and went to work for the state. Another went to work for an insurance company, and another left to do a cardiology fellowship. This isn't lost on the people in medical training today. They know what's going on. You read all the time that training programs are having difficulty filling their internal medicine slots because young doctors want to go into specialties that allow them to do some kind of procedure. They know that if they don't, they'll have a hard time surviving.

And what's replacing us are HMOs, which are trying

to make money, and these "doc in the boxes," the street-corner care centers. It's business people who are making money off this. So patients won't get continuity of care, or night coverage, or emergency coverage—none of that feeling of having a doctor when you're in the ER with chest pains, or when you go into one of these places and have a chest X ray that shows a lung cancer. Who's going to be there to give you comfort and support? But that's what is happening all over the country, because when primary care doctors balance it all out, you see you can't make it and still do what you thought you wanted to do.

As hard as my practice became, I still miss it and some-times I think, "How could I have given it all up?" But then I remember what it was really like, and I realize it was just not possible anymore.

I dread intensive care medicine, and I almost never send my patients to the ICU. I always sit them down and talk to them ahead of time if they have an incurable disease and tell them that I really think we should not go to the ICU for something that can't be readily reversed.

I had been taking care of a young woman who had leukemia when I was attending on oncology-hematology. She had failed multiple courses of chemotherapy, and she was very ill and in the final stages of dying. There was nothing more we could do to save her.

In the hospital she suffered a cardiac arrest from peri-cardial tamponade, a condition brought on when the peri-cardial sac around the heart fills with blood and constricts the heart's ability to beat. I think it may have been caused because her leukemia had begun to invade her heart. They rushed her to the ICU and began giving her drugs and put-ting in many intravenous lines. They couldn't revive her, so they cut open her chest and began doing open-chest cardiac massage.

They continued to work on her, and when I came back

into the ICU later, I saw what they were doing, and I yelled *"Stop this!* What are you people doing here? This girl has leukemia. She is never going to recover."

The anesthesiologist yelled back at me, "We can't. We've gone this far. We've got to keep going."

I said, "You haven't had a blood pressure for three hours. She has dilated pupils. She has lost central nervous system functions. She has flaccid paralysis. What are you doing?"

Even if they had revived her, she would have died from leukemia within a month.

The anesthesiologist became quiet and they stopped, and later the ICU attending came up to me and said he was sorry for what had happened. I don't think medicine is very good at teaching physicians how to stop, so I could understand how they became caught up in what I call "black box medicine." But when that happens, we can lose sight of the humanity of the person.

One of these peer-review organizations that keeps statistics for Medicare and is supposed to "assure medical quality" sent a letter to my hospital that said, "We think you should be aware that one of your surgeons has a higher mortality rate in coronary bypass surgery than any other surgeon in the area, by far." The letter contended that in an eighteen-month period there had been five deaths under my care, and no surgeon in the area had anything approaching that death rate. I really felt blind-sided.

The hospital administration wanted to know my response, so I reviewed the cases. One had been a patient who'd come to me from the catheterization lab who was in effect dead already because they had torn up his heart doing an arterial study. I had known that if I didn't operate, he'd die, so I had given it a try, and he had died anyway. Another hadn't even been a coronary bypass. It had been a complicated valve replacement. Another had involved a sixty-eight-year-old man who had lots of medical problems. It turned out that of the five deaths, only one could be considered unexpected, and even that one involved an older man in very poor shape.

I answered the letter and noted that the eighteen-month period that had been selected was not the most recent period. I said I found it curious that this time frame had been selected to look at me. In fact, I was damned angry with the way they had chosen to analyze my surgery. I also asked an independent medical statistician to look into it, and he concluded that my mortality statistics were as good as anyone's and that the only conclusion that could be drawn was that I was willing to operate on sicker patients than many other surgeons were.

Even though an accusation like this is baseless, it has a chilling effect. I'm now acutely aware of my statistics and very concerned that they not appear assailable. Because even if they are defendable, I can really be hung out to dry in this new quality-assurance climate.

I have since turned down patients that I might otherwise have operated on because I thought their chances of survival were so poor. In the past, if there had been a 100 percent chance of death if I didn't operate versus an 80 percent chance if I did operate, I went ahead and operated to give the patient a chance. I was willing to take the risk. But I can no longer afford that luxury. Now I tell these patients to see another surgeon.

Maybe someone like Denton Cooley, who has a huge volume of heart patients, is less vulnerable to this kind of statistical scrutiny than I am, but I know I personally cannot afford to disregard it. And it's not with any particular pride that I say this.

I feel miserable every time I tell a seventy-two-year-old Medicare patient that he has to show up at the hospital at six in the morning for his preoperative tests—chest X ray, electrocardiogram, blood work—so I can operate on him at ten that morning.

By twelve thirty that afternoon, an hour and a half after I started cutting on him, the poor guy—if he is like most people his age—can't urinate because of the combined effects of a benign prostate enlargement and anesthesia on top of that. By two that afternoon, he is barely awake, he is moaning and groaning. By six that evening, he knows where he is, he can stand up, and I have to send him home because that's all Medicare will reimburse, and he can't afford $600 or $800 on his own to stay in the hospital an extra day.

So the old guy goes home, and his wife is putting ice bags on the incision, and she's worried to death about him. Every time he moans, she slips him another pill.

This is not the way the people who live in the richest and most technically advanced country on earth should recuperate from illness. And I don't want them to recuperate this way, but that's what government regulations force us to do. Yet if I have a forty-five-year-old with the same problem and a generous insurance company, I can keep him in the hospital for five days.

So all I can do is write in the chart that this seventy-two-year-old man has an irregular pulse that needs monitoring. Or I can ask for a cardiology consult. The cardiologist will come in the next morning and won't find very much, but he might say something that justifies another day in the hospital for this old guy, which may be enough time for him to recuperate as he should.

In plain English, this is cheating. And if you want to do the best for your patient—and any doctor worth a damn does—you are practically *forced* to be dishonest if you want to keep that patient in the hospital long enough to recover properly.

And it's galling to see all the money that is being spent on a bureaucracy to try and save money on patient care by making sure the Medicare patients get out of the hospital when they're supposed to. To see the additional staff necessary in every hospital to look after these patients, the forms that have to be made out, the people who evaluate those forms, is disheartening. We have lost good bedside nurses who are now making more money being Medicare technicians.

My God, for every little dog, we've got two other dogs watching the little dog, and three more to watch the two that are watching the one. It's unbelievable.

Seeing this, I'm beginning to appreciate that Maurice Chevalier song that goes, "I'm glad I'm not young anymore." I say, let the young doctors deal with all this. It won't hit me much longer.

Civil rights have impeded the work of psychiatrists with psychotic patients—made it damned near impossible to help many of them. I've seen a lot of people die because of civil rights. We just couldn't institutionalize them because they hired a lawyer who did what the patient asked and kept them out of the hospital, not realizing that the person was very ill and suicidal. I'm angry at lawyers because of this.

I had one patient who we thought was clearly suicidal. He was a professional man, in his midthirties, and very depressed. He wanted to get out of the hospital, presumably to commit suicide, so he hired a lawyer who was very unsophisticated, and he got the patient out. This was against our medical advice. This patient went home and committed suicide within twenty-four hours. With treatment, I think we could have gotten the patient out of his depression.

The twist in this case is that the lawyer's wife committed suicide just a short time later. It just shows the stupidity of this lawyer. He didn't have the slightest idea this guy was suicidal. He didn't even know his wife was suicidal. Quite frankly, I was delighted by this turn of events.

There is a lot of doctor-bashing, a lot of hostility expressed by the media and fanned by the government. In my state, a physician-review organization puts out a patient guide to physicians that lists some questions and answers. One of the questions is, "Why is the allowed charge by Medicare lower than the charge my physician has billed me for?"

And the answer is, "Most doctors charge more than the usual reasonable and customary amount." Besides being inflammatory language, it is internally contradictory. How can they be charging something beyond usual and customary if it's what most doctors charge?

There's another question about quality of care, and this guide says that the review organization and the federal government want to make sure they get good care, and the implication is clear that if the government weren't looking over the doctors' shoulders, patients would really be getting terrible care. It's no wonder that poll after poll finds that the public believes we make too much money, that we don't care about patients, that we're greedy.

My real beef with the government is the way it's trying to cut medical care costs by going after doctors and making doctors unattractive to patients so the patients won't use the services and spend less of the government's money.

Doctors aren't the driving force behind higher medical costs. The Canadian government published an analysis of what really affects health spending. The first factor is genetics, meaning the individual's predisposition to certain diseases. The second is behavior, such as drinking and smoking. The third is environment, and medical care is a very distant fourth. So if the federal government really wants to save money on health care, it should put emphasis on behavior, like ending the tobacco subsidies and tripling the tax on cigarettes.

It should support prenatal services for pregnant women who don't have access to them or can't afford them. It's been shown that these services can get expectant mothers to stop smoking and drinking by aggressively attacking these behaviors. They can also help these women eat a correct diet. This results in much-less-expensive deliveries because you have far fewer babies in the ICU due to prematurity, or low birth weight because of smoking, or other problems caused by poor prenatal care.

This would reduce health care spending more than all these damned regulations that are harassing doctors. And that's what is so frustrating.

✐ One area of medicine that distresses me constantly is the way we abuse old people who are in the process of dying. In the past twenty years we have made dying the most expensive and painful process we could possibly imagine. I see these elderly people in the intensive care unit all the time. They are brought into the hospital for a procedure and don't do well, so we put them in the ICU and keep them there for this interminable period of time.

> *"We've gotten so entangled with medical technology that we don't see the difference between maximum care and optimum care."*

So here's some poor little pretzel of an old lady curled up in her bed and tortured with IVs, a respirator, and so forth. I sure as hell hope they have the problem solved by the time I reach that age. Money comes in as well. I have seen nephrologists want to give people who are almost in rigor mortis kidney dialysis because they can charge for the dialysis.

Somehow we've got to figure a way out of this. We've gotten so entangled with medical technology that we don't see the difference between maximum care and optimum care. There are no clear ethical guidelines, and a lot of docs just shrug away from it.

But the whole situation changes when a physician is the patient. There is no fear of malpractice, and no one is going to rip him off, and doctors rally around and close the doors and inject him with morphine. They let him go quietly and peacefully. I've see it happen time and time again.

✒  I went into neonatology because I was fascinated by the physiology of little tiny babies. It gave me an ability to get in there and save them. And I felt if I made a special effort, I was able to save a special person and that this person would be intact and able to live a normal life. But I also felt that I would be able to use my own judgment if the prognosis for that baby was not good, and if that baby would not have a good quality of life.

I still manage to believe that I went to medical school to learn an art. There is science to medicine, but it is not essentially a science. To me it is an art. And I do believe there is something called medical judgment. There will always be doctors who don't have any judgment about anything, but I believe that I have learned judgment.

But now I feel that my ability to use my judgment with parents and their babies has been taken away from me, in part by the government and the law but mostly by the machines, by the shiny promise of what they can do to keep not just life going but also existence going. This feeling that medical technology has run over my ability to use my medical judgment makes me uncomfortable and unhappy. If I were a resident now trying to decide what area of medicine I wanted to go into, I would really think hard about whether I wanted to go into neonatology.

I've thought of moving into something else, but I haven't. This is going to sound hard-nosed and maybe even a bit callous, but if all the people in neonatology who think about and agonize over the issues we are involved with moved out of the field, we would be left with the people who think it is perfectly okay to keep anything alive on the ventilator for years. And there are plenty of those.

This doesn't mean I'm a trigger-happy doctor who

wants to stop treatment at the drop of a hat. But I think I've learned from several babies that I now think I was too aggressive with. You have to know when to stop, to draw the line between sustaining life and prolonging death.

For parents, it can be a nightmare to deal with a doctor who refuses to see both sides of this issue, who insists on keeping a baby alive with all hope gone. I know several of these physicians. They sometimes say they're following their religion. But you would be hard put to find where it actually says anything in their religion about what they are doing. I think they're using their religion as an excuse for the way they're behaving. Knowing there are a lot of these people around has deterred me more than anything else from leaving this specialty.

I'm a third-generation doctor. My grandfather, my father, and me—all the same name, all physicians—but I don't want my son to go to medical school. The way medicine is going today, I think it would be irresponsible to encourage a bright kid to go into it.

The quality of life is terrible. You take huge responsibilities, you sink a lot of your life and money into it, and it's very hard. If you go into research, even though you might not be paid well, I can see there are rewards and satisfactions. But if you're going into practice, which most doctors end up doing, it's become intolerable. People are angry at you. Your judgment is doubted. You have to pay a fortune in malpractice insurance. People look at you funny if you take a vacation. You get no feedback—not financial, or emotional, or anything else. I mean, you can't do that!

My wife's niece is considering medical school. I think of medicine as a kind of a guild, and years ago if someone's child was interested in medical school, all the other doctors would come around and help ease the way. They'd help teach and encourage that kid to get into medicine, telling them it's a great idea, a great life. But no more! Now what you hear is, "Forget it! Don't do it!" And I must admit that is what I am telling my wife's niece, and it's what I'll tell my son if he shows interest.

✍ I took care of a patient who had a problem with fluid retention after surgery. This is a very common event in these particular cases and is manageable in a number of ways. Somehow the term *fluid overload* got entered in the chart. All it meant was that the patient wasn't able to get rid of the fluid he had been given, because you can't *not* give fluid.

A week later I got this letter from the quality assurance people saying, "Occurrence: Fluid overload in your patient," as if this were some sort of grave complication. It wasn't a complication at all. These things have occurred in the normal course of patient care for years, and they are not going to change, no matter what you do.

Getting that letter really lit me off. It's so dumb. We have these quality assurance people all over the hospital poring over patient charts to come up with so many complications a month, or what they perceive is a complication. It's like cops giving out traffic tickets. If they don't meet their monthly quota, then they haven't done their job.

All this has been mandated by a bunch of do-gooders around the country who say that in order for Medicare to pay, or for health insurance carriers to pay, or for hospitals to be accredited, we have to assure that quality care is being rendered. It's like apple pie, motherhood, and the flag. Who will deny that quality assurance is a good thing? I would support it if it were reasonable. But they don't know what they're doing. The only thing they're accomplishing is encumbering physicians and taking up a lot of their time—and taking the fun and satisfaction out of medicine.

✍ The stalemate is the hardest thing—the preemie who doesn't get well enough to come off the ventilator but doesn't get sick enough to die. This child is dependent on the titanic care effort that surrounds him. All this equipment, all this technology—and yet his medical problems fail to yield to the solutions we're offering. His heart is beating, his brain may be all right, but we can't make any progress.

If you take him off the ventilator, he will die. But by keeping him on, he lives, but he will never be able to breathe without the ventilator because his lungs can't sustain life. You are caught in this terrible ethical dilemma.

*"You tell yourself, 'I'm doing harm to this baby. There is no way that I'm helping this baby, or the family, or society.' "*

Everybody is trapped. The family can't just go away; it's their child. The medical team is trapped, and the nurses who see this little baby suffer every day are very hard hit. Everybody looks for a way out. You call in the chief and ask, "What do you think?" And there isn't an answer, and you go on and on for months.

It never changes. And it's right in front of you, every day. You and the family become locked in a dance. After a while you don't know what to say to them anymore. You can't figure out how to make things better, and you're out of ideas, and the family is exhausted, and their patience is at an end, and the bill is going up and up, and you can't get off these machines. You can't get off!

In death there is pain for everybody—you share that pain with the family. But you get through it. There is a beginning, a middle, and an end. But when you're in limbo, you just go on. If it were some inanimate things, you could say, "That's a bad one. Throw it away." But it is a person, a tiny baby, and you can't do that.

You tell yourself, "I'm doing harm to this baby. There is no way that I'm helping this baby, or the family, or society." And you try to convey this to the family, and sometimes they finally say, "Enough is enough." But most times they don't. They want to continue. They want to believe in miracles, and I understand why.

You can only search for a tie breaker, some type of surgery or procedure that will get the baby off the ventilator. Perhaps a tracheotomy. Sometimes one of those maneuvers helps—for a while, anyway. Sometimes the baby contracts an infection, and you can't control it, and it's taken out of your hands. That is all you can do.

When I was growing up, my family would go out to the local Italian restaurant on Sunday night, and people would come up to my father and kiss him and tell me what a wonderful surgeon he was and how he had saved their life. So I had a notion that being a doctor was fighting death, saving people's lives, outthinking disease.

It turns out that's not what happens in medical practice —at least, not in internal medicine, which is what I'm in. Being a good doctor means being incredibly compulsive. It has nothing to do with flights of intuition or brilliant diagnoses or even saving lives. It's dealing with a lot of people with chronic diseases that you can't really change or improve. You can help patients. You can make a difference in their lives, but you do that mostly by drudgery—day after day paying attention to details, seeing patient after patient and complaint after complaint, and being responsive on the phone when you don't feel like being responsive.

And you also know that most of your patients who have some medical illness will get better despite what you do or don't do. Being a doctor is no different from being Joe Six-Pack slogging it out at work. Medicine isn't what I thought it would be. It's not the pleasant, rewarding experience I had envisioned.

*"We have recently seen reports of the high incidence of suicide, substance abuse, and marital failure among physicians."*

> "Watching the Doctor"
> *New England Journal of Medicine*
> June 23, 1983

DOCTORS, FIGHTING THE WAR ON AIDS,
FIND THEY ARE AMONG THE CASUALTIES

> Headline, *The New York Times*
> April 11, 1987

*"All of us who attempt to heal the wounds of others will ourselves be wounded; it is, after all, inherent in the relationship."*

> *Healing the Wounds*
> By David Hilfiker, M.D.
> 1985

# 4

## Hidden Costs,
## Private Losses

"He came home with bruises on his arm. He didn't say anything about them until one of our children noticed them and asked him what had happened, and he kind of shrugged and said, 'One of my patients attacked me, that's all.' Nobody has any idea what he goes through, the risks he takes, caring for his psychiatric patients. He's gotten whacked more than once."

The doctor's black-and-blue marks were only the most visible evidence of some of the hidden costs of being a doctor. The same wife who feared for her husband's physical safety also said he was so devoted to his patients that she felt like a single parent. "My mother told me," she said, "never marry a doctor or a sailor because you'll be alone all the time. And she was right."

While most doctors consider it a privilege to practice their profession, they recognize the risks. Not only can their work be consuming, but many worry deeply over patients. They suffer burnout, grief, guilt, anxiety, and high levels of stress because of their work. But I was most struck by one thing—the haunting guilt that many doctors feel over harming a patient. One physician buried his head in his hands and said in a heavy voice, "Just talking about it makes it all come back." And then he shuddered. The incident had happened nearly twenty years earlier. No doctor I spoke about his or her mistakes with could talk about them without expressing sorrow.

Most doctors can endure the darker side of their profession; some cannot. Many studies indicate that doctors have a higher suicide rate than the rest of the population.

There are other hazards. It has always been a tradition in medicine to serve patients, even at risk to yourself. Doctors and other health care workers have historically exposed themselves to viruses, bacteria, radiation, and other occupational hazards. The list of physicians who have contracted work-related hepatitis and other infectious diseases is long. Many have died from these infections. And for the foreseeable future there is the specter of AIDS, a disease that burdens many doctors as they have never been burdened before.

My ten-year-old son began to have bloody noses, then weight loss, and he looked terrible. I thought it was sinusitis for a while, but I took him to another physician—an ear, nose, and throat specialist—who examined him and found a nasal obstruction. We took him to a hospital that night and a friend of mine was running the CAT scanner. My wife was with me so there were three of us watching as these CAT pictures came out showing a very big malignancy in the back of his nose.

I remember thinking, "Oh my God, this is my son. He's got cancer, a terrible cancer." He is our only child, and I thought he was dead.

We staged the cancer to find out if we could detect any spread. When you're staging someone, everything is heart stopping. You never know when you're going to run into something that tells you it's all over. At one point they thought they found something in his chest. They X-rayed it ten different ways and couldn't decide. It was very frightening, but ultimately we discovered through another CAT scan that it was nothing. But the staging process is horrendous. I was petrified the whole time.

We found a doctor at a university hospital who was noted for his work in this type of cancer. We brought my son over, and the doctor said the cancer was treatable, which was a huge relief to us. My son was randomized into a big national study on this kind of cancer. This was a real interesting experience for me because I am always randomizing people into trials in my research. But now I had to randomize my son into one, which was very hard to do, because one of the limbs of this trial involved using a very toxic drug. By the grace of God, he was not randomized into that limb.

But he still went through hell, absolute hell. He lost forty pounds and his hair. For a long time he could barely talk or move or eat. He suffered excruciating pain from the radiation burns. He almost died countless times from the low white counts he had from the chemotherapy. Many times I thought, "We are killing him!" And of course we were killing him with the treatment. The question was, would we kill the tumor before we killed him? He sank so far and hurt so much, he even wanted to commit suicide at one point, and we had to find him a shrink for that. I remember I was at the hospital once, going down an elevator, and I thought, this is how I feel, that I'm just falling through space, as if the floor had been pulled from under me, and I figured I was going to crash into the ground. I'd get very depressed, very upset, and got a little crazy. My wife remained very steady, very solid, like a rock.

I guess for me the pain had a different edge to it because up to the time of my son's illness, I had spent most of my career working with tumor-causing viruses in a biochemistry lab. I was awash in these viruses, which produce tumors in animals—monkeys in particular. I undoubtedly became contaminated and carried the virus home. I'm sure it was all over my hands, my clothes, the furniture—everywhere. I was doing this while my wife was pregnant and for years after that. I was studying cancer.

But we figured it was a simian virus and was not going

to infect humans. But now we have an AIDS epidemic, and the possibility remains that the AIDS virus may have originated from the green monkey, so we're not so sure that animal viruses can't infect us or can't mutate in a way that will cause human disease. Who's to say that in some predisposed patients these viruses can't be transmitted and cause cancer?

It's also not lost on me that my son had a very rare type of tumor. I was working with a virus that produces tumors in cell cultures that were similar in many respects to the specific kind of tumor my son had. Very similar! So it's possible, even plausible, that somehow I was the cause of my son's disease.

I feel a very exquisite, special kind of guilt about that. My son is alive now and doing well, with no sign of recurrence, so I guess it's easier for me to deal with my guilt. I've talked to him very openly about this. He's a bright kid, and he understands everything I'm saying. We have a very close relationship; nothing has gotten in the way of that.

But I'm not the same. I used to think I was thirteen; I had a very young outlook on life. Even going through medical school and becoming a doctor didn't change that. I could still go out and play ball and feel thirteen. But I've aged now. I don't feel like I'm thirteen anymore. Now I'm fifty.

Most people spend their lives walling out death with denial. But when you spend your life treating cancer patients, you know one morning you can wake up with a stomachache and that's the end of it, the end of life as you know it. No more good times. Done. It is totally arbitrary. Totally out of your control. Totally chance.

Denial begins when a child has to confront a world that is uncontrollable, irrational, and all-powerful. And he somehow has to feel safe in that world. That's the thing we all solve by adopting a series of delusions. You know, if we play our cards right, we'll get our raises or our grants funded, and life will get progressively better until we get to a ripe old age and just drift away.

But those illusions are often called into question when you do what I do for a living. Every day I come to work, I walk past a bunch of victims that I know are going to die, despite all I do. There's no escape from this stress, from the constant feeling that life can all be over in an instant. It can be unbelievably distressing, and anyone who tells you it is not is a sociopath.

I spent years in group therapy sessions for physicians to help deal with the stresses of taking care of very sick patients. I spent a lot of time trying to learn the difference between grief and depression, and why horrible things happen to perfectly nice people, randomly and uncontrollably, and feeling somehow that it's my fault. I've learned to take satisfaction in the things I do well, in bringing comfort to a lot of people, even if they die horribly.

Unless you have some other outlet, you can get into a lot of emotional trouble. So some doctors become entrepreneurs or real estate agents and become something that physicians are justifiably criticized for. I think they should be criticized for those things, but I think it would be nice if people understood a little bit more why physicians get driven to that.

Taking care of AIDS patients is something I do because I am a division chief in a major university hospital, so I have to take it on. A lot of people don't want to take it on, and they don't take it on. But I didn't have much choice.

It's difficult care, very work-intensive, very hard. AIDS patients are *never* well, and they just keep coming at you. They are sick in the morning and sick at night and they get sicker until they die. It's morbid. There aren't very many victories. You get someone over a little crisis, and everybody is happy. But it's pretty devastating to the staff when the patients come back a little later with a more advanced disease and they look awful. I feel bad for the nurses because they never get a break. They spend all day every day with AIDS patients. I can at least come up for air.

The time devoted to a single AIDS patient can be extraordinary. You have to take care not only of the patient medically but of their situation as well. They tell you their dentist won't see them anymore because of AIDS, and they want to know who you can get to be their dentist. What if they're eligible for a drug that costs ten thousand dollars and they don't have it? How can you tell a patient that he ought to take AZT when he doesn't have any money to pay for it? Are you supposed to say, "Listen, you figure it out?" You can't do that. So I find myself in the clinic spending half my time taking care of people in serious medical trouble and half my time trying to solve their problems from the society around them.

For people like me who specialize in infectious disease, AIDS care is a lot different from what we've done in the past. Most infectious disease specialists do consults—they don't have a group of patients that they see on a regular basis. But once you've got an AIDS patient, you have that patient for the rest of his life, usually as a primary care physician. What's also different is that we can't cure AIDS as we can most other infectious diseases, but a major reason why many of us went into this specialty is because we could cure people. So a lot of people in my field are not prepared to do it, and many people in practice are avoiding it. They just don't want to deal with AIDS because they don't like the patients who have it, or they don't like the possibility that they will get it, or they don't like the intensity of the work involved. Even a lot of hospitals in my area won't take AIDS patients.

And on top of everything else, I go to committee meetings all the time because when you have AIDS patients in a hospital, you've got a hospital full of nervous people. One week I went to twenty-five meetings about AIDS. And once a week I sit on the governor's task force or the county task force on AIDS and hear about the laws and the confidentiality issues, and the policemen who are afraid they will get AIDS if they are bitten by prisoners, and the medical examiner who is furious at us because we don't write AIDS the way he wants to see it on death certificates.

It just keeps coming at me. And I get constantly badgered in the hospital's hallways. I get a stack of telephone messages an inch thick every day. I can't possibly answer all of them. I had a group of a hundred people waiting for me to give a lecture the other day. I missed it. I was tied up with an AIDS patient. Tomorrow I have four lectures to give—all on AIDS.

Nobody pays you to give a lecture. Nobody pays you to do a hallway consult. Nobody pays you to go to all those committee meetings. And the pay for taking care of AIDS patients is awful. Almost half of them are on Medicaid and medical assistance, and that pays very low, which is why a guy trying to make a living in private practice can't take care of AIDS patients.

*"What's also different is that we can't cure AIDS as we can most other infectious diseases, but a major reason why many of us went into this specialty is because we could cure people."*

Our fee for daily care, which includes rounding twice a day with my team, is forty-five dollars. Medical assistance pays ten. You can't make a living doing that. And yet they expect us to settle for 20 percent of our charges for a disease that is more demanding in terms of time and attention than any other. Although nobody in academic medicine really worries about earning money because we are all salaried, I have to worry about it because I'm a division chief, which means that any revenues we get are how I support the faculty.

My life used to be peaceful. Now it's chaos. I now come to work at three in the morning because it's the only time I can get my administrative work done, and I never get out before six or six thirty at night. And even though taking care of AIDS patients is incompatible with my research interests and the research interests of a lot of people in my field, we can't walk away. We cannot!

I saw more death in my first three months on an experimental pediatric oncology ward than I had in my whole three years of residency. It's hard to see anyone die, but it's very hard to see somebody young die, somebody who has not even had a chance at life.

At first I tried not to show how much it affected me. I was not openly emotional about it. I became very angry about cancer and the fact that it is such an ugly disease, so unfair to children and adolescents. The pain and hurt I felt became so severe that they began to overwhelm me. I took care of a young boy of about fifteen, a warm, lovable boy with a wonderful family. His father had died a few years earlier, and he had become the "man of the house." We tried everything we could think of, but he didn't respond, and he knew he was dying, and he was scared. But what worried him most was how well his mother would get along when he was gone. He died at home, and when he did, it hit me hard. Very hard.

I'm not unique. Every oncologist I know is affected in some way by the death he sees. I haven't consciously tried to maintain a distance from my patients because that isn't the way I want to practice medicine. I always want to be close to them and their families. But I'm not sure how much I can endure of this, and I am now planning to leave patient care, as much as I like it, and go into research so I can escape the suffering.

My assistant had been up all the night before with another delivery, so she asked me if we could get this patient delivered quickly. The woman had already begun to dilate, so I ruptured the membrane to try to speed up delivery.

Forty-five minutes later my assistant called to tell me the baby's hand had dropped down and through. I knew this was a problem. By rupturing the membrane too early, the baby's head was not engaged down in the pelvis. This allowed his hand to drop through.

I examined the woman, which I never should have done because the umbilical cord was hanging. I think my examination allowed the cord to drop down and out, too. When it did, I pushed the cord back up. Right after that, the baby's heart sounds got terrible, and although the mother had not fully dilated, I reached in and pulled the baby out with forceps. But the damage had been done, because the baby suffered severe brain damage. Unfortunately, the baby survived.

The parents didn't fault me. They thought I did a good job, but I know I never should have examined the woman after my assistant saw the baby's hand. I should have propped her up on pillows and monitored the heartbeat and never touched that cord, which I think caused the baby's distress. I think it was a double error, because I should not have used forceps, either.

I feel terrible. As a doctor, you're given a tremendous trust. This family had entrusted me to deliver their child, and I screwed up, and now they have to live with it.

I was working with a very distinguished surgeon, and we had just completed a complicated operation. He was sitting exhausted in the surgeon's room, and he asked me, "Was I all right?"

I told him, "I think you did a terrific job."

He looked up and said, "You know, I really struggled. I

wonder if I'm losing it. Can I rely on you to tell me when I am losing it? Will you promise me that?"

I told him I would.

I never had to tell him because another surgeon a couple of years later told him before a major operation, "Doctor, I think you are too tired to do this. Maybe Dr. Green ought to do it for you tomorrow." He got the message. He didn't operate from that day on.

I hope I can do what he did with that kind of grace. In some ways, being a surgeon is like being an athlete. You even have a locker room. And I've known a number of distinguished surgeons who ended their careers just like some old ballplayers, thinking they still had all the skills and judgment that they did before. I sometimes wonder if I will be able to recognize in myself when I am slipping. At what point will I throw in the sponge?

When you have a baby in an intensive care nursery and you visit him or her regularly, you begin to see little things not get done, like the baby's diaper doesn't get changed when it should, or maybe the baby's feeding is a half hour late. That's what happens in an institution, even a very well-meaning one.

And if the baby's course becomes chronic and tortuous, the mother gets a terrible, agonizing feeling that she has to be the child's advocate, that she has to be there to make sure her little baby is well cared for. I have had mothers of very sick babies stay in the nursery for months and manage to remain pleasant to the staff through all the ups and downs. The fathers don't seem to be able to deal with it. They withdraw from the situation very early on. They don't visit. And I don't know if they are even involved in hearing about the baby many times. It is just too much for them. It's very obvious that the woman is the tougher one when it comes to something like this. But many of them eventually take their child home to cope alone because their marriage has been

destroyed. Some of these women lose their husbands emotionally, and others lose them altogether.

It makes me feel ashamed sometimes, what we make
parents put up with. I could not deal with this, I know that.
The prospect of having a child in an intensive care unit fills
me with fear. If I were presented with a twenty-seven-week
premature baby, I would probably disintegrate the first day
because I know what is ahead.

I had a case of a stepfather and a kid going to the
zoo on a Sunday afternoon. They got into an argument over
whether they would see the elephants or the lions, and they
shot each other. The kid was paralyzed.

A sister and a brother had a fight, and the sister threw
lye in the brother's face, blinding him. I've seen kids raped
by their mothers' boyfriends, by their stepfathers, by their
uncle.

When you work in the emergency room in a bad neigh-
borhood of a big city, you see everything. You see people
who abuse their children. You see people who can't even
take care of the children they've already got having more
children. You see people who feel entitled to get everything
for free—not just medical care but everything. They are perfectly able to work, but they won't work. And they want
you to take care of them. You see such awful things that are
totally beyond any experience you have ever had. You ask,
"How can people live like this?"

Your liberalism goes out the window. Gone. It really
changes your attitudes about people who live in the inner
cities, about minorities. And when people are sick or in
need, they're scared, and whatever control they have is
gone. So we end up seeing life like the cops do—raw. Cops
and ER doctors get along great because each understands
what the other is going through.

One of my patients is a woman on welfare who is
always running out of money. She can't pay the bills for her

kids, and at the end of the month they barely eat. Her husband left her a few years ago. She's depressed, and she's been in psychiatric care a number of times, but she doesn't stay in because she doesn't like her psychiatrist. She's afraid to leave her house at night because of the crime.

She comes to see me a lot. I've encouraged her to, but her problems don't go away. Sometimes she can't even get out of bed, and she calls me and wants a solution, and I don't have any. I can't find a medical illness to treat. What can I do?

You're always confronted with problems you can't solve, at least in primary care. Besides dealing with this woman's dilemma, I also deal with chronic illnesses. Although I think I'm pretty good at it, I can't help these patients. All I really do is juggle their medications, try to balance off the side effects, and make their lives a little happier. I can't give them a new heart. And with cancer patients, often I make the diagnosis and then help them die. I'm not saying that's unimportant, but I am not fundamentally changing the course of an illness.

I have a patient who suffered a severe stroke. He will never walk out of the hospital. In truth, he's a vegetable. And I have to go in and see him day after day and provide him with good, ethical medical care, knowing that it makes no difference. After months of this—and I've gone through the same thing with other patients—you dread going in and seeing that patient. I reach a point where I can't take it anymore.

A lot of my practice is taken up with this kind of never-ending, insoluble problem. I feel inadequate because I can't effectively help my patients medically or with all the non-medical problems they tell me about—family problems, financial problems, social problems.

Besides this, I'm faced day after day with hospitals that aren't functioning right or something else that has been screwed up. Not long ago, I reached the point where I became too angry and frustrated to be of any use to my patients. I was taking out my anger on people who didn't deserve it. I was burned-out and I knew I needed to get away, so I took three months off and thought about things. Now I structure my professional life so that I don't put in forty-five-hour weeks as most physicians do. I do two-thirds or even half that and spend the rest of my time on other projects. I understand that I need to continue to be fresh and caring and concerned about the patients I do see.

I don't know to what extent I am typical or not. There are some doctors who seem to live for practicing medicine. Overtly, at least, they don't seem to suffer burnout. My guess is that there are fewer of that kind of doctor than there used to be. I know that when I talk to other doctors about opportunities in other areas—such as administrative health care or entrepreneurship—they all say, "If I could do something like that, I'd get out of practicing medicine immediately."

I had been seeing a patient every week for nine years. She was a young woman who was schizophrenic but functioned pretty well. As her family practitioner, I was providing her primary care. I had gotten to know her well and I cared about her, even though she could be a pain at times.

On one of her weekly visits I was in a rush to leave my office, and she asked me if she could take her diuretic for some ankle swelling. I said yes, but I told her to be sure to take an extra potassium pill for every diuretic she took. She had previously suffered a cardiac arrest from low potassium when the diuretic had flushed too much potassium out of her system.

*"It was my error, pure and simple, and I had made it because I was in a hurry. In fact, I had been rushing off to a meeting about malpractice."*

Because I was rushing, I didn't have her chart when I answered her question. She even questioned me by asking, "A whole packet every time?" I said, "Yes, take a whole packet of potassium whenever you take a diuretic."

After she went home, she took an extra diuretic or two and, just as I had told her, the potassium. The next thing I knew, she was in the hospital emergency room in cardiac arrest. She'd also suffered brain damage, and she made noises like a wild animal for weeks, nothing coherent at all.

I then realized that I had been under the impression that she had one type of potassium, when she actually had had a different dosage of potassium that was three times stronger than the type I'd thought she had. She had done exactly what I told her and put so much potassium in her body that it interfered with the electrical conduction of her heart, and she had had an arrest.

When I saw her in the intensive care unit, I was devastated. Absolutely devastated. I told her husband what I'd done, that I had told her to take the potassium incorrectly. It didn't seem to fully register with him, and that was the last that he or I said about it. After three months in the hospital, she recovered and became a human being again. She eventually returned to her previous level of functioning and is now my patient again. But it was an enormously expensive and upsetting experience for her.

It was my error, pure and simple, and I had made it because I was in a hurry. In fact, I had been rushing off to a meeting about malpractice. I could forgive myself if I had just made a mistake. I am careful and do the best I can, but I have made mistakes, including some whoppers, and I've gone up to the patients and told them what I did wrong. What I can't forgive myself for is not giving this patient the time she deserved to answer her question correctly. I had broken my code of how I deal with patients. It was a horrendous experience. I'm still whipping myself for it.

Why is it that a big segment of the public expects a physician to be an impeccable, shining individual? Human beings are not to be tolerated when it comes to doctors. If he's a human being, he's just no damned good. Why doesn't the public expect that of lawyers or teachers or policemen?

I think what happens is that when people turn to doctors, especially a surgeon like myself, they're scared. They either know or believe something is seriously wrong with them. I think they really want their doctor to be larger than life because he is the guy who is going to save their life.

Sure, doctors have contributed to the creation of that image. Who doesn't like to be lionized and looked up to? But I think the greater factor is that when people are in trouble with the most valuable possessions any of us have— our health and life—we need to believe that the guy who's going to get us through is somehow more than a human being.

But do you know what that puts on doctors, all the stress and anxiety that go with living up to that ideal that so many patients construct for us? Goddamn it! I wish the public would give us a little credit for being nothing more than human beings who have learned their profession and use what they know to try and make people better.

I'm one of those people who always wanted to be a doctor, ever since I was ten. I sawed off all my other interests in pursuit of that goal. I crammed in college to get straight As so I could get into medical school, and I did the same thing in medical school, and then in residency. In all, I spent eleven and a half years in medical training and am boarded in general and thoracic surgery.

I entered private practice thinking it would be the light at the end of the tunnel after the pure, unadulterated hell of residency. At first I enjoyed it. I was the junior surgeon in a busy private practice. Thoracic surgery is high intensity, high involvement, if you do it right—which is the only way to do it, or you'll kill the patient or be sued for malpractice. It will absorb all your time if you're an obsessive-compulsive, which you have to be in the first place to be a thoracic surgeon.

I was on call a lot, and when I was, I couldn't go out and have a drink with a friend because I could be called at any time for an emergency—a ruptured aneurysm or a gunshot wound to the chest. And I was always afraid to stay up late because the next day I might be working all day and all night.

I'm a runner, and one day it was in the nineties. I was so dehydrated, my resting pulse rate was a hundred and forty. When I walked in the door, my phone rang, and I had to rush to the hospital because a patient had a ruptured abdominal aneurysm, and I ended up being at the hospital for twenty-four hours straight. I had to sip fluids through a straw during surgery.

Inviting people over to my house and leaving in midmeal became routine. It seemed that every time I planned anything, it was interrupted. It got old very fast, as bad as my residency. It became very isolating. I almost felt in exile, cut off from my past.

If I had drawn the satisfaction from surgery that I had thought I would, I could have tolerated it. But there was so much grimness and ambiguity in what I did. In medicine, especially chest surgery, you are surrounded almost constantly by suffering and death, an endless trail of tears. I began to question whether I was doing many patients any good or not. I made some good saves and they were satisfying, but they didn't outweigh my growing dissatisfaction and uncertainty about what I was doing.

Many times I'd open a chest and find an inoperable lung tumor. Or I'd do a bypass graft on somebody's legs. They might be in the hospital for three weeks and I'd get them through, and then they'd go out and go back to smoking three packs a day, and I'd feel as if it were a waste of time. Even though I did the operation, they were no better than they were before. I didn't feel like I was curing anybody, and making the money for the surgery didn't come close to compensating for that feeling.

I had one patient with a ruptured aneurysm. He was very ill to begin with. I operated, and he ended up with multisystem failure and eventually died after three weeks on the respirator. He suffered a lot, and so did his family. I also suffered and did a lot of soul searching.

There were so many patients like this. One man was in his fifties—a nice man, a real fighter—who came to me with a lot of problems. He ended up undergoing multiple operations. He developed every complication possible and eventually died of heart failure and infection. His wife was torn apart. She wanted it to end because she didn't want her husband to suffer. I thought over everything I did with this patient, and I could medically justify every step I had taken, but I still felt like a hatchet man and questioned what I was doing to patients under the guise of medical care.

My ability to exercise my medical judgment was also curtailed by the economic pressure of the practice. A local internist referred a man in his late seventies with claudication, a blockage in one of his legs. I worked him up and found he had serious cardiac problems. I'd seen too many people have heart attacks or strokes right on the OR table because they have big-time coronary disease like this man. In my opinion, surgery was too risky.

I sent the patient back to the internist and explained this in a nice way, and he seemed to understand. But my senior partner was upset that I had decided not to operate. He argued that this was a subtle insult to the internist, and he was afraid the internist wouldn't refer to our office anymore if we continued this. My senior partner was a good surgeon and wasn't unethical, but he had a real desire to make money. I had gone into private practice thinking—naïvely, I guess—that one does what one thinks is medically correct. But he was more concerned about the business side than I was.

I knew I couldn't go on like this. I was making more money than I knew what to do with, and I had achieved my dream of being a doctor, but it was becoming intolerable to me. I felt I was living in a nightmarish present, with a future that looked much the same. When I talked to my senior partner about this, his only message was, shape up or ship out. I thought of going to another practice or back to academic medicine, but I knew it would not be substantially different from what I was doing. There would still be the ambiguity and the grimness.

I began to feel that I could not be happy being a doctor, but I didn't know what in the world I would do. I felt trapped. I began to look into the ministry. I took some night courses at a local seminary and enjoyed them tremendously, and I began to think of going into the ministry.

As I considered leaving medicine, it did seem to me to be a waste of my talents and training. I had always thought I was a good and conscientious physician, so I went through endless self-questioning. Is this my fault? Wouldn't it be different somewhere else? When I finally decided I had to leave, I experienced stages of grief. I'd be sitting in the ICU, taking care of a patient, and I'd become sad thinking I wouldn't be doing this anymore. It took a while to work that through.

I quit the practice and began going to the seminary full time. I had several other good job offers to practice surgery but turned them down. I went to work part time with a local emergency room group to pay my bills. There are a lot of refugees from other specialties in emergency medicine. You work regular hours, you aren't on call, and most of the medical problems you deal with are minor. The only thing that helps me stay in medicine at all right now is my theological training, which is energizing and helps make up for the emotional drain of medicine.

There may be some way I can creatively link the medical with the theological someday, but I don't think I'm going to be in active practice when I finish my theological training. I've thought it over and over, and I always come to the same conclusion. I don't want to be there anymore.

✐ Nobody wants to perform abortions after ten weeks because by then you see the features of the baby, hands, feet. It's really barbaric.

Abortions are very draining, exhausting, and heart-rending. There are a lot of tears. Some patients turn on you. They say, "Let's get out of here," after the abortion, as if you're some dirty person. It's vicious. Then you get these teenyboppers in the office who laugh their way through it. It doesn't mean a thing to them. That bothers me. Then you've got the right-to-lifers calling you on the phone, coming in the office, preaching, threatening to picket your office.

*"I've delivered enough babies, seen enough divorces, and seen enough abused kids to do abortions with a clear conscience."*

I do them because I take the attitude that women are going to terminate babies and deserve the same kind of treatment as women who carry babies. So I started doing abortions on an altruistic basis. I've done a couple thousand, and it turned into a significant financial boon, but I also feel I've provided an important service.

The only way I can do an abortion is to consider only the woman as my patient and block out the baby. I've delivered enough babies, seen enough divorces, and seen enough abused kids to do abortions with a clear conscience. This may be some kind of mental gymnastics on my part, but I really feel that parenthood is so tough that people shouldn't back into it.

I don't feel I'm violating my trust as a doctor by doing abortions, but I don't want to do them anymore because you can do them to a certain point, and then you get overloaded. I'm at that point.

✐    I was in the second or third month of my pregnancy, working in the emergency room. I had an elderly patient in respiratory distress, and we needed a portable chest X ray in the ER. The X-ray technician came in, and she was this snitty young woman.

She told me to hold the patient because she wasn't sitting up straight. I said, "I don't want to get near the X-ray machine because I'm pregnant."

She said, "This little amount of radiation won't matter."

We had to have the X ray quickly, so there I was, during my child's embryonic development, holding up this patient. I wasn't directly in the X-ray beam, but I was scared about it. Well, my son was born two months premature and had two serious congenital abnormalities of his penis, which had to be corrected surgically, and he also had bilateral inguinal hernias.

I can't help wondering if that incident or some other exposure to an infectious agent in the hospital might have been the cause. I have found among my medical colleagues what seems to me to be an abnormally high incidence of illness and congenital malformations in their children. There have been published articles in medical journals about the high incidence of abnormalities in the offspring of hospital workers, nurses, lab technicians, nurses' aides—anyone in contact with patients and patient materials.

You can't help but feel deficient as a parent when this happens because your role is to protect your child, and here you are dragging him off to multiple surgical procedures, exposing him to anesthesia risks and other risks that you may be responsible for. You feel guilty and incredibly helpless.

Sometimes trying to save a baby's life can last for months, even years. Families run out of hope. They finally ask me, "When is enough enough?" They're frustrated and worried. It isn't that they want to put a pillow over the baby's head; they just stop coming to the nursery to see the baby. I think that's their way of saying, "We've had enough."

It's so hard dealing with these families because as a doctor I would like to tell them, if not good news, at least a solution. You know, "This is what we're going to do, and this is what the end point is going to be." But I can't because I don't have any answers, so I do everything I can to save the baby.

Some of these families are wonderful. I talk with them for hours and become emotionally involved with them and go home every night very upset because things are so terrible for them, and I know I can't make a difference. I think that's the feeling that bothers me most—knowing I can't make it better for people I think deserve it. Sometimes I would like to do a baby shuffle: take the nice healthy babies from the families who don't seem to care and give them to the families who care so much but can't have their baby.

I sometimes wonder what we're really doing here when we send home a baby who's going to spend the rest of his life blind and retarded, and you know that family is suffering. That's why I have a serious problem with people who think they have to pass laws to stop doctors from willy-nilly killing babies in the nursery. I think people who mandate that we need to have life at any cost should know what it is really like to have life at any cost. These people need to know how hard it is to care for these children. I'd like to see some of these right-to-lifers take one of these chronically ill, severely damaged babies home and see how much it costs them, see how much it takes out of them, see how few facilities and people there are to take care of these children after we save them.

✍     I had operated on a man three times and had gotten
to know him so well that he became a friend. He was sixty, a
wonderful guy, full of spirit, a salt-of-the-earth type of fellow. He had serious circulatory obstruction in his leg caused
by atherosclerosis. I had put in a bypass graft five years
earlier, but it clotted and he came in with an extremely
painful foot because of lack of blood flow. I didn't want to
amputate his leg, so I said, "We've got to give it one more
crack before we quit."

When I opened up his leg, I tried to find an artery
somewhere in his thigh to which I could attach a bypass and
bring circulation to the lower leg. I searched and searched
and finally I found a very small artery and thought I could
attach the bypass there. But then when I tried to open the
old existing graft I had put in, I couldn't get the blood clots
out of it. I should have quit right there because this meant
that I had to re-operate on the upper part of that earlier
bypass graft. This was a *major* operation. And in retrospect,
I don't think that the little artery I had used for the bypass
would have carried enough blood flow to the leg.

After the surgery, this fellow developed gangrene of
that leg, which was followed by the failure of the other leg.
He was losing circulation in leaps and bounds. He clotted
everything.

He ended up with amputations of both his legs; then he
developed kidney failure and had to go on dialysis. He was
fully with it, knew everything that was going on, yet still
had a kind of blind trust and faith despite everything that
we were doing to him. But he kept slipping and died after he
was in the hospital for about six weeks of pure hell. It was
an absolute horror story.

I classify my patients who die into three categories. The
first are those who die from clear-cut errors in technique, in
which something I do falls apart. The second is those who
die from overwhelming patient disease, where no matter

what I do, the case is hopeless. The third category is those who die from my own errors in judgment. This case was my error, and that is what I said at the mortality and morbidity conference, which is kind of a confessional for physicians.

There is no good surgeon who can't think of something that he should have done differently at some time. When you make a mistake like this, it just stays with you. I can now see that I had become too attached to the man's leg rather than to the patient. I was too protective of the earlier operations I had performed, and I wanted to make them work. It was a hard thing for me to quit on because of all I had invested in that leg.

There is no question in my own mind that I should have quit when I could not find decent arterial outflow in the thigh area. Then the next morning when he was awake, I would have told him that we had lost and that we needed to do an amputation. He had a strong family and a lot of determination, and he would have done all right with the amputation. I think if I had done that, he would be alive today. The only thing positive to come out of something like that is that it teaches you never to do it again.

My sister was voted most outstanding in her high school class. She was talented, athletic, attractive—a really outstanding person, and the sibling to whom I felt closest. She graduated from college and had done some work toward a doctorate. She married and went to live in Hawaii. Her husband had some financial reversals, and her marriage fell apart. She also began to drink a lot and to suffer from schizophrenia. We had both alcoholism and mental illness in our family history, and in her the combination proved terrible.

She returned home from Hawaii to visit my parents for Christmas, and at that point she was hearing voices, and a voice told her to kill our mother. So she got a big kitchen knife and stabbed my mother, who was a wonderful mother and a fascinating person, right through the heart. My father, who was also a doctor, was two rooms away and ran in and saw this horrible, bloody scene. My sister put the knife down and said, "God told me to do it." At this point my father was trying vainly to resuscitate my mother, who had died almost instantly.

In one moment my father was faced with the loss of both his wife and his daughter. He was a super helper, someone totally devoted to medicine and saving lives, but he found himself helpless to save two of the people he loved most deeply.

My sister was taken to jail, and my father was more shaken than I'd ever seen him. This was something he could not fix. He had never ever expressed words of sadness or fear in his life before this, and now he was crying virtually all the time.

Six days after my mother's murder, Dad was preparing to testify before a grand jury. We were in the district attorney's office when he had a heart attack and died right in my arms. I did everything I could do medically, and we got him to an emergency room, but I couldn't bring my dad back. I had been trained to be the great fixer, a medical star, but I couldn't save my father, whom I loved more than any person in my life.

My sister was found innocent by reason of insanity and was sent to a mental hospital. A few months later, she was given a one-day, unescorted pass to go into the city. She never returned, and I became worried because she had said God told her to kill me and my first child. Sometime later, they found her body in the river. She had leaped off a bridge and killed herself.

I got a call at three in the morning that a twenty-four-year-old woman had come into the emergency room. This was the middle of the flu season, and the junior resident told me he thought she looked blue and dusky. As senior resident, I was in control of admitting patients, so I left the residents' quarters and went across the street to the hospital.

I looked at her in the ER, and she did appear dusky blue. Her lungs looked reasonably clear on X ray, but her blood gases, which measured her blood's oxygen content, were terrible. They were so bad that I thought blood had been drawn from a vein instead of an artery. I drew some more blood and ran it up to the lab, and the blood gases were just as bad in this one as in the first one, but this time I knew the blood came from an artery.

I admitted her to the unit, but I still did not believe she was very sick. I thought she had the flu, and of course I had no memory or knowledge of how serious earlier influenza epidemics had been. I only admitted her because of her blood gas readings. I had even convinced myself that the fluorescent lights might have given her the dusky blue color.

After I took her up to the unit, I ran another blood gas, and it was still terrible so I put her on a little oxygen. Then I told the junior resident that I didn't think she was all that sick and to check on her when he had a chance. Her husband and parents were in the waiting room talking to her attending physician, who was telling them she was gravely ill. But when the family asked me how she was doing, I told them she looked all right to me.

I returned to her room. She told me she had a lot of pain in her side. That didn't sound alarming to me, so I prescribed some morphine and went back home. I hadn't been out of the hospital for five minutes before I had a stat page to return. I rushed back and found this woman in full arrest. They were pumping on her chest, but they could not resuscitate her, and she died.

It turned out that she had had horrendous influenza pneumonia. Her pain had been caused when something ruptured in her lung, causing air to escape and get trapped between her lung and chest wall and collapsing her lung. I had completely misjudged how sick she'd been.

We talked about her at the mortality and morbidity rounds and at the infectious disease rounds. We must have had ten reviews of her case. Every time I saw her X rays and her blood gases put up on the screen, I wanted to look away.

No one ever stood up and yelled, "You're a fool," at me. They didn't have to. They all knew how much this upset and depressed me. I couldn't get her out of my mind at all for weeks. Almost all the experts who reviewed her case thought this young woman probably would have died no matter what we did, but that was by their standards, not mine.

She was only twenty-four, and I keep thinking, if only I'd stayed with her she'd be alive. If only I had put her on the respirator, then at least I would be comforted by the knowledge that I had done everything I could for her.

*Part of my work is designing trials for new drugs, which means I get involved in the introduction of a new drug into human subjects.

This one drug had been developed years earlier as an anticancer drug but had been found to have no antitumor activity, so they shelved it. But they brought it out again to test its antiviral activity. It appeared to be effective against hepatitis B. Because I'm a gastroenterologist, which involves the liver, I was asked by one of the major teaching institutions to look at it. I examined the data and found that there was some central nervous system toxicity in the animal studies, but it had also been given to a limited number of cancer patients in high doses and they apparently had suffered no such effects.

I designed a trial for this drug for people with chronic, active hepatitis B. These are people whose livers are slowly deteriorating. I happened to be talking to a friend of mine who had to leave his practice of surgery because he had had a needle stick and developed chronic hepatitis B. Because of the risk to the patient—surgeons breach their gloves all the time when they operate—he couldn't be a surgeon anymore. So he had reluctantly taken an administrative job.

"I want to be your first subject," he told me.

He lived in another city, but we arranged it, and he signed the informed consent agreement. While he was getting the drug, cases were reported from a center in Texas that two patients had died from a stupor-coma death syndrome—central nervous system deaths—while taking the same experimental drug.

We told my friend this and asked him, "Are you sure you want to continue?"

He said, "Yes, give it to me."

We gave it to him, and two months later while I was visiting him, I noticed he had a foot drop.

"What's going on?" I asked him.

"Oh, I got a little weakness, a little numbness in my hands and feet. Nothing."

A month later he was in intensive care because all his neurological functions had collapsed. He was so bad, he couldn't breathe for himself and they had to put him on a respirator. It was almost surely drug related.

We still don't know how he's going to turn out, and it's been many months since he became so sick. He's off the respirator now, but he can't eat because he vomits everything. So he gets his nutrition intravenously. He has no use of his legs or his left arm. It's been terrible, just terrible, to see a very bright doctor who knows what is going on reduced to this.

I feel guilty about it. If he hadn't been a friend of mine, he probably would never have taken the drug. I can tell myself that he had chronic hepatitis that was likely to chew up his liver to the point of killing him. And it had destroyed his career as a surgeon. So there was a high ante for trying to cure him. But that can't erase the sadness I feel about him.

I visit him and talk to him. He says, "Look. I wanted it. I knew there were risks. Don't flagellate yourself." But it is uncomfortable to carry this around. It's an object lesson of what can happen in drug development.

The patient was a child from Belgium who had come to our center for complicated heart surgery. He seemed to do fine immediately after the surgery, but very early in the morning he developed some problems that I felt were caused by blood collecting around the heart. It collects in the pericardium, the sac which surrounds the heart, and constricts the heart contractions. It is called pericardial tamponade.

The child was still unconscious, so I opened his chest in the intensive care area—the same opening we had used earlier to operate. There wasn't any blood in the pericardium, but I saw that his heart blood flow was impeded in one of his ventricles. Pressure was building inside his heart, and now that his chest was opened, his heart began blowing up like a balloon right in front of me.

I couldn't get his chest back together, and I kept pouring saline on the heart and trying to empty the ventricle of blood, but I just couldn't stop it. Right in front of me his heart got bigger and bigger and finally it ruptured. It split open just like a watermelon. Blood exploded all over my face, the wall, the nurse, and the bed, and the child just died right in front of my eyes.

I had to go tell the chief, who was a demanding taskmaster. It was about six thirty in the morning, so I went down to the hospital garage to wait for him at his parking spot. He always got there at six thirty, and when he arrived I told him. And I thought he was going to get in his car and drive home and chop wood all day long. That's what he usually did when a child died on his service. He would just cancel his cases for the rest of the day. Even when he performed an exquisite operation and the child died, he always considered it a failure.

For whatever reason, that day he didn't go home. He just sort of looked at me and said, "What's on the schedule for today?" I told him both of us had to work all day long on two other hearts.

He didn't beat on me. He knew I was beating on myself pretty hard. I wish I had not opened that young boy's chest. I think if I hadn't, the child would have died anyway because of his ventricular problem. But that's the only consolation I have.

Probably the hardest part of my work as a general practitioner is having to work at the limits of my competence. Three or four times a day I have to do something that I really am not exactly sure how to do or take care of people when I'm not quite sure what is going on. Every night when I go home, there will be three or four patients out there in the hospital or somewhere in the community who could possibly blow up on me. And that's just the way I feel about them—that something I have done could come apart.

I've never talked to patients about these feelings. It's too threatening to me. It brings up my own uncertainty about being a doctor, and I'm not sure how they would feel about me. A newspaper columnist once wrote that everybody thinks it's good for doctors to share their feelings and be open, but my doctor should be someone who really knows his stuff. We want our physician to be somebody who is very certain.

For all I know, I could really be off the curve, I could just be one doctor who shouldn't be practicing medicine for thinking like this. There is no way of checking it out because doctors don't talk about their mistakes or about this level of uncertainty. If a doctor is open, he may tell you about one case that was awful, but the conversation stops. He'll never tell you about sixty others that didn't get quite that far because he wasn't sure what he was doing.

Even to mention the notion of acceptable error is foreign to doctors because no errors are acceptable. They almost freak out when you talk to them about how many or

what kind of mistakes are acceptable, because we're taught
from medical school on that no mistakes are acceptable. In
our training every patient is examined a minimum of four
times by different people. Charts are reviewed three or four
times. Residents go to the library to read medical journals
about the case. You are inculcated with this sense that everything is done perfectly and mistakes are not tolerated.
And if a mistake is caught, there is a dressing down by
whomever is next up in the pecking order. We use *LMD* for
"local medical doctor" in our mortality and morbidity conferences as a term of scorn to characterize some jerk out
there who sent in his patient without ever knowing what
killed the patient.

The best doctor I know once said, "I don't think you
can be a good doctor without being a little bit of a sociopath." He meant that you have to be willing to blame other
people when things go wrong to avoid blaming yourself. I
think this is what is happening when doctors try to blame
patients for their illnesses. If the patient gets better, the doctor is delighted and they both feel good. But if the patient
gets worse, the doctor has to somehow make the patient
responsible because there are only two possible options.

But it seems that mistakes and uncertainty are intrinsic
to medicine. Somebody ought to be doing research on what
level of uncertainty produces mistakes, or how many mistakes it's normal for doctors to make. But we don't have
anything that tells us what incompetence is or what is the
difference between a mistake and incompetence. All these
things are totally murky when you're out in practice, left for
the individual practitioner to kind of work out on his own.

So it ends up that doctors often make these judgments
based on their own personality, and I happen to be a personality type that looks at what I do very suspiciously.

✒  I knew that the patient going into surgery had no
better than a fifty-fifty chance of making it. She was a sixty-

six-year-old woman who had had at least two heart attacks, and the catheterization lab results showed that besides a blown mitral valve and severe blockages in her coronary artery, she also was in congestive failure. The drugs we had given her weren't stabilizing her condition, and I knew she'd never leave the hospital alive unless we tried surgery. A lot of heart surgeons I know would have refused to operate on her. We're judged on our statistics, and the most important one is how many people you lose in surgery. If you take enough tough cases, your statistics can end up looking pretty bad, and that makes you look bad. That's one of the problems with our profession—everything has gotten so damned quantitative that we sometimes forget what our job is.

We brought her up to surgery at about four in the afternoon, only a couple of hours after she'd left the cath lab. There was no question we had an emergency on our hands with this woman. I had to put in three bypasses and a new mitral valve. Just as we opened her chest, the ST wave on her electrocardiogram peaked and at the same time her blood pressure dropped. I was pretty certain she was having another heart attack right there on the table. We finished hooking her up to the heart-lung machine as fast as we could to take the load off her heart and minimize as much as we could any more heart damage, but I knew her chances had sunk even further.

At about midnight, eight hours after we had begun, the surgery was finished. I've always thought that a surgeon at times needs almost as much stamina as skill. Standing over someone for eight or ten hours cutting and sewing can wear you down. The operation had gone beautifully, but when we warmed her blood and unclamped her aorta to get her heart started again, it wouldn't beat. I glanced over at the EKG, and it appeared to be normal. Finally her right heart began to pump, but her left heart—the side that had taken all the damage—just quivered, like jello shaking in a bowl. We tried everything we could to get it going, but it still wouldn't beat.

It was a total, abject failure of her heart, something we call electrical-mechanical disassociation, which means that the heart's electrical activity is normal but does not translate into mechanical pumping. It also meant the woman was dead, medically and legally.

I hated the idea of quitting on her. I thought there was an outside chance that her left heart was only stunned from all the diagnostic tests we'd run on her and the surgery itself rather than permanently damaged from her heart attacks. I wanted to try the left heart bypass device on her. This was new to our hospital and had never been used on a patient before. It works on the same principle as the heart-lung machine, but instead of bypassing the entire heart, it just bypasses the left side. We were in the OR until 2 A.M. hooking it up, and then we wheeled the woman to the intensive care unit. I knew that if her left heart didn't start beating in forty-eight to seventy-two hours, it never would. That's what all the studies have shown so far, anyway. I told all this to the woman's daughter and husband. I didn't pull any punches or try to give them false hope. I think people want honesty from their doctors, and that's what I try to give.

The next three days were probably the hardest I have ever endured professionally. The day after surgery, there was still not a flicker of life in her left heart. I knew that her chances of coming off that bypass device were just about nil, and I knew I would have to turn it off sometime. I had turned off ventilators for people who were brain dead before. It's tough, but you do it knowing that whoever that person was is gone. This was different. This woman had a good brain. She could think and feel and see, but her heart was gone. She'd blink her eyes and write notes to us in the ICU. She recognized her daughter and husband. You knew there was a person there.

We had taken this woman about as far as medical technology could and had extended her life beyond the time it was really over. On the one hand, it's wonderful that we have machines that can do all this, but on the other, it makes our work harder and harder. We're really off into an area where we don't have any rules because we're not sure what we're dealing with. The line between life and death can become very confusing.

The thought that I would have to turn off the machine on that woman haunted me. I could think of little else for those three days, and it got worse as the deadline drew near. Even as I was performing surgery on other patients, I thought about her. People think doctors are somehow inured to death, but we're not.

Three days after I put the woman on the left heart bypass device, I knew we had to take her off. Her family came in to see her in the ICU. They knew it was the end, but they didn't say good-bye to her or in any way let her know her life was ending. We tried everything we could to get that left heart to kick in—stimulants, drugs to get her heart to contract, dopamine—but nothing worked. Then we gradually turned down the bypass device in our final attempt to see if the heart would take over its pumping function. We all knew it wouldn't, but we had to give it this one final try. Even though she was heavily sedated, you could see life slip away from her.

One of the young doctors working with me had grown attached to the patient. She began to cry a little, and she asked me if it was easier to lose patients in the operating room than this way. I told her it was never easy.

Any neurosurgeon who's honest will admit that he's on edge when driving to work in the morning before an operation. He's also doing some praying. We all know that things can go wrong. It's not like taking a car motor apart. There, if you strip a bolt, you get another one.

But we're dealing with delicate tissues, separating a tumor from a blood vessel in the brain or peeling a tumor off of the optic nerve—places where a mistake means the patient won't survive, or will end up like a vegetable, or will be blind. So you're constantly on edge, constantly tense, and a lot of times you're really not sure where you are in the brain, whether you're in the area that controls speech or somewhere else. Most neurosurgeons are prepared for the strain, and if they're not, they retire early.

Every patient, including me, is scared to death before surgery. But I don't think patients understand what the surgeon goes through, the stresses we feel. Partly that's our own fault, because after surgery we tell the patient that everything went fine. And of course before you operate, you don't want to give the patient the impression that you're really worried.

She was a beautiful little girl from the Midwest who had developed normally in the early months of life, but a spinal cord tumor caused her intense pain. As the tumor grew, she could no longer walk, and finally she couldn't even crawl.

She was fifteen months old when her family came to me. I knew before I began that this would be especially risky surgery, but I also knew she had a grim prognosis if I didn't operate. I felt I had to try, and when I finished, she looked like one of the ones who walk away. But a little later, I got a call that she was not moving her legs. That's the worst possible news. I knew then that she would never walk . . . because I had made a slip somewhere during surgery and injured her spinal cord. Then I had to face her family— lovely, religious people—and tell them that their little daughter's legs would be permanently paralyzed.

Operating on spinal cord tumors is the most exhausting and demanding procedure I do. Operating on the brain is much less demanding. Spinal cord surgery is difficult because the cord is so delicate that the slightest error can cause permanent paralysis. That happens in about five percent of the cases I do. That may not sound like a lot, but I operate on one hundred of these kids a year, which means that every eight or nine weeks disaster strikes. It's the one procedure where I don't allow a resident to operate. If a mistake is going to be made, I want to take responsibility for making it.

*"Of course, I'm very happy when a little child who came to me paralyzed goes home walking on both legs, or writes me at Christmas to tell me how well he or she is doing. That keeps me going."*

But the hardest part of my work isn't the technical or intellectual commitment to it; it's the emotional commitment I feel for my patients and their families, and the utter desolation I feel when I fail them, as I did with this little girl. The victories I forget. Of course, I'm very happy when a little child who came to me paralyzed goes home walking on both legs, or writes me at Christmas to tell me how well he or she is doing. That keeps me going. But the five percent that I fail with stick in my guts because I know I made a wrong movement somewhere.

I try to protect myself against the hurt of these failures as much as I can. I never allow myself to get emotionally close to the patients or their families before surgery. I even refuse to go into the operating room until the child is asleep. I just can't face it! They scream and cry and are in pain, and I have to handle all that I handle, and I can't bear to hear them suffering. If I'm in a room where a pediatrician is taking blood from a child, I walk out because I don't want to hear that child cry. I love children. That's why I became a pediatric neurosurgeon. But it upsets me too much to see them hurt. I won't even take splinters out of my own children. My wife has to do it because I can't handle it.

I finished an operation on a beautiful, two-and-a-half-year-old boy—another risky case. After I finished, some OR nurses rushed over to me and asked me how he was going to do. These were experienced, strong-minded nurses, and their faces were all distraught. I told them I thought he was going to do fine, and then they told me he had come into the OR holding his doll, patting it, and saying, "It's going to be all right."

I just about broke down when they told me that. I am so glad I wasn't there to see him do that because it would have destroyed me. It's only after surgery that I can allow myself to get close to the children and their families.

*"Admitted or not, the fact remains that a few patients kindle aversion, fear, despair, or even downright malice in their doctors."*

"Taking Care of the Hateful Patient"
*New England Journal of Medicine*
April 20, 1978

*"Practicing medicine would be a great life if it weren't for patients."*

An old joke still told by doctors

# 5

# Patients

Patients evoke any and all emotional responses from doctors. They amuse, for one. A psychiatrist told the story of a man who came to his office complaining of severe stress. The psychiatrist asked why. The patient explained that it resulted from an attack by a lion. The psychiatrist asked where the attack had occurred. The patient told him it had happened while he was walking downtown. The patient and the psychiatrist live in a big city, so the psychiatrist thought the patient was delusional. The patient sensed that and took off his shirt to show his scars.

"It turned out that this guy's story was absolutely true." The psychiatrist laughed. "He was walking downtown when he felt this big weight on his shoulder. He immediately thought some drunk had stumbled into him, so he turned around. He was staring into the face of a full-grown African lioness. He could even smell her hot breath.

"What happened was that some gas station owner had kept the lion in the station. He'd left the door open, and the lion escaped and wandered downtown, where she jumped on this guy."

There are patients who vex. One doctor I spoke with had just seen a patient who came to his office with two problems. The first was that he believed he had a melanoma, a virulent form of cancer that arises on the skin but can spread throughout the body. The second problem was that this man had a phobia about doctors and adamantly refused to allow the doctor to examine his suspected melanoma. Caught in an ethical dilemma, the doctor didn't know what to do.

Patients provide a never-ending display of the human condition. They are the sources of doctors' greatest professional rewards and often of their biggest frustrations.

Doctors fit patients into categories. There are the self-pitiers, the help-rejecting "crocks," the dependent clingers, the self-destructive deniers, and the entitled demanders, to name some of the major groups. There are even some patients who, for lack of a better name, can be called sexually alluring. Many doctors I spoke with admitted to being attracted to patients of the opposite sex, and some even admitted to acting on it.

> *"Many doctors I spoke with admitted to being attracted to patients of the opposite sex, and some even admitted to acting on it."*

"I think it's improper for a doctor to see a patient socially for the purposes of romance," one doctor said, "because of the great imbalance of power between doctor and patient. But I have been attracted sexually to some patients, as I'm sure most doctors have, and in one instance I did ask a woman out after she was no longer my patient. I think that was proper, but I know of doctors who don't play by those rules."

Different doctors have different styles with patients. Some are manipulative, others are authoritarian, and others act only as advisers and encourage the patients to make their own decisions after they have laid out the facts. Some doctors also adopt different styles to suit different patients.

"Some patients want you to tell them what they should do, and others bristle if you even try, so you figure out each patient and try to adapt your approach to their personality," an internist said. "Of course, there are some doctors who don't give a damn about the patient's personality and are authoritarian with all of them. Their patients either love them or hate them."

Like any relationship, that between doctor and patient is nurtured by mutual trust and respect—commodities that seem to be diminishing on both sides.

I get a call in the emergency room. It's some guy with a southern accent. He tells me he's a sheriff from somewhere in Texas and that his brother-in-law is coming into the hospital soon. He says his brother-in-law is a deaf-mute and has a painful kidney stone. He tells me he's had them before, and he asks me to treat him right. He explains that he is calling me because the guy's wife has just had twins.

"You've got to tell him that," he says.

I said great, and I tell the nurses, and they get all excited that we're going to give this guy such great news. A few minutes later, in rolls this guy doubled over in pain, moaning and moaning. I ask him if he has a kidney stone, and he nods. And one of the nurses tells him, "Your wife just had twins." He smiles and looks real happy.

We give him pain medication, Demerol, and he begins to feel better, and then we tell him we are going to get a pyelogram on him—a test to run a dye through him and see what is going on with his kidneys. He writes out a note that he is allergic to the dye, so we can't do it. Of course, because this guy is a deaf-mute whose wife has had twins, we can't do enough for him. We treat him like royalty.

We admit him to the urology service and put him on the ward, but we notice after a little while that every time his pain medication is about due, he orders it right away. This goes on for a couple of days, and we all get very suspicious of this guy. We try to locate his brother-in-law, the sheriff, but we can't find him. We do some checking and discover our deaf-mute is an escapee from the local mental hospital. He's also a drug addict. He'd concocted this idea to get into our hospital and get drugs. He also isn't a deaf-mute. Turns out, he's the "sheriff."

🖋 I grew up helping my uncle, who was a doctor in a poor area. On Saturdays I'd act as his receptionist or clean up the office. From this experience I developed the idea of helping poor people, so when I came out of my medical training, I chose to work in an emergency room in an inner-city hospital. I've been there a few years, and I've reached a point where I don't feel I'm helping anything; I feel I'm just perpetuating things. So I treat someone's venereal infection. So what? They're just going to go out and do it again.

Patients who really get on my nerves are sexually active adolescent girls, sixteen-year-olds who've been pregnant five times and keep getting venereal infections. They're such a drain on the health care system, I want them to die.

I tell them, "You ever think about using birth control?" And they answer, "Pills are dangerous." I tell them there are other methods, but if I get too outspoken, they become sullen, and I can't reach them at all.

I feel the same way about alcoholics or drug addicts. They lie all the time. When they come in with a bad drug reaction like palpitations from cocaine and they're very anxious about it, I could give them Valium to help them relax. But if I know they're not in a life-threatening situation, I let them suffer. Maybe they'll remember.

🖋 I was moonlighting in an emergency room near Philadelphia when this big, fat woman came in and complained of abdominal pains. She was huge, about forty years old. I examined her belly, and I felt this rock-hard thing in there, and I thought, oh my God, she's got a tumor.

I sent her over to X ray, and they came back with a report that they had found a Coke bottle in her abdomen. I thought they were playing a joke on me, so I walked over there, and there was this big crowd of people around the X-ray light box, and I looked at it, and sure enough, there was the outline of a Coke bottle right there. You couldn't miss it.

I went over to her and told her there appeared to be a Coke bottle in her abdomen. She didn't seem fazed when I told her that. She admitted to masturbating with the bottle. I told her we would have to operate to get the bottle out, and she agreed. She apparently had pushed so hard on the bottle that it had gone through the posterior wall of her vagina. Quite a trick with a family-size bottle.

I operated on an adolescent boy who had a brain tumor. I was able to get it all out and the operation went well. During his recovery in the hospital, he was a little weak on his right side, so he kept his right arm kind of folded against his chest. And because the tumor was on the left side of the brain, he also had a speech impediment.

He was a kind of bizarre boy to begin with, and he loved walking around the hospital corridor with no head bandage, so his head was shaved like a ball and had this long row of stitches. A weird sight. He would always say to me that he wanted to be a neurosurgeon.

While he was in the hospital, I had another patient come in from a foreign country, a young girl. Her family had come over with her, and on the night they arrived, I went to her room to talk with her and her family. When I got there, I found they'd suddenly fled the hospital. All of them were gone without a trace. I couldn't figure out what the hell had happened.

I looked around and finally found this young boy. He had on a white house officer's coat; a stethoscope was hanging out of one pocket, he had no bandage on his head, and his arm was all bent up. It turned out that he had gone to the foreign girl's room and told the family he was a neurosurgical resident who'd come to work up their child.

We located the family and convinced them to come back. I still see that young boy. Every time I do, we laugh about it.

We had a guy in his midsixties brought in who had been riding his motorcycle one Sunday morning at about eight o'clock and ran into a parking meter. He suffered very bad injuries. He had been quite sober; he might have had a heart attack before the accident.

He had a head injury and was in a coma. We kept him in the intensive care unit, where he became jaundiced because of liver failure. He was completely unresponsive for weeks, and the nurses thought he was brain dead. They kept him in one of those cubicles where they keep people they've given up on. Everybody was down on him, and I held conferences with the nurses to reenergize them to care for this guy. Our medical director came around every day, and he seemed amazed that we had kept this guy in intensive care for so long. The clear implication was, why are we doing so much for this guy when he isn't going to make it anyhow?

I told him I was surprised to hear him say that. I said I've got the resources, and this patient has got the potential to function again. I mean, you give a broken leg three months to heal, but people get disappointed when the brain, which is a whole lot more complex than a bit of bone, doesn't respond in a couple of weeks. We're dealing with so many intangibles here.

After about eight weeks, this guy came out of his coma. He had a complete recovery. After he was discharged, he came back to thank everyone for taking care of him. As he walked through the door, he was flipping peanuts in the air and catching them in his mouth.

A patient came for an office visit, a middle-aged man whose daughter had a fatal form of cancer. He told me he felt a lump on himself that was similar to the one his daughter had noticed on herself when she had discovered her cancer.

Feeling this lump really heightened the anxiety and depression the man was already feeling. I examined him and knew the lump was benign, but I also knew that the man was feeling all of these terrible emotions. I really felt that I should take some time with him and talk things through, but I had other patients waiting to see me.

A lot of nasty things are said about doctors because we are always late—that we're rude and arrogant because we keep patients waiting. I'm very sensitive to that and try to run on time, but it's not always possible. Sometimes I see a patient like this man for what I think is going to be a routine call, and I find out it isn't routine. Am I supposed to tell him his time is up when I know he's suffering and wants to talk? If I did that, I'd be called uncaring and insensitive to his needs.

So I did talk with him because I thought I could help him, and maybe the patients who had to wait awhile were angry with me.

The one thing I kept telling myself was that this was a seventy-year-old man with a gunshot wound. I didn't dwell on the fact that he also happened to be the President of the United States. The emergency room was controlled chaos. It was almost deafening at times. I knew I would have to operate when we couldn't stop his chest bleeding, and I could tell by the rich, red color of the blood seeping out of his chest that it came from an artery. I knew that if we kept waiting, he'd bleed to death.

I told him I'd have to operate, and he said for me to do whatever I had to do. We wheeled him up to the operating room. As we were ready to put him to sleep, he made his famous remark, "I hope all you guys are Republicans." It was another surgeon, a liberal Democrat, who said, "Today we're all Republicans, Mr. President."

After we opened him up, I kept probing around in his left lung for the bullet. It wasn't that I had to take it out for any medical reason. In fact, we seldom ever remove a bullet from a chest wound because it isn't necessary. But I knew the whole world was watching, and if I didn't get that bullet out, there'd be a million questions and headlines saying the President's doctors left the bullet in the President. Also, none of us knew at that time what had happened. I thought the bullet might be needed for evidence, and I wasn't about to leave it in there and then have to go back in later and take it out.

I kept squeezing his lung tissue, but I couldn't locate it. I had to order another chest X ray. We did it with a portable machine right there in the OR. The film came back a few minutes later, and I could see the bullet in the shadow of his heart, not more than an inch from his aorta. It was that close.

I began looking in the lung near where the X ray told me it would be. President Reagan's lung felt like that of a much younger man. As I kept looking I wondered if I would find it. Then I finally put my fingers on something hard; it was the bullet. It had been flattened like a dime from where it had glanced off the limousine before entering the President's chest.

I squeezed it out with my fingers, and there was a Secret Service man right there with an envelope. He took the bullet and sealed it and wrote something on the envelope. That was a real good moment.

✒   I worked at a hospital in the South Bronx. A wild, wild place! There were street gangs with names like The Savage Skulls. Shootings all the time. A lot of the patients who came into the hospital were abusive. They were drug addicts, street people, criminals, cursing and screaming.

I had a kid there, he was dealing drugs and got shot. We had opened him up to fix the wound, and after that I was in his room when he suddenly yanked his lines out. He pulled out his naso-gastro tube, pulled out his IVs, pulled out his catheter.

I went over to him and said, "Look, I have to put these tubes back in."

This kid said, "No honky Jew doctor is going to lay a hand on me."

There was a rule that every criminal had a police guard, even if they were in a cast and unable to move. So the next thing I saw was this policeman who's guarding him move to the other side of the bed. He pulled out his gun and pointed it at this kid's head and said, "Are you going to let the doctor put in the tubes?"

And the kid looked up at me and said, "Do whatever you want, doc."

✒ One of the most amazing phenomena I have ever witnessed happened while I was on the orthopedic service. This patient was about fifty. She was floridly psychotic. If you got near her, she'd spit and curse at you. Real nasty. That was her hallmark. She also had delusions.

She had broken her hip and needed surgery. But after she came out of surgery, she was a rose, an absolutely terrific person. You could not believe it was the same woman. I have no idea why that happened. Something in the anesthetic process may be like shock therapy to these people. A form of sleep therapy is used in Switzerland, and it may be that something happens to dopamine, which is a neurotransmitter, during anesthesia that puts these people into remission. As long as this woman remained in the hospital, which was four or five weeks, she was wonderful.

I saw a similar change with a friend's grandmother.

This was a real depressed, nasty woman. I think she'd been depressed her whole life. When she was in her seventies she had a stroke, and within the space of two days her demeanor and personality changed entirely. And for the rest of her life, which was about eight years, she was the most pleasant, sweetest little old grandmother you could ever imagine.

These things are still mysteries. My suspicion is that her stroke was her own form of electroshock therapy. We know that in shock therapy there is a tremendous alteration in neurotransmitters. It's like a massive influx of antidepressants. And this is probably why these patients recover after shock therapy.

This very attractive and charming woman came into the hospital. She was about my age and had an abscess that had to be surgically removed. It was a very messy operation, and later that day she was taken back to her room.

I came in at about ten that night on my sign-off rounds. I chatted with her a little bit to put her at ease, and she was very pleasant. Because she had had general anesthesia, I had to check her lungs, and as I bent over to put the stethoscope on her chest, she suddenly reached up and grabbed my tie and pulled me into bed with her. I really didn't know what to do at that point. Nobody had trained me for this.

I extracted myself and said, "Must be the result of anesthesia," or something like that and left a little more quickly than I normally would have. I saw her for the next couple of days before she was discharged, and she continued to be very flirtatious with me. I pretended not to notice.

There is a good amount of sex in medicine, between doctors and nurses, doctors and patients. I think it's much more common than people talk about. It certainly happens with male gynecologists and their patients, with internists and their patients. It's usually a male doctor and a female patient. I knew of one ophthalmologist who had his female patients strip and wear nothing but a see-through plastic apron when he did his eye examinations.

I think that when therapists are involved with their patients, it is usually associated with anger and disappointment and hurt. I think it's a very serious violation of medical ethics, as well as a danger to the patient. That isn't necessarily the case with other kinds of doctors, but I think we have to admit that the problem exists.

This guy's biceps were bigger than my thigh, and it was not fat. I knew he was psychotic, and he looked at me and in a voice that was convincing said, "You know, doctor, I could tear you limb from limb."

I unfortunately had been stupid enough to seat myself so that he was between myself and the door. I didn't see how I could get out of that room without getting myself beat to a pulp. I tried to think of what to do. He had already told me that one of his fantasies was that he was a great opera singer. He said he knew all the operas. So I said to him with great enthusiasm, "You know, I really like music, and I'd love to hear you sing. But if you start singing, the aides and nurses are going to get upset and think something strange is happening. If you just let me step out into the hall for a second so I can tell them you are going to be singing, they won't be upset."

He said okay to that, and I stepped outside, leaving one foot in the room so he wouldn't think I was trying to run away. I motioned to an aide and told him that my patient was going to be singing, and then under my breath I said that this guy was really dangerous and that I wanted the aide to get every giant aide and cop in the hospital and signal me at the door when everyone had arrived.

Then I stepped back into the room and the guy started to sing. I don't remember him having much of a voice, but I was close to hyperventilating because I was so scared that he might suddenly try to tear me limb from limb.

In a couple of minutes the aide signaled me. He had four other aides who all looked about six feet four and three policemen with guns.

I told the patient thank you and said his aria was wonderful. I walked a little bit out of the room and asked him to come outside. There he saw everyone.

I said to him, "I think because of things that are going on, it would be good if you would let us give you some medicine and get you to bed."

He looked at the cops with the guns and said, "You know, I could take you all on, but three of you have guns and I can't yet stop bullets."

Then he went very quietly, and we strapped him into bed, and I gave him an injection. Things seemed fine until late that night, when I was asleep in the on-call room. I heard this fierce banging. I didn't know what was going on. It turned out that this guy had completely upended his metal bed, to which he was strapped at the ankles, chest, and hands, and had walked the goddamned bed across the floor and was banging it against the steel door. That's how strong this mother was.

✎  I'd learned that my wife had an affair with a friend of mine, and I was devastated. I guess after that I was ripe for the picking. Years before, I had treated a woman patient after her husband had committed suicide in a particularly gruesome way. After I'd learned of my wife's infidelity, we met again. I fell in love with this woman, and we had an affair. I don't think any harm came of it, but it was foolish, a mistake.

She entered into our affair with the idea that it would be temporary. She was more of a sexual instigator than I was, and in fact I didn't want to get involved sexually, but I think I had a need then to love and be loved. It lasted five and a half months, which is just about how long the average affair lasts.

As the affair was ending, she accused me of taking advantage of the therapist-patient relationship, even though she had pushed for the sexualization of it. I guess she had to make me the villain.

Until then, I'd always stayed away from romantic entanglements with patients, even though there are a considerable number of patient-doctor affairs. I think the psychiatrist-patient relationship can create a very tempting sexual situation for psychiatrists because of the level of intimacy you reach with a woman patient. And it's tempting for them, too, because they can't reach real intimacy with other men, so they bare their souls and reveal themselves to you and get to feel that you are so wonderful.

I also think the loneliness of the therapist is a factor; psychiatry is a very isolating profession. Many patients are also lonely, which helps create the illusion that the closeness of the therapeutic situation can be transposed to a real living situation; it can give patients the illusion that they are experiencing the essence of love. I was lucky that my affair ended as well as it did and didn't blow up in my face.

A woman came into the hospital complaining of terrible stomachaches. I took her history and worked her up. She told me the stomachaches had started when her son married a shiksa and moved to Pennsylvania.

We gave her a full GI series, parasite tests, blood counts, barium enemas and colonoscopies, but we never found anything wrong with her. Nothing.

One day I get a stat page to her floor. I go in to see her, and she says, "Doctor, a worm came out of me. It was in my bowel movement."

I said, "Is it still in the toilet?"

She said, "No, I flushed it down."

"What did it look like?" I asked.

She said, "It was swimming and squirming around."

I said, "Did it have fins?"

She said, "Yes, it did."

There is no parasite in the world with fins. She was describing the Loch Ness monster. So I tried to use a little cheap psychology. I said, "Well, that must have been the cause of your problems. If you got rid of it, you must be better."

She'd have none of that. "There is one of those things in me that's ten times larger," she said.

I said, "Well, I don't know if I can do anything for you."

We finally discharged her. The only thing wrong with her was her son marrying the shiksa and moving to Pennsylvania.

A fourteen-year-old boy was playing on a railroad car. He grabbed hold of a line and took a huge jolt of electricity. It could have killed him, but the electrical surge went through him and then exited. I have seen all kinds of electrical exit wounds, but this youngster's were the worst. His wounds dessicated his legs below the knees. They were absolutely dead, and we had to remove what was left of them. He had also lost part of the hand that had grabbed the line.

He was a tall, rangy black kid from the inner city and had been a very good junior high school basketball player. All he ever wanted to be was a basketball player, and I think that that young man took this news with more hurt, more disappointment, and more disbelief than any child I can remember. He fought the truth of it for days. He just kept the sheets up and said, "I'm going to be all right. I'm going to play basketball. I gotta play basketball. I'm going to be the best there ever was."

Finally, there was nothing for him to do but look at the stumps immediately below his knees and deal with them. I think it was one of the most crushing truths to come to a young person that I have ever seen. He just had no preparation for that kind of devastating injury. But finally, with the same energy that he had used to play basketball, he began to adapt and learn to do things remarkable for a double amputee. I think it's possible that he might be using his brain more than he might have used it if his legs were still good. But that is little consolation.

*   You can become weary of people's vanity if you are a plastic surgeon. Some people imagine they need surgery to improve features that appear completely normal.

But one time I had a man come into my office holding a picture of W. C. Fields. He had a normal-looking nose, and he pointed to the picture and asked me to give him a big, bulbous nose just like W. C. Fields'.

I asked him why, and he told me he was a comedian and that he wanted to put on a W. C. Fields act. I told him makeup could do the same thing without making any permanent changes.

That request and one by a very proper elderly woman who asked me if I could make her vagina smaller are the two most bizarre requests I've ever had in plastic surgery.

*   When I went to work full time in a public mental hospital, people were incredulous that any psychiatrist would voluntarily work there unless he was a drug addict, an alcoholic, had lost his medical license in at least two states, or, like the guy I replaced, was a foreigner who turned out not to have a medical degree and was being deported.

The strangest aspect of psychiatry is that the most highly skilled psychiatrists almost invariably treat the patients who have the least illness. These patients have various kinds of intrapersonal and interpersonal problems, but we call them psychiatric patients for insurance purposes. They include everyone from a bored thirty-five-year-old housewife to a middle-aged man with an existential crisis because he was passed over for promotion.

But the sickest mental patients—the ones with schizophrenia, bipolar disorder, and other serious conditions—are usually treated in public hospitals and community health centers. They're cared for by some competent doctors, but most of these doctors are foreign trained and are usually not very competent. It doesn't make any sense.

It's like taking all the surgeons in the United States and having the best-trained ones lance boils, while importing Filipino and Indian surgeons with very little training to do the quadruple coronary bypass operations. But that's what we've done in psychiatry. So if you say, "I'm a very good psychiatrist and I take care of people with schizophrenia," other psychiatrists will laugh at you because that's a contradiction in terms. I find that very sad.

It comes out of the influence of psychoanalytic, insight-oriented talk therapy, which beginning in the 1940s attained the highest status within the profession. Psychoanalysis attracted, and continues to attract, the best psychiatrists. It is high-prestige psychiatry. During my training, virtually every psychiatric residency had a psychoanalyst in charge of it. If you wanted to get into academic psychiatry, you had to have psychoanalytic training.

But the problem is that people with schizophrenia or bipolar disorder don't respond to psychoanalysis. In fact, many people with schizophrenia get worse with it. So the best psychiatrists have had no contact with these seriously ill people.

In a broader social context, I think this has had an impact on the problem of mentally ill people living on the streets of this country. About a third of these homeless are seriously mentally ill; most of them have schizophrenia.

The problem stems from the *King of Hearts* decision to open the gates and let the mentally ill out on the streets so they could live happily ever after. But there were no bright, thoughtful psychiatrists involved in the public system, and so no one insisted on a pilot program to evaluate whether or not the community health centers across the country, which were to take the place of the mental hospitals, would work. Well, it turns out that they did not work because these centers were not interested in picking up these seriously mentally ill patients.

So you had no one recognizing that these seriously ill patients coming out of the hospitals were falling between the cracks. If there had been a pilot program, they would have been saying, "Hey, this thing is not working," by 1973 and 1974, because it was very clear by then that it was a failure.

But all the best psychiatrists were in the high-rent districts doing talk therapy for the worried well, and there really wasn't anyone to say, "Let's stop and rethink this policy." So the exodus continued right through the 1970s, and it wasn't until you got three hallucinating, homeless, mentally ill people per twenty square feet of many downtown streets that the general public looked around and said, "Hey, there's something wrong with this."

A reasonable estimate is that one-third of the 450,000 or so homeless people in this country are seriously mentally ill. In the state mental hospital system, there are about 75,000 patients with schizophrenia or bipolar disorders. This means that there are twice as many seriously mentally ill people on the streets today as there are in our public mental hospitals.

So if you look at psychiatry and ask, "What kind of a job has it done?" and juxtapose it with the homeless situation, you have to say very modestly that for the past twenty to thirty years, psychiatrists have not done a very good job. They've deserted the patients who needed them most and betrayed the implicit trust they accepted when they went into medicine.

After their baby was born, the wife didn't want their baby circumcised but the husband did. Unless people have religious convictions about it, we don't recommend circumcisions for babies anymore, so I spoke to the husband about it once when I got him alone.

"Why do you want your son circumcised?" I asked.

He said, "Isn't it true that circumcised men are more intelligent than uncircumcised men?"

I couldn't laugh out loud, because he was serious. So I said, "No, that's not true. How could a little piece of skin on the end of the penis have anything to do with intelligence?"

"I read it somewhere," he said.

I asked him where.

"In the *National Enquirer,*" he said.


Three of us were taking care of a patient, a young, attractive woman who was seriously ill with cancer. I used to round every third night at about ten just to make a final check and talk to patients, and after a few weeks I got to know her and like her. One night when I came in to see her, she said, "You know, when you're on call, I feel particularly safe. It's not that the other two doctors aren't terrific; it's just, when you're on, I feel a special sense of safety. I'm very grateful for your concern and knowledge."

Of course, I loved it. Secretly, I knew she was right. I was better than the other two doctors. And I loved it that she appreciated that I took extra care, which I knew I did. I really enjoyed this little secret that I kept from my colleagues.

We had a group of doctors who met once a week. It included doctors from our ward, as well as those from other wards. We talked about various problems and issues raised by patients. For whatever reason, I brought up this woman patient and repeated what she had said to me. Well, it turned out that she'd told the other two doctors exactly the same thing, that they gave her a special feeling of safety.

At that moment, if anyone had suggested we walk down the hall and strangle her, we would have done it.

That's how stupid she made us all feel. But once we thought about it, we realized how perfectly this woman had sized us up. Three young, competitive guys, well trained, wanting to do good. She figured out at some level, unconsciously I think, what it would take to get us to pay special attention to her needs.

What I learned from that—and have since seen many times in caring for very sick patients—is that all of them to a greater or lesser extent try to seduce the physician. You know, if you have acne, you don't need the doctor to be there with you all the time. But if you're seriously ill, you want a lot from your doctor. In some childish sense, they wouldn't mind if you dropped everything just to take care of them. So there's a lot of seductive behavior. It's not necessarily sexual, although that has happened, too. What you hear is, "You're so young to be a doctor." Or, "Your mother must be very proud of you."

I think that believing things like this from patients is one reason why doctors who take care of seriously ill patients burn out. They make themselves more to those patients than they really are.

I was seeing a mental patient in the outpatient clinic when he heard a fire truck coming down the street. He jumped up in the middle of my talking to him, ran out the door, hopped on the fire truck, and rode off to the fire. A very dramatic exit from a psychotherapy session!

I saw him a few days later, and he explained that he had wanted to ride on the fire truck—that was all there was to it. One of the absolute essentials for working with seriously mentally ill patients is to keep a sense of humor.

A patient complained to me that he left his other psychiatrist. "He just raised his fee to a hundred dollars," this patient said, "and he sleeps throughout the goddamned sessions."

He said he had challenged the therapist on this, and the therapist had said he wasn't sleeping, he was "reflecting."

I can understand why this therapist was nodding off. You get certain patients who are quietly, chronically unhappy and anxious. They don't have personality disorders or any serious emotional problems. They're the kind of person to whom other people say, "You have no spine. Pull yourself together, and stop whining."

If you accept this kind of patient and don't set up a defined treatment plan, you have open-ended therapy. Usually these patients don't like defined treatment plans, so the sessions can go on and on, and all you hear is how these people are unhappy and worried and how they think everything is wrong with their life. I've got scars inside my mouth from biting my cheeks to keep myself awake listening to these patients. Sometimes you find yourself busily writing notes, but it's usually a grocery list.

We had a young girl in our intensive care unit. She was a wreck. Everything was falling apart. She had a disseminated fungal infection, hemorrhaging in her lungs, and a pancreatic cyst that was about to erode. She had bleeding ulcers and increased intercranial pressure, and she was in kidney failure. She had high fevers, and her platelets—clotting factors in the blood—were dropping, so she began to bleed from everywhere.

It had all started with a kidney problem that we treated, which then suppressed her immune system, and she was overwhelmed with just about every infection you could think of.

Her parents were there keeping vigil, and I told them their daughter would not survive. They were there with their minister, and they seemed very stoic and said, "It's okay. We appreciate that you're doing all you can."

Later that same evening, I went out to talk to them, and I told them that she would not survive the night. The next day she was still alive. Then she started to rally and get better. Today she is a healthy teenager, suffering only from some minor kidney problem.

How she lived is a complete mystery to me. I've seen people die who have far less wrong with them than this young girl. She is one of those patients who refuses to die. They will themselves to live. I've even seen it in people in comas. They're sick as hell, but you can see they're just not ready to die. And there are other patients who conjure up buzzards at the heads of their beds, and no matter what you do, it won't work, and whatever can go wrong, does go wrong.

*"This rush toward what some have termed the 'commercialization' of medicine and others have called the 'industrialization' of medicine has bewildered physicians, perhaps because we instinctively sense that although there have always been some business aspects to medical practice, medicine, in the most fundamental sense, is not a business."*

"Medical Practice in the Competitive Market"
*New England Journal of Medicine*
February 5, 1987

*"Everywhere one sees the growth of a kind of marketing mentality in health care. . . . The 'health center' of one era is the 'profit center' of the next."*

*The Social Transformation of American Medicine*
By Paul Starr
1982

# 6

## Money

The doctor who told the story had herself experienced financial problems. "A young husband and wife, both doctors, moved into our city a few months ago to set up separate practices," she explained. "She was an obstetrician-gynecologist, and he was in family practice. They went to the local bank to get a loan to start their practices, and the bank refused. This couple was stunned. Doctors getting turned down for bank loans? But I'll tell you, the bank knew what it was doing. Being a doctor today is no longer a guarantee that you'll have money."

Long accustomed to economic privilege, today many doctors are worried about money. For many of us, like me, who have grown up believing that all doctors are rich, the idea of doctors complaining about money is like the idea of Saudi Arabia complaining about oil. But for many doctors today, the worry is real. Money considerations are forcing them to practice medicine in a way they don't want, and for a few, they are threatening their economic survival.

The problem isn't reflected in the average annual income for American doctors, which the American Medical Association calculates was just over $119,000 in 1986—a good living by almost everyone's standards. But this statistic hides important truths: the enormous and growing disparity among physicians' incomes. The disparity is becoming so divisive among doctors that it is pulling at the fabric of the medical profession.

A quarter of all physicians made less than $70,000 in 1986, and a quarter made more than $150,000. General and family practitioners averaged a little more than $80,000 a year, while radiologists averaged nearly $169,000 a year, according to the AMA. Although even the lower salaries are high in comparison with many salaries in the country, as one doctor remarked, "For well-trained professionals in responsible positions, $70 or $80,000 a year is no longer a lot of money."

*"Some cardiac surgeons, perhaps the highest-paid specialists, earn in excess of a million dollars a year, and some general internists earn $40 or $50,000 a year."*

But within these averages are even wider disparities. Some cardiac surgeons, perhaps the highest-paid specialists, earn in excess of a million dollars a year, and some general internists earn $40 or $50,000 a year. One doctor who works in a small city said, "I hear nurses complain about their salaries, and they have a right to, but they're catching up with the money some general practitioners are making. I accept that there's always been a gap in physician incomes, but the way medical reimbursement is geared toward procedures and surgery today, it's gotten out of hand."

There is also the incursion of commercialized medicine, the for-profit health maintenance organizations that sweep into areas and enroll patients by the truckload and threaten doctors by taking their patients away. Doctors must also compete with the new walk-in care centers that are springing up in shopping centers and other well-traveled areas.

Beyond the growing competition from corporate medicine, hassles over reimbursement from private insurers and the government in the continuing fight to keep health care costs down are increasingly nasty. The economic warfare is getting more intense. As one internist said, "I didn't go into medicine to make a lot of money, but I didn't think it would become a financial sacrifice."

✒ Sure medical costs are going up. But so is everything else. The press tells you the costs are going up because doctors have increased their charges, and doctors are all rich. It says we all want to live in posh neighborhoods, have our own swimming pools, have lighted tennis courts behind our homes, and belong to the best country clubs. It says we are cheating and milking the public. I guess we make an easy target.

Well, I'll tell you why the cost of medicine has gone up. The reason is medical technology. We are doing things today that ten years ago nobody dreamed possible.

Every day we have helicopters flying to this hospital carrying someone who was lying on the floor somewhere with crushing chest pain a half hour earlier. Within minutes, a doctor will have a catheter in his coronary arteries shooting dye in there and taking X-ray pictures. An hour and a half after that, this patient might be on the operating table, getting a bypass for the vessel that occluded and caused his heart attack. Four hours after that, he'll be in the recovery room, and within twenty-four hours, he'll be out of intensive care. In a week he'll be home feeling comfortable, and in six weeks he'll be playing golf again.

You know where he would have been ten or fifteen years ago if he'd had that same crushing pain? In the cemetery, that's where.

✒ The entire payment system is so atrocious that you play incredible games with medical insurance companies. There is no more conscience among doctors! You are dealing with an impersonal third party, and if you can get away with something, terrific! So you have doctors committing fraud left and right against insurance companies. It's only a question of how brazen you are.

Take blood tests. You order what is called a Smack 24. This is a series of twenty-four different tests done on one centimeter of blood. The lab charges us twelve dollars. Most doctors double that when they bill and make a nice profit. Some doctors actually go so far as to bill for several separate tests. They charge eight or ten dollars each for an iron, plus a thyroid, plus a this, plus a that, and the total comes out to seventy dollars for this one twelve-dollar test. And some insurance companies pay it.

It used to be that a physical was just a physical. Now doctors bill every single item. If you do a rectal exam, that's a separate bill. So instead of eighty dollars, you charge a hundred and fifty dollars. The insurance companies also have these rigid limits on office visit charges. There are five levels, each with a code. So what doctors used to call a limited visit is now called an intermediate visit. You just check off a level higher than what you did.

To some extent, the insurance companies deserve what they are getting because of all the stupid exclusions they have for preventive or routine care. So most doctors I know lie. A patient comes for a routine physical, and they'll put down four diagnoses. I find myself doing it. To justify a Pap smear for healthy women, I've put down a vaginal infection so she'll be reimbursed.

If you come up with a diagnosis of some kind, even one that has nothing to do with any of the tests you've ordered, most of the clerks back at the insurance companies are instructed that the claim is valid.

Doctors and patients are in a conspiracy to get the insurance companies on this, because a doctor's relationship with a patient is much stronger than it is with the insurance company.

I didn't start a rural general practice because I thought I'd get rich. In fact, I knew I wouldn't. But it was something I wanted to do, to go into the woods and have the kind of practice that would mean a lot to people and be satisfying to me. But it's reached a point where my concern is survival—to have enough to raise my family and own a car that runs. It's a shame that young doctors will not be able to go into this kind of practice because it isn't affordable. They won't be able earn enough to pay off their medical school debt by practicing this kind of medicine.

I've found real joy in being a small-town doctor, in being an intimate part of people's lives. You go to school functions, you see all the kids that you've delivered and taken care of, and everybody wants to show off the doctor who delivered them. You're important to them, and it's really fun.

You walk down the street and see someone who was at death's door a few months before, and you remember being up all night and getting them through their medical crisis. And you go to people's homes when they're dying, and you try to ease their pain and the family's grief and help them feel they are doing the right thing. You feel very privileged and complimented to share those emotions and to be a part of that. It's a kind of satisfaction that you can't get in any other field.

But this is ending. Insurance won't pay you for what you do, and many rural people don't have much money. So I think the country doctor as we've known it is fading away. It's just part of the times.

The original idea for health maintenance organizations was wonderful. The Kaiser HMO—the first in the country—started in the 1930s as a liberal-left organization taking on the medical establishment. It began in California, and Kaiser hired doctors, paid them a salary, built a facility, and got rid of the shenanigans like overtesting and overbilling that go on in private practice.

But these new HMOs that are coming on the scene today have nothing to do with Kaiser's original idea. They call themselves HMOs, but they've perverted the original concept. They all have nice-sounding names that make them appear to be patient oriented, but they're operated by venture capitalists and business people who are cashing in on what for many of them is a real bonanza.

Instead of a nonprofit HMO like Kaiser, these new ones are profit-making. And instead of hiring doctors, they contract with them and give them incentives to keep patient health care costs down. The less you do for the patient, the more you make for yourself and the company.

Like many doctors, I'm threatened by these new HMOs because they're gobbling up patients. Doctors are afraid that if they don't sign a contract with an HMO, they'll be left without any patients because patients are enrolling in them so fast. So a lot of us ran around signing up without really knowing what we were signing.

When you take a close look at them, you can see what a scam these new HMOs are. They know that 5 percent of patients generate 50 percent of medical costs, so they do all they can to get rid of that unhealthy 5 percent. They try to enroll only healthy patients. It's called skimming. That way they get all the premium money but provide less care, which means more profit.

In Florida one HMO held a dance to advertise and sign up Medicare patients. So who comes to a dance? People who are healthy enough to dance. And where do you have to go to sign up? To a third floor walk-up, so no one who is in a wheelchair or has a serious illness can get there. If an ill patient somehow overcomes all this and gets there to sign up, they advise the patient that he or she should think very carefully about the fact that they'll have to give up their private doctor. Anything to scare a sick patient away.

✒ I had a patient, a man in his early forties, who called me up one afternoon complaining of chest pain that was radiating out to his left arm—a classic symptom of a heart attack. This guy is about my age, and I had been friends with him. He had become my patient through a capitated HMO that I had signed up with. They are called "capitated" because I got a monthly fee, a per-head payment, for each of my patients. My fee ran eight dollars per patient. The idea, of course, is that most patients don't go to the doctor, so it is supposed to average out.

I called the ambulance to pick him up, and I called ahead to the hospital coronary care unit. Then I phoned his wife at work to break the news to her, and I rushed over to the hospital to be there when he arrived. I made all the right moves medically. And at the hospital I also tried to calm his fears, as well as his wife's. That takes a lot out of a doctor's hide, trying to help people through the emotional side of this. There's a lot more to taking care of a heart attack patient than just prescribing the right drugs.

But something bothered me about this case, and that was my own realization that when he called to tell me he had chest pains, my first reaction—before anything else crossed my mind—was, "You can't do this to me. I only get paid eight dollars a month to take care of you."

I went home that night and thought about it, and the next morning I called the director of the HMO and told him I had been corrupted by the HMO, and I quit right then and there.

It was clear to me that I had been corrupted because I was upset that this patient had had the effrontery to take up a lot of my time for such a small amount of money. That meant—to me, at least—that I was corruptible, something I hadn't previously thought possible.

Let's face it; people think doctors order too many tests and perform too many operations. That's why the payment system has to be altered—I agree with that. But then you have to look at what you're replacing it with, which also has possibilities for corruption, except that now doctors make more money by *not* giving their patients the care they may need. The HMO corporation's bottom line is the bottom line, but the doctor's bottom line is the health of the patient, and that's a conflict that makes good doctors very uncomfortable.

Many HMOs pay doctors annual bonuses. These bonuses, which can amount to a sizable amount of money, come out of the surplus money in each doctor's patient account. In other words, the less money you spend on your patients, the more money you get. So is a doctor supposed to think he's taking food out of his child's mouth every time he orders a test or a consultation for one of his patients? If this isn't a conflict of interest, I don't know what is.

A local doctor-entrepreneur came by my office recently to offer me a share of his osteoporosis detection machine—which costs a few hundred thousand dollars—for a minimal investment. He wanted $2,000 from me and a number of other doctors.

His pitch was that I could expect to reap all kinds of income from this because the insurance companies reimburse osteoporosis screening. He said he would keep 60 percent of the screening income for himself and his partner and put the other 40 percent into profits for the initial physician investors. To me, if you charge 40 percent more than you need, you're overcharging.

The only reason he was asking for anything from other doctors was that he wanted to get us to accept the concept of sending patients over to his office to use this machine and getting the profits. He wanted us to buy in psychologically much more than he wanted us to buy in financially.

I consider this outrageous. First, I think osteoporosis screening is an inexcusable hoax, and an expensive one. It has absolutely no benefit for the patient because the treatment and prevention of osteoporosis—which is a loss of bone density—is the same. Whether a patient has or doesn't have it, you still want them to avoid smoking, keep up their calcium intake, exercise, and consider estrogen replacement therapy if the woman is postmenopausal. Secondly, there's an absolute conflict of interest. You don't order a test for a patient because you can make a profit on it.

I told all this to this doctor, politely of course, and he agreed that I was right. But he said that with all the publicity that osteoporosis was getting in the media, women would be asking for the test anyway. I said I knew that, but I was going to educate my patients not to ask for it.

That didn't stop him. He's in business now and has a number of doctor-investors.

Sure surgery is a high-paying specialty, but the risks are much higher than they are in internal medicine. Instead of saying, "Well, Mrs. Smith, we're going to push up your steroids," like you do in internal medicine, you actually make an incision in someone. That involves a lot of blood, sweat, and tears. And the risks you take are commensurate with the reward. It's why pilots get paid more than bus drivers.

Surgeons also have much higher stress levels than internists and other primary care doctors. The highest-paid surgeons are cardiac surgeons doing coronary artery bypass grafts. We call them "cabbages." The staff opens the patient, and the surgeon comes in and spends an hour doing the grafts and then goes to the next patient. They do four to six cabbages a day; some even do ten to twelve a day for a few thousand dollars each. They can make up to a million and a half to two million a year, and they earn every penny of it.

My parents were eager for me to become a doctor because they had lived through the Depression, and even during the Depression doctors did well. So they were so happy when I decided to go to medical school. But becoming a doctor was not the best thing for me to do financially.

I'm in a solo internal medicine practice, which is the way I like to practice medicine, but I can see the handwriting on the wall. I'm not going to be able to do this much longer. I'm getting close to the point where I can't make enough money as an internist to pay the expenses of running my office.

When my lease expires in two years and my rent increases, I don't think I'll be able to practice medicine as I do now. If my malpractice premiums take a huge jump, it might end sooner. Every time my premium notice arrives, I open the envelope wondering if I'm going to be able to stay in solo practice much longer. I'm paying about $7,000 a year now.

Right now I can meet my rent and my mortgage, and I drive a small car and live in a modest home. If no big bills come in, I can just about make it, but I can't absorb anything sudden or unexpected. I'm that close to the margin. It makes me lose sleep at night.

There are ways to practice medicine to make a lot more money than I do, but I don't want to do them. I like the fact that I can spend time with my patients. If I have to see patients every fifteen minutes and work in a big group practice or work for some other kind of health care provider, I don't know what I'll do.

✍ I guess I'm old school, but I think traditional medical ethics have gone out the window. I work at a hospital that participated in a prepaid health plan. It was an independent practice plan, an attempt to provide medical care as inexpensively as possible. But it had a lot of financial trouble, and it was bought out by a big health conglomerate because the conglomerate wanted to turn this around and make it profitable. One of the provisions of the buy-out was that the participating physicians were offered stock in the new plan.

I had participated in this plan for the benefit of patients. It was a health care payer, like Blue Cross. And here I was being offered a chance to earn profits off of it from some of the very patients I would be treating.

To me, it is unethical for doctors to own stock in health care plans. I shouldn't own a drugstore. I shouldn't patent a medical invention so I can make money off it. The ethics I learned was that doctors could own McDonald's stock or Gulf Oil, but you didn't own anything medical. You didn't send patients to drugstores you owned or get medicine from the drug company you had stock in.

I threw the stock offers away, but I don't think all the doctors did. I was going to raise the issue, but I decided that trying to do something about it was like pissing in the ocean to raise the water level.

Right now I'm dealing with the Internal Revenue Service. They're really putting the hammer to me. They're saying, "Look, you did this tax shelter and it went under, and you owe us $75,000. And I say, "Bullshit." And they say, "Oh yeah!"

Well, I got nailed because the tax shelter I invested in turned out to be fradulent. I didn't know that until four years down the line. These guys who started the shelter were filing for bankruptcy, and I was paying them every month, and all the time they were telling me everything looked fine.

Before I invested, I went to an attorney in town. We're talking about one of the best law firms in the city. This lawyer looked over this tax shelter and said, "It's legal. It will work."

Now, five years later, I'm sitting here holding the bag and this attorney says, "Well, I guess I made a mistake."

I hired another lawyer to look over the IRS claim, and

he said I better pay up because the IRS will win in the end, and I'll only end up paying more if I hold out.

If I screw up in surgery like the lawyer screwed up on the tax shelter, can I just say, "I guess I took out the wrong organ. Sorry"? I'd get sued for five million dollars.

I make the same income now that I made ten years ago. I don't mean in real dollars, but the same actual income. This means my purchasing power is half of what it was ten years ago, and I'm still working just as hard. My partner and I had to move to an office that is about one-third the size of our old office simply because we couldn't afford the rent anymore. So now we occupy a very small office.

There's no doubt that some doctors don't deserve what they're making, but I'm working harder now than I did ten years ago and my income is stagnating because of insurance reimbursement.

Medical insurance companies will come up with anything they can think of to deny legitimate claims, or they try to delay payment for as long as they can to sit on the float and make greater profits. They have a number of tactics. The first one is to say they never received my claim. You learn this when you call them weeks after you've submitted it. Of course, this is bullshit. The mail is reliable in other areas. When I send a check to someone, they always get it, but when I send a claim, they say they didn't get it. I've heard from a good medical company insurance source that one out of three claims is thrown away in the trash can. They just pick out one of every three mailbags of claims and toss it. I believe it.

They also look for any technicality to deny payment. They'll tell you that you wrote down the wrong code and you have to resubmit the claim. One time I had an anorexia nervosa patient, and they denied her claim because they found out that when she was covered by another insurance carrier four years earlier, she had weighed less than a hundred pounds. They maintained that she had a preexisting condition. What it forces me to do is to change medical histories. I had a patient with a drug problem who also was depressed. I don't know if they were related or unrelated, but I knew if I put down on his insurance claim that he had a drug problem, he'd be denied coverage, so I said he had depression.

I really got fed up with this insurance business, especially with Blue Cross/Blue Shield. So I collected enough cases among my colleagues to show that there was a pattern of nonpayment and slow payment that constituted breach of contract. I threatened them with a lawsuit, and immediately after that they gave me the red carpet treatment, which indicated to me that they knew perfectly well what they were doing all along. They also knew they had gotten somebody angry enough to do something about it, so they accommodated me while continuing to screw all the other doctors who didn't fight them.

Money has taken over medicine. I practice in a teaching hospital. It used to be that talking about your money or your investments was taboo, bad form. You just didn't do it. But now I walk around and hear doctors talking openly about it. This attitude seems to have reached all levels of medical care.

## *"Money has taken over medicine."*

Not long ago there was a new, experimental medication that was made by genetic engineering. It's very important for some hemodialysis patients. But the drug company that developed it had not yet gotten approval to market it from the Food and Drug Administration.

I had a patient who really needed this new medication. In the past, drug companies would very often for humani-

tarian reasons release an experimental drug for a single patient—provided you followed the protocol—because the
company knew the patient needed it to survive.

But this company has made it very clear that under no
circumstances would it release any of this medicine for hu-
manitarian reasons, because it didn't want anything that
might slow up the FDA approval. It wanted to start making
profits on the drug as soon as possible.

*There are some things you are paid outrageously for.
I get $700 from medical insurance companies to do a D&C.
If I go slow, it takes forty-five seconds, maybe a minute. I
mean, I ought to be wearing a holster and a mask. That's
absurd.

A patient comes in for a vaginal infection. By the time
you charge her for the visit and the culture, the insurance
companies are more than willing to pay you this outrageous
amount of money.

Then you spend four hours in the OR doing a tubal
plastic surgical procedure that requires a considerable
amount of work, skill, and risk. If you were paid at the same
rate as you are paid for a D&C, you would get a quarter of a
million dollars. But the maximum is about $2,800 in our
area. We ought to be getting a lot less for D&Cs and more
for these other, more complicated procedures.

It's so confused. It doesn't make sense. Some guy from
Blue Cross once said to me, "We're not here for health care.
We want to use our premium money for investment. If we
get seven percent off our investment for an extra month,
who cares what you get for a D&C? We don't make our
money off that." And he's right.

*I am the only member of my family to become a
doctor and the first to attend college, so it's a big honor—or
at least, it used to be. Nowadays, my family is constantly.

complaining to me about physicians, and I can't defend some of the things they've complained about.

My grandfather was eighty-seven, an old Italian. He was a wonderful man, and I always felt very close to him. His mental faculties were terrific, but he was experiencing more and more pain when he walked, and he said to me once, "Joey, I've lived a good life. When my time comes, I want to die. Don't let them do anything to me."

When my grandfather went into the hospital, I called up his doctor. He said my grandfather was very sick and that he was going to give him kidney dialysis and put him on a ventilator. I said, "I don't want that done." He became very angry with me. He said I was just the grandson, and he told me he had already spoken with my grandmother and my mother and they'd given permission.

I rushed up to New York. My grandfather was in a private hospital. I reviewed all his medical records, and I knew it was hopeless. He had advanced kidney failure and congestive heart failure. While I was there, the cardiologist told my mother and grandmother that he had to put a Swan-Ganz catheter into my grandfather. This is a catheter that would monitor the fluid in my grandfather's heart. He said, "We can't manage him without the catheter. If we don't put it in, he'll die." That really angered me because it was as if he were saying, if you don't let me do this, you'll be the cause of his death. It also angered me because I knew it wasn't true. You can manage patients like my grandfather by clinical examination.

I brought my mother and grandmother together and told them of my earlier talks with Grandpa, and I told them that at best he could only survive a month or two with all this life support. "He will hate it," I told them, "and you will regret you ever did this."

They were angry with me at first because I guess they thought I just wanted to give up on him, but they appreciated the fact that I was a doctor and was giving them the best advice I could. They soon came around to my point of view and said—much to the chagrin of my grandfather's physicians—that they agreed with me. One of his doctors had actually dialyzed my grandfather two or three times already, and after my grandfather died, my mother received a tremendously large bill for that. I told her that if we hadn't stopped treating Grandpa, the bill would have been astronomical, and he would have died in agony.

I can't say that these doctors wanted to treat my grandfather only for the money they could get out of it, but I suspect that that was part of the reason. There is no question in my mind that avarice is taking over medicine, and that some doctors are more worried about their business than their patients. I don't think it's just the fault of the doctors. It seems to be the way our society is going, and doctors are part of it.

If you've done a procedure for years, you're locked into a fee range. But when you have a new procedure, you can set a high fee. I once asked a dermatologist how he set his fees for a new procedure. He said, "I set them ridiculously high and then the insurance company tells me how much they're going to pay, and that is what I end up charging."

So under a fee-for-service system you have urologists, orthopedic surgeons, and cardiac surgeons making out like bandits because they're always coming up with new procedures. Anesthesiologists and radiologists used to be at the low end of physician salaries, but in the last fifteen years they've climbed near the top because their hospital procedures are covered by insurance and they charge outrageous fees for them. And no one's stopping them.

Not that we internists are guiltless. Take the sigmoidoscopy, an examination of the colorectal area. It used to be that you inserted this rigid metal scope to do the exam. It was painful for the patient and messy for the doctor. Not a great test. It had an established fee of fifty dollars.

Then they came out with this new fiber-optic scope. It's more comfortable for the patient and easier for the doctor. This scope costs more for the doctor to buy, but not that much more, and you can depreciate it for tax purposes over three to five years.

Well, in any other business a new procedure that was quicker and better would be cheaper because of the downward economic pressure. But in the medical business, anytime you have a new procedure that may be more efficient, the charges become higher.

The medical profession decided that the fiber-optic sigmoidoscopy was a new procedure, and doctors now charge three times more for doing it than they did before, and it takes less time. And if you insert the scope more than twenty centimeters and go around a bend—which takes about twelve more seconds—suddenly it's called a limited colonoscopy, and you get $350 for it.

Insurance companies have set up a system to be gamed by doctors, doctors are gaming them, patients are getting a bad deal, and it's getting worse and worse.

I went to a dermatologist to have him look at something on my back. He said he thought it was a skin cancer. I asked if he could take it off, and he said yes. I thought I'd have to come back for another appointment, but he said he'd do it right then.

The whole visit, including talking and taking off the skin lesion, took fifteen or twenty minutes. And he billed Blue Shield more than $300.

We talked about that because he knows I'm a general practitioner. He'd been one for years, and he said he couldn't do it anymore. He couldn't stand the responsibility —all the calls, the worries, the breadth of the problems we have to take care of. So he became a dermatologist, where he can make three times what I'm making for less work and virtually no responsibility.

But primary care doctors aren't in the same league as doctors who perform procedures, and it's pushing doctors to do nonmedical things in their office to make money, like their own lab work. Well, I don't think doctors should do their own lab work. Also, doctors want to install X-ray machines, and I don't think anyone but a radiologist should read an X ray. And now physicians want to dispense drugs in their office. It's happening because primary care physicians have no other way to enhance their income, so they're looking for gimmicks to keep their office going.

There's also a lot of creative financing going on, and I consider it beyond anything I ever thought I would have to do to earn an income, but you have to do it to keep going. I had a patient who had some vaginal bleeding. When I examined her, I found a forgotten tampon that was the source of the problem. I removed it, and when I did, I thought, I can get paid for doing this. Before, I would have treated it as part of my twenty-five-dollar office visit and thrown it away. But when I did bill the insurance company for it, I got more money for it than I did for the office visit.

I had a patient with a finger infection. I stuck in a syringe and drained it. The whole procedure took a minute or two. Before, I never would have billed for it. But I billed his insurance company and got about fifty dollars, and the office visit was twenty-five dollars. There was no quarrel from the insurance company because this was a procedure.

This was never part of what I wanted or expected to do, but I understand very well why many general care doctors feel driven to do it. The system forces it on you. It may not be unethical, but it is unnecessary. If we were paid to do the real work we do, we'd never even have to think about these kinds of gimmicks, and we wouldn't have this ethical dilemma.

✒ I spoke before a group of conservative Christian doctors. Most of them were very wealthy—millionaires. I told them that accumulated wealth was wrong, that they ought to be using their wealth for other people, that the only purpose of wealth is to create justice, and that we have enormous injustices in this country.

They didn't openly react to my talk of money, and then I talked about my work, and after that they began to ask whether I evangelized in patient rooms when I went to see patients. I said no. They asked me if I was sure I was saved and basically got into questioning the validity of my own conversion. I am fairly sure that the reason they needed to do that was because I had presented them with something that didn't jibe with their interpretation of Scripture. So they needed to disqualify me as a person who had authority to talk about these issues.

It is my view that our attachment to money and our standard of living hinders our work as physicians. At a very simple level, the fact that physicians are so well paid augments the sense of them up there, of them being God, of them not making any mistakes. And when someone is paid $100,000 a year, and a patient makes $15 or $20,000 a year, that just exacerbates that sense of separation. It's only when we develop a better relationship with money that we will really be able to pursue our calling, pursue what is most deeply our own.

If you are going to be really attached to money, it's not possible to do the kind of work I am doing. Nobody pays $100,000 a year to come into the inner city to work with black people. So for me to follow my call means that I had to loosen some of my attachments to money and all the different things it can buy. And as I look at other physicians, especially nowadays, I see that this attachment to our current standard of living is preventing a lot of them from doing what they really want. To make the kind of money most doctors make, you have to see patients every five to ten minutes. You can't sit and chat with them. You can't get to know them as a whole person.

I also think that when somebody makes as much

money as a physician, nobody wants to hear him talking about his pain. The attitude is, "I come to you to heal me. Go to your shrink or someplace else with your problems."

This is not to mention the resentment people feel over physicians' salaries. Other doctors—caring, sensitive doctors—literally look at me like I'm crazy when I say this. They think I'm dead wrong. But as I talk to lay people, I'm convinced that those physicians are wrong. There really is resentment toward physicians over money. I think it is at least part of the reason for today's malpractice climate.

I also think the money issue underlies the conscious decision by our society to make medicine a business by insisting that doctors must now pay for their education, that it's a business investment. I don't think the huge debts doctors now incur in medical school—which are a relatively new phenomenon—have changed doctors' attitudes about money; I think their attitudes caused this change.

It's not that physicians are doing anything different from other people in our culture. I mean, the culture says you make as much money as you can. It doesn't make sense, according to our cultural values, to turn down money that is being offered to you. So physicians are no different from the rest of us; it's just that physicians have succeeded so well.

I can understand why physicians come to feel this way. The hard work and the concentration camp–like environment in the third and fourth years of medical school and residency give you the feeling that you are abused and that you are owed something.

I remember very clearly the first night that feeling came to me. I had been on for hours already, and I was called to see a patient, a woman with cancer. I wanted her to go down to the cancer specialist, and she said, "No, you can help me here." She was almost dying; all her veins were shot, and I couldn't get an intravenous line into her. I tried to make a cut down and couldn't get that in, either. Finally, after a long struggle, I got it in, and then something else happened, and I ended up spending all that evening and most of the night with her and several other patients. And when I came home at three or four in the morning, I said to myself, *Goddamn it! I deserve all I can get!*

It was a visceral feeling, and I could see that if you ran with it, there would no bounds to how much you thought you deserved.

*✐* Doctors who treat patients with runny noses, urinary tract infections, and other run-of-the-mill medical problems don't have the same risks or require the same skills as plastic surgeons, who move one part of the body to another part of the body, or cardiac surgeons, who take a big risk every time they operate.

Most surgeons are well paid, and I think they ought to be. I've paid a personal price to become a surgeon. I've paid a family price. My family hardly sees me. There are surgeons left and right who are divorced and their kids don't respect them because they weren't around when they were growing up. The surgeons weren't around because they have an intense, personal commitment to surgery. I'm sure high-tech surgeons have pretty low life expectancies compared with other specialists because of all the stress they go through. I think you've got to be compensated for that, for your initiative and skill. No risks, no rewards.

People are willing to pay for this expertise. When you go to a surgeon, it's a personal contract between surgeon and patient. It's not just to take a gall bladder out or open an obstructed artery; it's to make sure the right anesthesiologist is there, that the right medications are administered, and that the surgeon will be there for follow-up care.

I tell you, the surgeons making $800,000 a year are earning it. They're working their butts off.

*✐* I've talked to surgeons, and I know they think they're worth more than we internists are. They think they're invaluable because they wield that scalpel and that

what I do as an internist is nothing. The irony is that in medical training the most respected people are internists. We have always been the smartest ones, the ones who are able to figure things out. The jocks go into surgery. But when you reach the outside world, you find that your knowledge and skill as an internist are not really valued.

So there's money to transplant somebody's heart and money to separate Siamese twins. But try to get the money you need to keep an eighty-year-old woman in her home with the medicine she needs to live. There's no glory in that, and there's no money for the patients or for the doctors taking care of them.

A patient was hospitalized for a month by a very good internist who billed the patient about $1,000 for his care during the entire hospitalization. A surgeon had done a tracheotomy, a fairly minor procedure, on the same patient. The surgeon's bill was $2,400. It had taken only a few minutes.

When the patient received the bills, he wrote letters to both doctors and said he could not pay them in full right away. The surgeon wrote back a nasty letter and demanded full payment. The internist worked out a payment plan. The insurance company involved also told the patient to pay the surgeon. The internist asked the surgeon about it, and the surgeon answered, "Don't you think I should get $2,400?" The internist is still seething about it.

This is an example of the growing tension between the high-paid and the low-paid specialties. It's always been covert and smoldering, but it's more than smoldering now. There's real anger and a real feeling not only that the high-paid specialists—like surgeons, radiologists, and anesthesiologists—are screwing the internists and other low-paid doctors but also that they are blowing it for the profession by making us all look greedy.

It's a very divisive issue in medicine right now. I think

it could become the nail in the coffin of medicine because if you are a bureaucrat in some government agency trying to drive down doctors' fees, you don't have to divide and conquer. The profession is already divided.

FLORIDA MALPRACTICE CRISIS DEFIES CURE

Headline, *The Washington Post*
July 13, 1987

*"Professional liability is seen by our fellows as the most serious problem facing our specialty and the public we serve. It is a problem of crisis proportions not just in California, New York, and Florida, but throughout the country."*

1985 Presidential Address
American College of Obstetricians
and Gynecologists

*Q. What is brown and white and looks good on a lawyer?*
*A. A pit bull.*

Joke told by a doctor who'd been sued
for malpractice

# 7

# Malpractice:
# Fear and Loathing

"I've been in practice nearly twenty years and I've never been sued," the doctor said, knocking wood. "But I will be. It's inevitable. I have a little ritual I go through when I pick up my mail. Before I open anything, I sort through the envelopes to see if any of them have a lawyer's letterhead."

With medical malpractice suits up threefold in the past ten years, this is a ritual repeated in doctors' offices throughout the country. In my interviews with doctors I found malpractice suits, or the threat of one, the single most anger-provoking, fear-instilling part of their professional life. They hang over doctors like the sword of Damocles. "A goddamned curse," one doctor called them. They see malpractice suits as an undeserved and painful assault on themselves and on their profession. They feel that they are sued when patients have bad outcomes that are not the fault of the doctor but an inevitable consequence of illness.

The doctors I spoke with maintained that most malpractice suits are filed by women, and studies show that a disproportionate number are filed by the indigent. But they placed most of the blame on "ambulance-chasing" lawyers.

"We produce sixteen thousand doctors a year and thirty thousand lawyers," one doctor said. "And lawyers accuse *us* of generating work for ourselves. Much of the malpractice problem is at the lawyer's doorstep. There is a lot to be gained by filing a nuisance suit and getting paid five or ten thousand dollars just to go away."

This doctor said it's known that some lawyers call up people who have been discharged from hospitals—which is a matter of public record—and convince them to file a malpractice suit if they were unhappy with their hospital stay. Newspaper and television ads by lawyers that ask patients if they were satisfied with their hospitalization or if their child was injured at birth add fuel to this fire. As this doctor said, "There is extraordinary antipathy toward lawyers among doctors. Extraordinary!" This was a sentiment expressed by many, many doctors with whom I spoke.

Not only are doctors scared and angry, they're also being hit by increasing malpractice insurance premium costs. Internists and other lower-risk specialties may only pay $5 to $10,000 a year for malpractice insurance, but doctors in high-risk specialties can pay incredibly high premiums. One study found that malpractice premiums for Chicago obstetricians averaged nearly $175,000 a year and more than $2?0,000 a year for neurosurgeons.

In 1987, the Government Accounting Office, an investigative arm of Congress, studied the medical malpractice situation and found that in 1984 more than 73,000 malpractice claims were filed. But some insurance companies count a suit filed against several doctors as one malpractice claim, and others count the same suit as several claims. Because of this, there is no way of knowing how many doctors have been sued. But this many claims suggests that a sizable percentage of the more than 500,000 practicing physicians in this country are sued in any one year.

The total payout for these claims in 1984 was $2.6 billion, and the average settlement was slightly more than $80,000. Of all the suits filed, 57 percent had no payout at all, which doctors say substantiates their charge that many malpractice suits are unjustified.

Patients are affected by malpractice in different ways. Many doctors have stopped practicing or curtailed their practices in certain higher-risk areas of care because of the high premiums. Moreover, many doctors routinely practice defensive medicine by ordering tests that their best judgment tells them are useless medically but essential legally. The cost to patients and to the country is incalculable. Some estimates put it in the billions of dollars.

But malpractice does have a positive side. As one internist explained, "The one thing our lawyers tell us all the time is to be nice to our patients, so one of the virtues of the malpractice climate is that doctors are more concerned about being courteous."

For certain doctors, the malpractice climate creates a nearly intolerable burden. In one study 39 percent of physicians who were sued showed symptoms suggesting major depression.

It's not the bad doctors who get sued for malpractice. The doctors around my hospital who couldn't find their way out of a paper bag are the ones who patients say are such wonderful doctors, the ones they say are so concerned. Well, these doctors have a lot to be concerned about, but they aren't the ones getting hit with malpractice suits. It's the point men, the leaders, who are getting nailed.

I'm an academic, an innovator. I've done things to try to advance my field, but now I've lost my virginity. I've been sued for malpractice, and it hurts. I've been sued by someone who alleged that an operation I do best, I did for the deliberate purpose of doing them harm. Those are the lawyer's words.

*"For the people suing me, it's a ticket out; the lawyer—who gets a third to a half of the settlement—will do whatever he can to destroy a professional reputation."*

I did the operation on a Friday. It was a surgical procedure for which I am known. It was totally uneventful; there were no problems, no complications. The patient returned to work the following Thursday and subsequently did well in her job. Two years later, I was served with a subpoena. Her suit claimed that somehow my operation had contributed to her losing her marriage, job, and everything else.

I know many malpractice suits are brought because of communication problems, but I have always taken time to talk to my patients and answer their questions. In fact, my only fault is that I sometimes take too much time with them.

The case went to trial, and the jury awarded her a big settlement. I think it was a simple case of an affluent doctor, a medical leader, from a big medical center against this poor, downtrodden woman. The medical witness against me was a doctor who makes his living testifying against doctors.

When the jury came in with its verdict, the woman's lawyer called a press conference and said, in effect, "Look what I'm able to do." The fact that the judge subsequently said that the award flew in the face of reality and rolled it back wasn't mentioned, of course. Since then, other people I've operated on have found their way to this lawyer, and I've been sued again and again. Some of these suits are dismissed almost immediately, but others are pending. For the lawyers, this is a bloodless sport.

So what does this all mean? It means that for the foreseeable future I have to deal with dreck until these cases, one after another, are overturned, and that will be at an enormous personal and professional cost. For the people suing me, it's a ticket out; the lawyer—who gets a third to a half of the settlement—will do whatever he can to destroy a professional reputation. It's a free-floating crapshoot that doesn't relate to the real facts of the case. It's a system completely out of control. It's very disheartening.

I still love what I do. I thrive on it. I'm not too tired to get out of bed in the middle of the night to try and help solve a problem. But if I ever come close to saying that every one of those bastards out there is a potential litigant and I have to guard my flanks, then I'll have to leave medicine. Right now I've accepted malpractice suits as an extraordinarily high cost of doing business.

A young woman who had miscarried in her first pregnancy came to see me for routine pregnancy care. She'd been told that she had an incompetent cervix, a cervix liable to dilate abnormally early in pregnancy, resulting in the premature expulsion of the fetus.

There are two theories on how to treat this condition. One is that the cervix should be stitched to strengthen it. The second theory, the one I had been taught, is that stitching the cervix during pregnancy is very risky.

The woman said her first obstetrician had told her she should have stitches. I neglected to write this obstetrician about her case, but even if I had, I don't think it would have changed my mind. It's a question of judgment, the way you've been trained.

Things went well for a while, but when she came to see me in her fourth month, her cervix was dilated three centimeters, which I knew was a serious problem. I sent her right away to a specialist, which is exactly what I should have done. He eventually delivered the baby, who turned out to have severe cerebral palsy.

The woman is now suing me for more than $3 million. It's just an awful feeling. This is a case in which I don't think I made a medical mistake.

When I first got the summons, I was so shaken, I spent a week unable to think of anything else, of fantasizing revenge. It dominated my thoughts. Whenever I would try to take some quiet time, it would be there. I felt such anger at this woman and her husband. And I felt guilt at the mistake I had made in not writing to the obstetrician.

I had a sense of being completely isolated and alone. I just couldn't get anyone to sit with me and listen to what had really happened. Other doctors would kind of pat me on the back and say, "I'm sure this is going to be all right," or they wouldn't listen at all.

And I have since learned that my malpractice insurance company has gone bankrupt, so I am completely naked in this suit. My one solace is that I haven't spent the last twenty years trying to make a lot of money, so there isn't much they can get.

The malpractice climate in south Florida is considered the worst in the country. To practice obstetrics, the premium costs for a million dollars' coverage—which isn't a lot of coverage—run from $160,000 to $200,000 a year, depending on which of four insurance companies you go with. And the premiums are going up. Minimum coverage is $250,000, but the premium for that is $117,000 a year. All you have to do not pay in for two years, and you can cover the coverage. So as a result, most of the obstetricians have dropped their malpractice insurance coverage and are putting their money in a pot to help them withstand a lost malpractice suit.

Because of the problems here, hospitals will allow you privileges even if you're not insured. A state law requires that you either have $250,000 coverage or sign a document that you will cover that much yourself.

The insurance costs drove me out of obstetrics, which I had enjoyed. But the premiums are still high for gynecology, so I've gone bare. There are laws that allow you to protect your assets if you're sued, but if a judgment goes against me for a big sum of money, I'm not sure what will happen because I haven't been there yet. It only worries me when I think about it, so I just don't think about it.

I dropped my medical malpractice insurance for about seven years because of the high premium costs, but that situation became increasingly hard to tolerate psychologically, knowing that a mistake could take away all I'd worked for. I also knew it was beginning to interfere with my relationships with my patients.

If they questioned something I did or recommended or if they had a complication of some kind, I found myself becoming extremely defensive. It wasn't conducive to a good doctor-patient relationship. A physician should be supportive and do all he or she can to make things right for a patient, but I was feeling more like an antagonist to my patients because I felt so exposed.

There apparently are services that doctors can buy that research patients' backgrounds and tell you if they have a history of suing, but I don't want to be involved in that kind of paranoia. It would totally destroy my ability to function as a doctor.

Finally, I couldn't withstand the pressure of going bare anymore. I realized that I had to get malpractice insurance again so I could relax and get back to dealing with patients as I should.

Physicians don't separate what they are from what they do. So when a doctor is sued for malpractice, it's a direct attack upon him or her as a person. And it's a devastating one.

As I am chief of staff, every time a doctor is sued, the law requires that I get a copy of the complaint. So I know every doctor who is sued; but in general, physicians who are sued do not share that information with anyone other than a close circle of friends. They isolate themselves. As a result, they get very little support.

Many doctors who've been sued become suicidally depressed. Doctors have high suicide rates anyway, and malpractice suits are one of the factors. Doctors don't rise above them well. It's why I've become involved in trying to reform malpractice laws.

The majority of bad medical care in this country goes

unnoticed because it's committed in doctors' offices. Yet most of the malpractice cases involve hospitalization. For the most part, the wrong doctors are being sued for the wrong things.

The physicians sued most often are those most highly trained; but they have the shortest and least intimate contact with patients and their families. They often meet the patient in a crisis situation. It may be that they're highly paid and they may sometimes be arrogant, but that is not what causes them to be sued. They're sued when something doesn't turn out the way the patient wanted it to turn out, even though it might be completely out of the doctor's control. The doctor is the identified cause. And if that patient also perceives that the doctor is not caring, then you're almost certain to have a suit on your hands, regardless of whether or not malpractice was committed. It makes doctors cynical to be accused of things that aren't true. It would make anyone cynical.

So you take a bunch of people who are highly motivated and sue them all, and you get a bunch of unhappy, sour, not-as-good physicians. That's just what we're getting in this country.

Doctors will talk about the cost of the defensive medicine that has been made necessary by malpractice suits, and the money wasted on needless tests, and that sort of thing. All that's true. But the real cost is a change of attitude, a loss of enthusiasm. That is unmeasurable. It's the price the American public is paying and will continue to pay—the loss of the physician as their advocate.

You hear people say it's not true, that doctors are overstating the case and that they will still care. *Well, it is true.* I see it. Doctors are caring less. Talk to a physician who's been sued, and ask him how he feels about being a physician.

A doctor in California, a very bright guy and an excellent surgeon, went bare because he was paying an astronomical amount of money for malpractice insurance. When he gets sued, he sends the suing attorneys a letter saying he has no malpractice insurance and if they want to proceed with the case, they can contact his attorney. So far, not one case has proceeded.

He's devised real clever schemes to protect his assets. The law only permits the garnishment of salary and wages, so he pays himself and his staff wages in the form of a quarterly bonus from his corporation, and bonuses cannot be garnished. So he's protected there. And he's put his property in his wife's and children's names, so no one can get at them. This isn't a game with him; he's dead serious about it, and so far it seems to be working.

✎  This patient wasn't psychotically depressed. She was a very angry, manipulative person. I had hospitalized her, and one particular day I knew something was upsetting her, so I visited her room twice, which is unusual. She didn't indicate what the problem was, but later that day she jumped out the hospital window, which wasn't high. She suffered injuries, but nothing catastrophic happened, and she survived. She'd jumped to make a point about something.

I think people should be held accountable for their own actions. There is a reasonable need for the hospital to protect patients against themselves, but at the same time this woman was sane, and it took her nearly a minute to demolish the window before she jumped. So it's not as if it was an open window inviting her to leap out.

But she sued the hospital anyway, and what I resent is that she also sued me for malpractice. She sued despite the fact that for months after she jumped, I continued to be her psychiatrist. So she had not lost confidence in me at all. Nothing ever came of the suit because she never showed up for depositions. But my malpractice rates increased because I had been sued.

This woman later successfully committed suicide. I'm sorry to say this, but I have no pity for someone who sues me for such frivolous reasons.

I went to a medical school where we were imbued with a sense of responsibility and service. So when I moved to the South in the early 1950s, I looked for a way to serve. There was a hospital in the southern part of the county, a two-story, wood-framed building that was way out in the woods and served indigent, mostly black people. It was a very primitive facility run by the county.

My partner and I each gave three months of coverage a year to this hospital. We'd do elective surgery and be on call for emergencies. I did this for seven years and never got a penny for it, nor did I expect to.

In the late 1970s there was a story in the paper about a woman who had been found to have a hemostat in her abdomen. It turned out that she had been operated on at that county hospital twenty years earlier. Although the hospital had been closed for years, the records were discovered in a basement, and I was the doctor of record in the case.

According to the records, she had had an ectopic pregnancy and had been operated on at about midnight in what was clearly an emergency. She had had a quart and a half of blood in her belly, but we had stopped the bleeding, and she had recovered and gone home. I had no memory of the case at all, but as compulsive as I am, I'm sure I got there while the resident was doing the surgery, if not before. I imagine what happened is that we tried to get a hemostat on a bleeder and didn't get it on firmly, and it slipped under the intestine. She had felt fine for twenty years, but she developed severe high blood pressure and her doctor had ordered a kidney X ray that revealed the hemostat.

She was operated on, and the hemostat was removed, and she then sued both myself and the county. The suit was dismissed summarily because of sovereign immunity, which means that you can't sue the government. Her attorney took it to an appellate court, which said that the county was protected but I was not, so my case went to trial.

I don't think my lawyer did a good job. He didn't try to find any other people who were at that hospital at the time who could have told the jury how difficult the circumstances there were. I went through the guilt, the cynicism, the soul-searching, the depression—all the horrible emotional things you go through in an ordeal like this. I think the woman deserved something for the surgery to remove the hemostat, but it was devastating to me because this had happened when I was making sacrifices for the community.

I was hit with a $135,000 malpractice judgment. I think the jury saw this as a contest between a nice, grandmotherly woman and a rich doctor. But the malpractice insurance that had covered me during the time of her injury reflected the 1950s. Its limit was $5,000.

The attorneys negotiated the settlement down to $55,000, of which I had to come up with $50,000. Friends of mine wanted to petition the county to pay the settlement, but this case had gotten a lot of publicity and I had already taken as much emotionally as I could, so I agreed to pay the $50,000 over a period of eighteen months.

I did a lymph-node biopsy on a woman with Hodgkin's disease, and after the operation, the patient was fine. I mean one hundred percent fine!

This woman had a chronic arm and shoulder problem that had been diagnosed earlier by an orthopedic surgeon. But after the surgery, she claimed she had suffered weakness in her arm, and she sued me for a half million dollars. Her suit alleged that I had injured a nerve during surgery. Incredible!

There is a nerve in that area and I may have cut a branch of it, but even if I did, I don't think it would have caused the arm weakness she claimed, and I had a neurosurgeon who would testify to that fact. Also, this patient never returned for follow-up visits, even though I had told her a number of times that if she had any problems to come back.

The case was eventually settled out of court, more for nuisance value than for anything else. And because the settlement was for so little money, it didn't change my malpractice rates. It was just a frivolous suit. You know, give me something for nothing.

I see this woman sometimes and when I do I want to spit in her face. It takes all the restraint I have not to walk up to her and ask, "How's your arm feeling now?"

Ever since I've been in medicine, I've heard about the malpractice crisis in capital letters. I had always felt that doctors who get sued for malpractice in one way or another deserved it. Either they are too quick, see too many patients, are too callous or uncaring, are not up to date, or are not interested in the patient's problem. That was my view, and I deemphasized the malpractice issue to the residents and medical students that I taught. I told them, "If you do the job the way we teach you to do it, if you take precautions and are doubly diligent, you should not have to worry about malpractice."

But in the past six months my opinion has changed. A number of physicians who practice good medicine, physicians who are clearly above average, have been either sued for malpractice or threatened with a suit. In my view these are completely frivolous actions and amount to nothing less than harassment.

A cardiologist I know saw a patient who had been hospitalized for a number of weeks. He identified the problem, which had been overlooked by the patient's previous doctors, and took over the case. He set things right as best he could with the patient and got him up and out of bed and eventually out of the hospital and functioning.

Six months later, the patient died of a a heart problem

related to his original condition. The family of this patient turned around and sued the cardiologist because of a very minor drug-dosage change that had happened while the patient was in the hospital under this cardiologist's care. The suit alleged that if the medications had been adjusted properly in the hospital, the patient would not have died. It flew in the face of logic. The cardiologist who was sued had saved the patient's life, and the doctors who had really screwed up and misdiagnosed the problem were not sued.

I know this cardiologist well. He is exemplary, one of the most caring, thoughtful physicians I know. And I also know he is not motivated by money because he's independently wealthy. He practices medicine because he enjoys it. He's absolutely wedded to it. He's been emotionally demolished by this suit and was hospitalized for depression as a result.

Doctors find it very hard to admit their ignorance or their mistakes in the first place, and now with the malpractice climate, it's almost impossible.

What the hell is a doctor going to say—"Oh, I'm sorry, I made a mistake"—so he can then get sued? You just do not do that.

The lawyers tell us all the time not to admit mistakes. "Whatever you do," they say, "don't tell the patient you made a mistake. Cover it over! Couch it in other terms! Whatever! But God forbid you should ever admit that you made a mistake!"

A woman in her forties, perfectly normal, had a sudden convulsion late one night. She was taken to a local hospital emergency room, where they took a CAT scan and noticed something abnormal. They admitted her and the next day took another CAT scan. This time they used contrasting dyes. The scans suggested a brain abscess. It didn't *have* to be an abscess, but the scans suggested it.

A couple of days later, they did more scans. The lesion had become a lot bigger. This clearly pointed to an abscess. The neurologist called in the neurosurgeon, who looked at the X-ray studies and said that the woman's problem had been caused by a stroke. By this time, the woman was doing better. They'd been giving her medications but not antibiotics, which would be indicated for an abscess. They sent her home and told her to come back in another two to four weeks for another scan, but she was dead thirty-six hours later.

I'm asked to review a lot of potential malpractice cases, and many of them look to me like people trying to win the lottery by suing a doctor. I tell the lawyers beforehand that I hope I don't find anything wrong. That's my bias, and I'm very open about it. I've been sued twice—both times unjustifiably, in my view—and I know how agonizing it is for a doctor to be sued for malpractice. I ended up with coronary bypass surgery after one suit against me. But if I agree to review a case and find negligence, I feel compelled to speak out.

In this case, I brought the woman's X rays to my hospital and put them on the light box. I had people read them without telling them what was going on. I had attendings, senior residents, and junior residents look at them, and I asked, "How would you read these X rays?" Every one of them came up with an abscess. I took them to a neuroradiologist and asked him. Same thing—an abscess. This was also my opinion. The case was open and shut, as far as I am concerned. If she'd been diagnosed, in all likelihood she'd have been cured.

I sent the lawyer representing this woman's family a letter indicating this, and the case was settled out of court.

✦ We called this doctor 007—he seemed to have a license to kill. He was one of those guys who really doesn't give a damn. A pregnant woman came into the hospital in labor whose cervix was fully dilated for ten hours. Any doctor knows this is much too long a time without delivery, but he didn't do anything. He was in the hospital the night this was happening and the nurse kept updating him, but he wouldn't act.

He finally delivered the baby by forceps, and he rotated the head as he did so. Delivering a baby like that is like what supposedly happened in Detroit when that airliner took off without extending the flaps. The doctor hadn't done the most basic things, and now he was adding insult to injury. The baby came out floppy, looking really terrible.

The mother was very unsophisticated, and she had told this doctor before the delivery that she wanted her tubes tied. Although this was her first child, the doctor never even told her how difficult the delivery had been and didn't really give her time to think about what was happening so she could reconsider. Twenty-four hours after the delivery, he tied her tubes.

The next day, the baby started having uncontrollable seizures. She went into kidney failure and had one complication after another. That's when I was called in—to pick up the pieces. We were in a small, local hospital, so we transferred the baby to a neonatology unit at another hospital. But the end result was that the baby had suffered serious, irreversible brain damage. She was very retarded and spastic.

The parents brought the baby in for checkups, and the mother kept asking me, "Why did the doctor wait so long? Why didn't he deliver the baby sooner?" I told her I didn't know, but for the only time in my professional life, I suggested to a patient that she should talk to someone about the matter. She knew I meant a lawyer. This was not easy for me to do. There are a lot of gray areas in medicine. Some doctors do things differently from other doctors. Some are unorthodox. And there's always the feeling, "There but for the grace of God go I." But I felt that this was egregious.

The family filed a suit and asked me to testify, and I

did, willingly. It may be easy to file malpractice claims, but they are hard to prove in court. You have to find that the doctor is really below the standard of care. But this case was clear-cut and was settled out of court for the largest malpractice settlement in the history of the state.

*✐*     I've been in practice about fifteen years, and I have patients who love and adore me, patients for whom I can honestly say I've made a major, positive difference in their lives. But I wonder what would happen tomorrow if there was a malpractice suit on the horizon?

One of the worst things I've ever heard happened after an obstetrician in town committed suicide. I overheard two women talking about it. One said, "Did you hear that Doctor So-and-so committed suicide?"

And the other one said, "Yeah. I can't get my diuretic prescription refilled yet." That was her level of concern for someone who had been her doctor.

> *"I've been in practice about fifteen years, and I have patients who love and adore me, patients for whom I can honestly say I've made a major, positive difference in their lives."*

I thought to myself that although there was a warm relationship between me and my patients, I should not play it up to be more than that. I am delivering a service, and in return for that they owe me a payment.

The fact that I think this way bothers me.

*✐*     Nothing in medical school or residency was as enjoyable as obstetrics to me. It gave me the chance to do primary care as well as surgery, and I liked the doctor-patient relationship. You get to know the patient very well over the course of the pregnancy, and I liked women pa-

tients better than men. With modern Dopptones you get to hear the heartbeat together for the first time. The patient gets excited, and you get excited with them. It gave me a lot of personal satisfaction. Putting the baby in the mother's arms is always an emotional moment, and you know that throughout their life, the couple will associate that baby with you. There's nothing like it in medicine.

I went into private obstetrical practice with a partner, and we became successful. Although neither one of us was ever found guilty of malpractice, our malpractice insurance rates kept climbing like crazy every year because obstetrics is such a vulnerable area. Settlements for injured babies can be very high.

The insurance company that covered us pulled out of our state, so to keep my partner and myself protected against any future lawsuit while we were covered by this company, we had to buy out what is called the tail. This amounted to 150 percent of our annual premium.

We had been paying $60,000 a year, which meant that to buy the tail, it cost my partner and me $90,000. On top of that, the only other insurance company that would cover us wanted $150,000 a year for coverage. That meant that we'd have to pay $240,000 for our obstetrical malpractice coverage in this one year. We couldn't go without it because it's inevitable that you're going to be sued, and you can't get hospital privileges if you don't have coverage.

We charged each obstetrical patient $2,000 a delivery. In our busiest period we did about twenty deliveries a month, or about 240 deliveries a year. We could survive, but it meant that half the year, staying up all night and working weekends, we would be working for free, in effect working only to pay our malpractice insurance.

I had thought that at the age of forty I would give up obstetrics and concentrate on infertility and gynecology, because getting up in the middle of the night to deliver babies gets wearing after a while. But when we were hit with these insurance premiums, I said what the hell, and my partner and I quit obstetrics. I figured that if we waited for another three or four years, the way the premiums were climbing it might cost us $350,000 to buy out.

I am angry that this decision was forced on me, but knowing what the alternative would have been, the decision wasn't even close.

The patient was a fourteen-year-old boy whom we strongly suspected had an adrenal tumor. These children have only a five percent survival rate, so we had to confirm and image the tumor as well as we could to give the surgeon all the guidance possible.

We first tried an intravenous pyelogram and saw no tumor, so we had to do angiography. The evening before, I spoke to the boy's parents and explained that this was a big deal because there was a possibility that their son could die or lose a leg because the femoral artery could shut down. Other potential complications included an allergic reaction to the contrast dyes and a blood clot. But we were between a rock and a hard place because we had to find that tumor if the child was to have any hope of survival.

The next day, we did a test injection and all went well. Then I injected contrast dye as we took X rays. Five or six minutes later, the child suffered a grand mal seizure. We gave him some phenobarbital to control the seizure, and he woke up and was all right. The film was high quality, but we couldn't detect any tumor. In my own mind I had no hesitation about trying to find the tumor with angiography again. So I gave him another injection, and he had another seizure. We got him out of it, and this time we could see the tumor clearly. But I also knew that the only real chance for the surgeon to remove the tumor completely would be to know the tumor's blood supply—the bleeders and the drainers. If the surgeon knew which ones they were, he could control what was going in and out of the tumor and have a better chance at cure.

I was worried about the seizures, but I had been trained at an institution where children had seizures all the time. They were no big deal because we could always bring the child out of them. So I did a third run, and this time we visualized everything perfectly—the tumor and its blood supply—and although the boy was drowsy, he was aware when we were finished. I spoke to him, and they took him to the recovery room. But a short time later he developed generalized seizures that didn't stop. He just kept seizing. Finally they were brought under control, but by that time the child was almost comatose and had suffered severe, irreversible brain damage. He became profoundly retarded. This was the ultimate complication—far worse in my view than killing a child. I'd never had anything like this happen in years of practice, and I called every angiographer I knew around the country to see if any of them had ever seen or heard of anything like this, but no one had. No one!

A few days later, the child was operated on for the adrenal tumor. I was beginning to sense that I would probably be sued for this, and a few months later I was. I'll never forget going in for my deposition and seeing the father there. I extended my hand to him, and when he wouldn't shake it, I almost became unglued. It really said to me that this guy hates me and that what had happened to his son was not just the result of something that had gone wrong but something he blamed me for.

They had found an expert witness who I don't think had had any experience with cases like this but who nonetheless testified that I had committed malpractice because I had repeated the test after the first seizure. That was the crux of their case against me. But if I had stopped, there would have been no diagnosis. And to my mind, that meant that the child would have had no chance of survival.

Throughout this time I kept digging deeper and deeper into the medical literature, trying to find out why this boy had suffered such an injury, trying to find something that might help me in my legal defense. I found one study that

suggested an association between adrenocortical hormones
—which this patient had been putting out in abundance because of his tumor—and central nervous system disease.

Finally I found a case study in the literature in which a
young boy with adrenal cancer who had gone into the hospital slipped into a coma, and had never had *any* angiograms.
I knew that if I had found that one case, there had to be
others in which children with adrenal tumors went into
comas spontaneously. So I went back and dug out twenty-
two others that had been reported. None of these children
had had angiograms either.

What I suspect is that the seizures my patient suffered
were a natural outgrowth of his adrenal tumor and the over-
production of certain hormones. I won't argue that the contrast dyes had nothing to do with the seizures, but I don't
think they were the cause. Maybe they acted as a kind of
trigger, but nothing more. I knew that kids have seizures all
the time, but they come out of them and get better. This one
didn't, so there had to be a reason besides the contrast dyes,
and I think the reason was the disease itself. We asked one of
their expert witnesses about it. He said he knew nothing of
the relationship between adrenal tumors and central nervous system disorders, but he thought it had nothing to do
with what had happened to this young boy. Once that testi-
mony was entered into the record, I think it was over for
me.

My lawyers saw this through eyes different from mine.
They wanted to settle. The hospital, which had also been
sued, agreed, and so did another doctor who had been involved, but I refused because I felt—and still feel—that I
did not injure that young boy. The other side threatened to
sue for millions in punitive damages and word got to me
that they would go after my house, my bank account—everything. I still wouldn't sign.

The hospital turned its back on me, didn't support me
at all. I knew there was even a good chance that I could lose
my job. It got lonelier and lonelier. The pressure on me to

settle was intense. I finally agreed to consult with an older lawyer I knew, a very wise man. I told him everything. He agreed that I could fight it, but in his view I should settle because there was the possibility of medical disagreement, and more important, because the extent of the young boy's injury would have a persuasive impact on any jury even if they did not think it had been caused by my malpractice. He also told me that I wouldn't be accused of doing anything wrong in signing the settlement. So I signed, which was for a very high sum, and even though it said I'm not guilty of malpractice, it really says I am guilty.

I almost feel that I should be angry, but I'm not. There is just a lot of sadness. My life changed. I don't think I was as good a doctor or teacher when this was happening. It dragged on for years, and I went to just about every deposition there was. I know that my life did not change as much as it did for that young boy or his family, but I still don't feel any guilt over it. I've done things in medicine that I do feel guilty about; I've hurt people with my own misjudgments and mistakes. But I know I did not hurt this boy.

The ultimate irony, of course, is that because I imaged the tumor so well, the surgeon was able to get it all out, and the young boy has been cured of cancer.

I love *St. Elsewhere*. I think it's a little melodramatic, and some of the ethical issues it raises are overdone, but basically I think it was a pretty good show. I also liked *Ben Casey* and *Marcus Welby, M.D.* I think the image of doctors on these shows is great, but it's not always attainable. Unfortunately, everyone doesn't always get better by the end of the hour like they do on TV, which leads to unrealistic expectations and malpractice suits.

I've been sued for malpractice six times. I can honestly say that I have made mistakes for which I might have been successfully sued, but I never committed malpractice in any of the cases for which I was sued.

We all know there are screw-ups in medicine that hurt people. When a doctor screws up and causes real losses, we have a system to compensate patients. It's called insurance. I don't have any trouble with that.

But I think the system we have now is riddled with pitfalls. There are no standards of responsibility for attorneys. Everything they do is justified on the grounds that it's their job to advocate for clients. We all know that's nonsense, but there doesn't seem to be any control over what's going on.

I think the malpractice crisis will be solved in about five years, when legal malpractice premiums become onerous enough to produce tort reform. When some lawyers have to pay $150,000 a year for malpractice insurance, as I do, doctors will ride in on the coattails of the lawyers, who will be self-serving in these reforms. It won't happen before then because there is too much money in it for the lawyers now.

I took care of a depressed patient who was an alcoholic and who also had a congenital condition that caused her bones to be fragile. She got fractures very easily. She also did not pay her bills, even though she could afford to.

One day she had a fight with her husband and jumped from a second-story window. Of course, with her condition she broke a number of bones. She was taken to the hospital, where they treated her fractures. After she recovered, the doctors at this hospital felt she could leave, from a medical as well as from a psychiatric point of view.

She insisted on coming to my hospital to be under my care. Her wishes were conveyed to my senior partner. He looked up her records and saw all the money she owed us and said we didn't want her as a patient any longer. My partner reasoned that the doctors at this other hospital didn't feel she needed hospitalization any more.

The next thing, we were both slapped with a malpractice suit for patient abandonment—something like $2 mil-

lion. We went through depositions and all that, and then our
insurance carrier said they wanted to settle because it would
be cheaper than going to court. I was reluctant to agree to
the settlement, which was in the range of $30,000. I thought
it was just a case of someone trying to line their pockets.

At just about this time, I received a telephone call from
a sister of this patient. She told me she had heard what her
sister was up to. She said that she and her other sisters
would be willing to testify that this was the fourth time her
sister had sued a doctor after she'd jumped out of a window.

I thought, wonderful. I called the lawyer and said,
"Don't settle. We've got the perfect witnesses."

And he said, "That's totally immaterial. They'd never
be admitted as witnesses, no matter how many times she's
sued other doctors."

So we ended up forking out the settlement, and to this
day I regret it. We should have fought it. This was the beginning of my bitterness toward the whole damned system—
patients, lawyers, the judicial system. It stinks.

Two years later, this patient called and said, "You were
the best doctor I ever had. I want you to take care of me
again."

I came out with every swear word I knew. She wasn't
my patient anymore, so I really let her have it.

I was sued once by a patient for failure of informed
consent when he had a complication. He sued me even
though we had produced written informed consent that said
the complication could occur and even though he acknowledged that he had seen it and signed it before his surgery.
This was my only malpractice case that led to a settlement.
The hospital agreed that I had delivered excellent care, but
they had settled because they didn't want to take any risks
in court. That bothered me a hell of a lot at the time. It still
bothers me! Because I think it lets a lot of spurious and
marginal claims get pressed and ultimately paid off because

the lawyers know there is a value in filing a claim if *anything* at all happened to the patient.

A patient came to me with a leg that was bent in the middle. I asked her what had happened, and she told me that she had fractured her leg and that another doctor had performed a questionable operation on her. Then she had had a complication. He had continued to treat her for three months without—as far as I could tell—either doing a physical examination or taking an X ray. Her leg was bent nearly 50 degrees between the knee and the ankle. She could not walk on it, and this guy was charging her exorbitant fees.

I thought this was wanton disregard for the patient's welfare and for his responsibilities as a physician. I do not like the business of testifying in malpractice cases, particularly against doctors who practice in the same city as I do. Also, I am much more in sympathy with other practicing physicians who I feel are often sued only because someone hopes to gain something. Despite this, I agreed to testify against this doctor. I did it because I thought that what he had done was so outrageous.

I testified, and we got him to admit to malpractice, and the case was settled before trial. He had to pay personally with a judgment. The good thing was that because I had reoperated on her, she had regained full use of the leg. But the bad thing was that this SOB didn't have to pay nearly what this woman should have been paid for her suffering because we were able to make her leg better. So I'm not sure justice was served. But I had no compunction about doing it, and I would do it again.

This doctor is still practicing. I've never met him and wouldn't know him if I ran over him. But I'd like to try.

What bothers me most is that the public thinks doctors are rapacious, that they don't care, that their primary interest is in money. And also that we're incompetent, as reflected in the frequency and size of malpractice awards.

I see that attitude in the patients I deal with. A certain proportion of them make me very uncomfortable. They question my statements, which is all right, but it's done in an unpleasant, argumentative way. If they're ill, I don't care if they have a chip on their shoulder; it doesn't matter. But these patients I'm talking about aren't seriouly ill.

I get the feeling that the public thinks we're somehow impervious to all this hostility. My father was a neurosurgeon. This is a guy who used to live and breathe patients. He'd operate all day on cases, then stay at the hospital until early in the morning operating on trauma patients brought into the emergency room because that was what he thought he was supposed to do as a doctor. I remember that on the few vacations we did take, he'd get called about a patient, and we'd turn around and come back home.

But he was sued once. The case dragged on for four years, and he was devastated. He was an eminent, talented neurosurgeon, but he began to doubt his own ability; he lost the kind of confidence and trust that neurosurgeons need to have. He became severely depressed. Finally, the case was dismissed because there was no evidence of malpractice, but I'm not sure he was ever the same doctor or the same person he had been before.

I've never been sued—knock wood—but I've seen other doctors who have been sued since then. They look like ghosts.

I testified as an expert witness for an obstetrician who was being sued for causing a subdural hematoma, a hemorrhage over the surface of the brain of a baby. The obstetrician had used forceps to deliver, and the subdural was discovered six months after birth.

As a neurosurgeon, I knew it was not physically possible for the baby's subdural to have occurred during delivery but only show up six months later. I was certain that it had been no more than a week old when it was discovered, and I testified to that.

The plaintiff's attorney asked, "Well then, what do you think caused it?"

I said, "There is no question. This is an abused child. This is a shaken child. This is a case we would refer to child welfare."

You'd think that would have blown the case apart. But do you know what happened? The lawyers for the obstetrician's insurance company ended up giving the plaintiffs $35,000 to settle out of court. I find that unbelievable.

The problem stems from the fact that medical malpractice insurance companies usually hire second-rate attorneys to defend us. These attorneys don't give a damn, don't understand the case, and usually don't have the vaguest idea of what they're doing. The times I've been involved in malpractice cases, I've ended up being more resentful toward the attorneys they employ to defend us than the plaintiff's attorneys, who may be bastards but they're smart bastards.

If I were sued for malpractice tomorrow, I'd probably let the insurance company settle, even if I knew I hadn't committed malpractice. And the reason is that I don't want to get into court. Because if I get into court, I'm going to lose, no matter what the facts are. I'm going to lose because the six or twelve people sitting in the jury box aren't looking at my embarrassment, aren't looking at the emotional pain I feel because I've been accused of something I consider to be almost a criminal act. They are looking at the fact that a major medical insurance company will pay off. What the hell!

And the malpractice insurance companies will throw you to the wolves if it's in their best interest. Let's be realistic about the insurance companies. They do not have your interests at heart. If they can save money by settling a case rather than defending your honor, they will. They are profit-making corporations that deal in investments and money. Nothing more; nothing less.

I testified against a physician in another city. The patient had gone to him in early pregnancy and said she felt a lump in her breast. The physician had basically said, that's nice dear, and written it down but had done nothing else.

She kept reporting it until finally, in her thirty-sixth week of pregnancy, he said, "Okay, if you insist, we'll get a surgeon to look at it." It was malignant, and by then it had metastasized. She was delivered immediately and put on chemotherapy and died about a year later. They could get no doctor in that city to testify against him, so they came to see me. As far as I'm concerned, the case was clear-cut negligence that warranted compensation to the family and to the child who would never know his mother. It was eventually settled for a good amount of money.

It's easy for me to say that the doctors in that other city should have testified in the case. If that same case had happened in my city, would I have testified against the doctor? It's easy to say yes, of course, but I also have to be realistic. There's that old fraternal spirit that still exists. You know, once you swear to the mafia code of silence, you're in it for life. And there's no question that with the malpractice climate being what it is, doctors feel besieged. And I think if we all don't get together and protect our own profession, then we doctors will find ourselves in even more serious trouble than we are now.

But I also have to admit to financial considerations. Many of the cases that come to my office are referrals. So I can see some referring doctors saying, "That son of a bitch testified! We won't send any patients there again!" That's certainly a possibility, and I think a realistic one. And then what happens when the day comes that I do something wrong? Is there going to be a line of doctors at my door saying, "Let me testify first?"

I guess if a local malpractice case came to me that was truly outrageous, I would let my opinion be known that this can't go on. I would like to think that, anyway.

*"Most physicians work continuously in the fear of death or in its presence, but familiarity does remove its sting."*

"The Effects of Stress on Physicians and Their Medical Practice"
*New England Journal of Medicine*
February 25, 1982

*"Death is always the enemy."*

An internist
July 1987

# 8

---

# Death and Dying

The pediatrician is a thoughtful man, kind and caring of his young patients and their families. He is an oncologist who treats childhood cancer, the cruelest disease. His skill has helped save many of his patients over the years, and they have grown up to become happy and successful adults, but he and they have also lost. It is always painful.

"I go to the graduations and weddings," he said softly, "but I can't face the funerals."

For this doctor, and for almost every physician I spoke with, the death of a patient is the most painful and humbling experience in their professional life. It is the ultimate proof that the physician's art is limited and the human body and spirit are an untapped mystery.

Like the pediatric oncologist, many doctors confessed that they have a difficult time dealing with the death of a patient. Some admitted that they avoid patients who are terminal because they can't stand it. But others are willing to face it head on and absorb the full impact of grief.

"There is nothing you're taught in medical school or training that shields you from your own feelings," one doctor said. "You might crack some gallows-humor jokes about death that would shock people outside medicine if they ever heard you, but the humor is something you use to try to push the pain away, to deflect the madness and sadness of what you see.

"Not all deaths are sad or tragic. The death of an eighty-five-year-old man who has lived a good life may be poignant, but you know that that man has lived out his life. It's the young lives cut short that are hard to face. There aren't many doctors without a memory of a dying patient that will stay with him for the rest of his life.

"For me, the most difficult are men about my age who face a terminal illness with great courage and stoicism. They absolutely tear me up; they show such guts and courage that I question myself. I wonder if I will measure up to these men when my time comes. For every doctor there is usually a certain type of patient who will strike an emotional chord. I've known doctors who've lost their distance from these patients and begun denying death along with the patient. And when these patients die, it is hard—very, very, hard."

I operated on a little girl for a malignant kidney tumor. Six months later, despite X-ray therapy and drug therapy, she developed a metastasis to her lung. I removed a lot of her lung tissue, and although she was having a very hard time in the postoperative phases, I thought she was going to get better. I thought she had enough lung to make it.

Her mother and father were absolutely exhausted by this ordeal. They were very nice people—intelligent, thoughtful. They'd been with her almost constantly for the five days since the surgery, and that evening after I made rounds I told them that little Carolyn would need them to be fresh. So I said, "Why don't you go home and take a shower and eat supper, and I'll stay here with her?"

I had developed a very close attachment to this little girl. It seems that so often that children with malignant disease are really the most beautiful children. And she was. Five years old, blue eyes, blond hair, adorable smile. She seemed to love everyone. You couldn't help but be drawn to her.

Her parents left the hospital to go home, and I went in to sit with her. We were talking about lots of things—her favorite doll and what she was going to do when she got home. Her intravenous needle was hurting her; it apparently was rubbing on a nerve or something, and she winced over and over. So I went and got some Novocain and stuck just a tiny bit around the needle so she would feel better. The pain went away, and she was very happy.

We talked on for twenty or thirty minutes, and then she became quiet for a little bit, and I thought she was going to sleep so I didn't interrupt her. And then she opened her eyes and looked up and me and called my name and said, "I love you." And then she closed her eyes and died.

I have never seen a death like that before or since—not even in the movies. She was perfectly conscious, told me she loved me, and the next moment she died. I had to face her mother and father, who were coming back to the hospital and who had thought she would be well enough to go home in a little while. I don't think I have ever had such a wrenching experience in the practice of surgery.

✍ I was at New York Hospital on the consultation-liaison service, which means I would do consults for any psychiatric problems that arose among patients who were in for a medical problem.

I was asked by the nurses to look at one of the patients because they and the physicians had noticed a peculiar thing about him. He was about to undergo coronary bypass surgery, and there was also a valve replacement involved. It was risky surgery. The odd thing about this patient was that as the time of surgery grew closer, he became less and less anxious, even serene. This was very bizarre behavior for someone about to undergo that kind of surgery. Usually people become more and more anxious as surgery approaches, until you have to give them antianxiety medication.

I met him and interviewed him. His name was Alan. He was thirty-seven years old, but he looked much older. He was prematurely gray, and his skin was wrinkled. He looked like someone in his fifties.

He was very glib and expansive, almost high. When I asked him why he was getting calmer, he told me that his surgery was his trial, his test, and he welcomed it.

The more I talked to him, the more I learned about him. He told me that when he was eight his father, who had also had cardiac problems, took to bed one morning because he wasn't feeling well. He was a schoolteacher, and before Alan left for school, he had asked his father to look over some homework he had done. Alan lived close to school, and he walked home for lunch. When he arrived home that day, he saw his whole family there crying. He found out his father had just died. His father was thirty-eight at the time.

As Alan grew up, more and more he felt that by asking his father to look over his homework that morning, he had taxed his father too much. He convinced himself that he had really killed his father, as crazy as that might sound.

His serenity continued right up to the surgery. He didn't need any medication at all to control his anxiety. He did beautifully in surgery and for the next six days his recovery went very well. But on the night of the sixth day, which was the night before his thirty-eighth birthday, his vital signs began to go bad suddenly. His cardiac output dropped, and he had all the signs of cardiac tamponade, a condition in which the pericardium—the sac around the heart—fills with blood and puts pressure on the heart to the point where it cannot beat properly.

This happened about ten o'clock at night. They rushed him to the operating room and opened his chest, and they found no tamponade, no excess fluid in his pericardium at all. They looked around for other problems, such as bleeding, but found nothing that suggested heart failure of any kind. They did all they could, but Alan went into full cardiac failure anyway, and they never got him off the table alive. He died a little before midnight.

I am convinced that Alan willed himself to die because he could not allow himself to live as long as his father had. He could not live with that guilt. If that is an extreme interpretation, I plead guilty. But I have seen so much since then to convince me I am right. Every day I see patients where it is clear not only that psychological factors are an integral part of their illness but also that probably without these factors there would be absolutely no disease at all. I point this out to them, and they tell me they had no idea of the connection. But I know they are doing it to themselves because I know Alan did it to himself.

There are some babies who are such obvious fighters, who you know want to live. But others seem to beg us to stop treatment. I took care of a little girl who started off as a tiny preemie. She had multitudinous problems, and she ended up paraplegic from a spinal embolism.

Her parents had staunchly refused to allow us to stop treatment, although we had tried to persuade them for weeks. We told them she was suffering and that her prognosis was very poor, but it was hard to get that across. When she was something like five or six months old, she took another serious turn for the worse, and her parents wanted us to do everything we could for her.

I took them over to their baby and I asked them to look closely at the baby's facial expression. If ever I have seen a suffering face, that was it. This baby was in agony. Her parents looked at her, and they understood what I meant. I think they realized that their baby was asking for them to let go. They agreed to discontinue, and she died.

A woman in her late fifties came into the hospital emergency room because she was having breathing problems related to her asthma. Until that time, she'd apparently been in good health. She became critically ill quickly, and there was a long, complicated resuscitation. Although she was kept alive, she lapsed into a coma, apparently as a result of brain injury of some kind.

This was a deep coma, and she showed no signs of coming out of it. This is the time I talk to the family and try to discuss what to do. I will pull the plug in these cases if the family wants it. But this woman had been so alive and healthy such a short time before, that her family hadn't accepted the idea that she was gone, so they told me to keep her on the respirator.

Somehow she stayed alive. After a few months it became clear that she was also paralyzed from the neck down. She was totally dependent on us, and she received beautiful care. She never even had a bedsore.

The neurologists said she'd never come out of it. But after a year or so, she started opening her eyes. We got all excited and called the neurologists, but they said she was still in coma, only she had her eyes open. But they were wrong. Over the next several months she awoke and clearly had an awareness of what was going on around her.

By this time, we had detached the respirator from her mouth and had given her a tracheostomy to get oxygen into her. Although she couldn't vocalize words, she could mouth them, so we got a lip reader. The first thing she told us was that she wanted to die.

In the meantime, her family had stopped coming to see her because they couldn't stand it. She was in limbo, neither alive nor dead, unable to move. She occasionally got an infection; when she did, we treated her because there was no way not to at that point.

She remained in the hospital because she was a Blue Cross patient. Blue Cross wouldn't pay for her to go to a nursing home because they would have had to pay the nursing home more money because of the care she demanded. So rather than establish such a precedent, they paid the hospital.

Month after month, she continued to tell us that she wanted to die. I don't want to inflict harm on people, but it was perfectly obvious that if I were in her situation, I would want to be dead, too. I knew her wish to die was rational, but there was no way I could kill her ethically. I can't do that as a physician, I can't do that as a human being. It was a horrible dilemma.

Her family finally showed up again, and now they wanted us to take her off life support. I told them I would not and that they would have to go to court. They dropped the issue and never came back. So we just continued taking care of her.

She was bedridden like this for five years until she suffered a circulatory collapse, which was inevitable. I made the decision not to resuscitate as her condition grew more unstable. I felt I was carrying out her wishes. I wasn't on call the night she died.

When I came in the next day, she was already wrapped in a sheet, and they were preparing to take her away. I had seen her virtually every day for the last five years, so I went to her bed and unwrapped her and looked at her, just to see that she was really dead.

The man was in his late sixties, and he came into the hospital with massive gastrointestinal bleeding. He had been a drinker, so his liver was in bad shape, and he also had some kidney failure. He'd lost a lot of blood, so we worked long and hard on this man to pull him through. His wife was really supportive of him, always at his bedside.

We began making very good progress with him, getting things under control. We came in one morning on rounds, and he extended his hand to shake our hands and thanked us all for what we had done for him. Immediately I understood what he was trying to say, and I said to him, "No, no.

You're doing fine. You're going to get better." He was a gracious man and he smiled at me, and in two days he was dead.

He had given up. He'd apparently decided that life wasn't worth the fight and that it was too much pressure on his wife to come in to the hospital every day and see him so ill. I think he felt he was a burden to everyone.

What struck me is that it showed how people can develop the will to live or the will to die, and how that will can determine whether they survive or not. It's a strange thing to say, but when he died, he was in better shape physically than he had been when he first came to the hospital and was fighting to live.

Perhaps if I had been more perceptive at the time, I could have talked to him and helped him see the things he had going for him—his fine wife, his children. So what I learned wasn't a medical lesson but a human lesson that has had a profound effect on the way I practice medicine.

> *"What struck me is that it showed how people can develop the will to live or the will to die, and how that will can determine whether they survive or not."*

When people are seriously ill, I try to deal with where they are, and I try to let them see that they have a reason to keep trying and living. If we are effective in doing that, we give the medicines a chance to work because the medicines can only do so much—the rest has to come from us.

It keeps you humble as a doctor. You realize that you aren't really curing the patient. They are curing themselves, and you are just aiding in that cure.

The absolute hardest thing to do is to answer a young child who asks, "Doctor, am I going to die?" What do you say to a child who you know is terminally ill? How do you assess what he or she can take in the way of an answer? How do you say anything with a loving pair of parents who are just heartbroken because they know what the truth is? In some way or other, you have to be honest with the kids.

I was taking care of a ten-year-old boy, a very likable young fellow. He had had two operations on his abdomen for a malignant tumor and was treated with chemotherapy, which made his hair fall out. Children hate to have their hair fall out, so this young boy wore hats, and he had quite a collection. And you could tell how he was feeling by what hat he had on and by the way he wore it. Sometimes he would have the big bill of one of his baseball hats pulled way down over his face so you couldn't really see him or deal with him, and other times he'd have the bill up and be cheerful and talkative.

I think he sensed that we were losing the fight and that he was weakening and that that probably meant he was going to die. He couldn't talk about it with his family. He didn't want to broach it with them, and they didn't want to talk about it with him. That's not unusual. A mother and father can't sit down and put their arms around their child and say, "Now in a few days you're going to die." That's not part of being a mom or dad.

But he wanted someone to talk to him. A very alert intern sensed this and came to me and said, "Nobody is answering this child's fears. Everybody is avoiding it, saying he's going to feel better tomorrow, and nobody is dealing with what he is dealing with all alone."

I had been a part of that. I had worn hats when I came in to see him and had joked with him, and it was always jolly. But after the intern alerted me, I made a point one day while the family was out having dinner to come into the room and sit with him and see what was on his mind. It was something I had to steel myself for because it is so painful to deal with a dying child for whom I can't do anything. I closed the door and told the nurses that I didn't want to be disturbed.

I asked, "Do you know what's going on around here?"

And he said, "Yeah, I think so. I don't think I'm going to get well."

"Well, we've done everything we can, and whatever it is inside you seems to be winning," I told him.

It was clear that he understood this. He said, "I don't think I'm going to live a month."

I said no one could know for sure when, but it did appear as if he were going to die. I said I did not know why his life would be short while his mother's and father's lives were so much longer. There are some things we cannot explain. I told him I would do all I could to get him well enough so that he could go home and spend some time with his horse and do whatever else he wanted to do at home before what was going to happen happened. He said he wanted to do that.

He asked me what I thought about heaven, and I told him that everyone has a different view of heaven, and whatever his idea was was just as likely to be true as mine. I told him that my view of heaven is pretty pleasant and that I thought I would see a lot of people that I loved who have gone on, and I said, "I'll bet you're going to do the same thing." And with that, he started talking about his grandfather, and what a great guy he was, and how he had died, and that he hoped his grandfather would be on the other side.

We were able to get him home for a few days before he came back to the hospital for the terminal phase. He told me he was glad he had gotten home. Although I asked him from time to time if he wanted to talk about anything, we never talked about death again. He didn't seem to want to talk about it anymore, even though he knew he was weakening, and he knew I knew he was weakening. He lived for another month.

I took care of a little girl with a very unusual kidney problem. Over a period of several years she did reasonably well, but all of a sudden one summer her parents noticed a mass in her abdomen. She went to surgery, where we found she had an extremely malignant, highly unusual tumor of her ovary, which probably had been the cause of her kidney problem. Her chance of survival was nil.

We treated her for her tumor, and she seemed to suffer every side effect of every drug we used. She was in pain and very uncomfortable, when her parents decided they wanted to stop treatment and bring her home. One of the doctors had trouble with that. He thought we ought to do *everything* medically, even though everyone knew our treatment was only palliative. There are some doctors like that. They believe that science should be pushed to its very limit before a patient dies, and then when the patient does die, they die of some scientific malfunction.

I felt that we had done all we could, so I told the parents that another doctor and I would come by their home one evening a week to check on this little girl. I wanted the parents to feel comfortable in their decision to stop treatment.

We came by once or twice a week, but in truth we could do nothing for her. We would talk to her and ask about symptoms, listen to her heart, and feel her abdomen. We prescribed medications to keep her comfortable and reassured the parents that they were doing the right thing and tried to make them feel that they had not been cut off from all medical services. I also decided that when she died, I would go to their home and pronounce her because if I didn't, there would have to be a coroner's investigation.

On the night she died, I went and stayed with the family for a while after I pronounced her dead. Six of us went to her funeral a couple of days later. I know some doctors will not go to the funerals of their patients. I become deeply emotional at the funerals. I think not to go is failing to complete the circle of care.

Strange things have happened in my medical career that I cannot explain. I mean, I don't have any idea what went on in these cases!

At the City of Hope Hospital in California I examined a young boy suffering from neuroblastoma, a cancer involving the nervous system. We sat down with the boy's mother to explain what we had found and told her that children with this disease usually do not survive but with treatment can live a reasonably long time. She was an intelligent woman, very caring about her son.

During the course of his early treatments, her son shared a hospital room with a child who had been diagnosed with neuroblastoma a year earlier. We had brought this other child back to the hospital because we were having difficulty controlling his cancer.

The two boys became close over the ensuing weeks when they were in and out of the hospital for treatment. The mother of the young boy with the newly diagnosed cancer kept in close touch and always wanted to know how the other child was doing. During his first round of chemotherapy both he and the other child did quite well. One day while I was talking to the mother, she turned to me and said something I will never forget. She said, "I know that the same day the other child dies, my son is going to die."

I couldn't quite believe what I was hearing, but I tried to dissuade her. I said, "No, no. That's not so. The other child's cancer is much more advanced. It has disseminated, and he has a different kind of neuroblastoma. But your child is doing well and we are very encouraged. We can't even find evidence of tumor right now. We think we've got it under control." Everything I told her was true, but it did not dispel her premonition.

She just looked at me and repeated, "I know the day that child dies, my child will die."

About three months after she had said that her child was admitted for another round of routine chemotherapy. He appeared absolutely well. We could find no trace of tumor. But during this time the other child had gone steadily downhill and his condition reached the critical stage. I got a call one morning to come to his room and by the time I arrived there he had died. This child's parents had been prepared, so I went down the hall and put my arm around them to break the news. As I was walking with them a nurse came rushing over to me and said, "You'd better come right now. We're having problems."

*"Even at the cutting edge of medical science, we're only scratching the surface of what human life is all about."*

I walked into this other boy's room and although he had looked fine when he came in, he now looked terrible. I examined him and couldn't determine what was wrong. We ran a bunch of tests and still we couldn't find out what was wrong. He kept getting worse no matter what we tried. He died that night.

I went over to comfort the mother and she appeared completely calm, almost serene. She said, "It's all right. I told you he was going to die the same day as the other child."

We did an autopsy and could find no cause of death, and I have no idea why he died. There is so much in medicine that is absolutely unknown to us, and doctors are very uncomfortable talking to one another about these things. But events like this make you realize how complex we all are. Even at the cutting edge of medical science, we're only scratching the surface of what human life is all about.

A baby was born with a disease called spinal muscular atrophy, which is a hereditary paralysis. Sometimes these babies are not too badly off at first, but by three months at the latest they develop severe paralysis. It is absolutely lethal. No one has ever survived. They usually die from aspiration pneumonia; they can't breathe.

This little baby happened to be born with severe paralysis from the neck down. Knowing what was wrong, we knew that there was nothing we could do for the baby. She was an alert little girl with a normal brain entrapped in a totally useless body. She was already wasting away. The parents asked us if we could keep the baby alive indefinitely on the ventilator. I told them we could.

Those of us taking care of the baby told them that nothing would reverse their baby's condition. They were very accepting and knew there was nothing that could be done, and they didn't want their child to suffer. We told them that we should take the baby off the ventilator, and they agreed.

I removed the baby from the ventilator and was prepared to hold her for as long as it took, but she died very quickly in my arms. The parents could not stand to be there for this. But after the baby died, they came over and thanked me for holding her for them. I felt I had helped them.

This never gets any easier. It gets harder, if anything. We deal with a lot of uncertainty in our work. We remember the babies no one expected to survive who not only made it but turned out normal. But with this baby, I was absolutely certain. I mean, I knew this baby would not live, but I still feel terrible about it. I remember in graphic detail every single baby that I had to remove from the respirator after all hope was gone. There have been fifteen of them. Most of them had brain damage, so I knew they were not registering. That made my job a little easier. But no doctor ever does this without a feeling of sorrow.

I operated on a beautiful young girl with a brain tumor who initially did very well. After her recovery, she returned to high school and scored quite high on her college boards and was accepted at Vassar. She was a wonderful, charming girl with a warm family. But quite suddenly her tumor disseminated and accelerated, and within a short amount of time we knew she faced a hopeless situation. Her family decided that they would give her no more treatment, which was appropriate.

She had come in for a number of follow-up visits, and I had grown very attached to her. I wanted to see her before she died because I liked her so much, and I think I have an obligation to my terminal patients to help them leave the world any way I can.

When I visited her, she was very pleased. She couldn't talk, but she knew who I was, and I knew it meant something to her that I had come to visit. I just held her hand and sat with her for a while. She died the next day. This was hard to do, but it is part of what I have to face because I deal with so many children who are terribly ill, and many of them don't make it.

I don't tell a child he or she is going to die, and they seldom ask. If they do, I tell them everyone will die someday. I don't think it's my place to tell them they are dying. If they were adults and had to get their affairs in order, I would tell them, but children don't have the same responsibilities as adults and don't anticipate as adults do.

I tell the families when their child enters a terminal phase, and that is always painful because I know how hard and how much they have hoped. I've found that the one thing families want from me at that point is to know I care.

When the end is imminent, I let the family remain alone with their child as much as possible. I try to get all the IVs out, keep all the other doctors and nurses away, and just let them be together as a family to make their final peace.

I once had a mother with a beautiful baby who was
dying from a tumor. As the baby neared death, I said, "It's
time for you to hold him in your lap. We're going to leave
you alone." She held her baby as he died. I think parents
need to know that when the end came, they were there to
give their child comfort.

For me, the death of a child is always a terrible, painful
wrench. I'm filled with an overwhelming feeling of impo-
tence because I can't do anything to help.


When I was in the oncology section at a hospital in
San Diego, I saw a young man from Texas who had melanoma. Melanoma is a terrible form of cancer—my least favorite. It starts out as a kind of skin cancer similar to a
mole, but once it spreads, it can move throughout the body.

This is exactly what had happened to this young fellow.
It had spread into his brain. He had been to a military hospital in Texas, and they had given up and asked him where
he wanted to go to die and he had said San Diego.

When he came into my office that first time, he said,
"Doctor, I don't want to die. You have to do something for
me." That's very unusual. A patient almost never says that,
especially one who had probably been told numerous times
before that he was going to die. He had a young daughter
and a wife. He was a runner, just like me, and he was my
age. It was as if I were looking at myself.

I was at a total loss. I wondered, what am I going to do
for this guy? I told him I would look into his case and meet
him later that day in the hospital rotunda. I took his medical records to neurosurgery and asked if they could operate
on his brain tumor.

One of the neurosurgeons asked me if I was kidding.
He said the cancer had moved into the speech and motor
areas of his brain. If they operated, he would lose vital functions in his body.

Then I went to the radiotherapist. I asked, "Can you

radiate this?" Same answer. "He's already had 4,000 rads of radiation. If he's given anymore, it'll destroy his brain."

I went all around the hospital and received the same response from everyone I consulted with. There was nothing I could do for this young fellow except offer him chemotherapy, which doesn't do much against melanoma.

That afternoon I went to the hospital rotunda to talk with him. The rotunda is a beautiful place—lots of sunlight and palm trees all around. As I came in, I saw him across the way. He was completely bald from the radiotherapy, and he was embracing his wife. I could see they were both crying. Their little girl was with them.

I tried to approach them, but I couldn't. I felt as if I were frozen. I just stood there and watched them holding one another. I broke down crying, and I almost collapsed to my knees. I'm a Catholic, and I asked myself, My God, why is this happening, why do You do this?

Then I told myself, you're an oncologist and this is your job. Nobody likes to do this. That's why a lot of people don't go into this specialty. You went into it because you wanted to help people, to give them comfort even when you couldn't save their life. I came up with every rationalization possible so I could muster my strength to go up to them. As I approached them, I tapped them on the shoulder, and they turned and looked at me, and I was absolutely devastated by the expressions on their faces. I will never forget them.

The little girl kind of tugged at my leg and said, "Can you help my daddy?"

I did all I could to control myself, and I told them I would do everything in my power to help them. But in reality I could do little besides try to give them comfort.

He wanted to try chemotherapy, and I gave it to him, and he became very ill with it. He didn't live long, and I gave him morphine to ease his pain as he was dying—that was all I could do.

You lose patients in oncology. It's part of what you do, and when it happens, I feel grief for the people I've gotten close to. I usually become quiet and kind of withdraw for a while. I felt close to him and his family, and I grieved for a long time. I kept asking myself, what did I do to help this guy? And I came to the conclusion that I had done everything I could but that there was not much I could have done. That's the only answer I have.

✎   I took care of a man with cardiomyopathy, a condition in which the heart muscle weakens and deteriorates. We don't know why it happens. He was hospitalized, and I had done a lot to get him out of congestive heart failure and to get his medicines working optimally.-He was in his late sixties, and I had gotten to know him and like him.

While he was still in the hospital, he had a cardiac arrest and I was called to his room. We did a long resuscitation, but no matter what we did, he didn't respond. We thumped on his chest for forty-five minutes. There is no crisp end point to this kind of resuscitation, but we finally decided to stop because we knew we were not going to be able to bring him back. We couldn't get a spontaneous pulse or respiration. He was dead.

After it was over, this man suddenly sat bolt upright in bed. This was no reflex contraction of his muscles. His eyes, which had looked glassy all during the resuscitation, changed and appeared to be focused, as if he were looking at something. There was purpose in his gaze, and I expected him to get up and walk away. Then he just laid back down and was dead.

I've never seen anything like it before or since, and I never heard of it happening to other people. If it hadn't happened to me, I would have said it couldn't have happened. It is the eeriest experience I've ever had, and I had dreams and nightmares about it for months afterward.

✎   I served as a Peace Corps doctor in the Carolina Islands in the South Pacific. I was stationed on Yap, the big island, and from there we regularly took a boat trip to the other islands. We carried coconuts, canned goods, a priest, a storekeeper, myself, and some passengers. The whole trip covered about a thousand miles and took about three weeks.

Many of these islands are inhabited by only twenty people or so. They're out in the middle of nowhere. The people are very friendly, and our arrival always caused great excitement.

We came to one of the islands, and there was the usual excitement. The people there were also very anxious for me to see a young woman who was ill. They led me to a small thatched hut, where I saw her sitting on the floor kind of gasping and grunting. She was in her early thirties. Her family was around her rubbing coconut oil on her back. I examined her, and it was clear that she had an advanced case of pneumonia. This was during a flu epidemic on the islands, which is devastating because they have so few immunities to that kind of disease.

I was very worried for her. I gave her some antibiotics, brought her down to the beach, put her aboard the dingy, and took her out to the boat. I told the captain that we should head right back to the main island for treatment; there is a little hospital there.

We left right away. We put her belowdecks, where a medical aide helped me care for her. A group of island people had also come along with us, and they were with her every moment of the trip, saying rosaries for her and giving her all the comfort and support they could.

She was very weak and I knew she was getting weaker as the trip wore on, but I could do nothing more than what I was already doing. I couldn't give her oxygen or anything else to sustain her. I think she had a viral pneumonia, and the antibiotics were of little use. I felt incredibly helpless, even superfluous. We were only a few hours out of Yap; I was hoping she could hold on, but she died. I was stunned when she did, and I pronounced her dead. The ship turned around and headed back to this young woman's home island. When that ship came into the island's lagoon, even from a distance you could tell from the silence that the people knew something terrible had happened.

We anchored in the lagoon, put her body in the dingy, and headed toward shore. As we did, the women on the island standing alongshore began wailing. The chief also came to the shore to await us. As we came ashore, the island people formed a long processional line. They took her body, which we had put on a stretcher, and carried her over to a small thatched church and held a funeral service for her right there. Everybody from the island attended. Her family was well supported.

I had been trained at an academic hospital in New York City, and this was a view of death that I had never seen. There was acceptance of death in this culture, and I recognized that my role as a doctor had been virtually nil because it was the people themselves who had given her the care and the love she needed as she died. There were no tubes or heroics, no thrashing around over medical ethics.

We had a premature baby in the nursery—a "frequent flyer," we called him, because he was in and out of the hospital for months. He had multiple shunts because of water on the brain. Each time he came in, he went back on the ventilator and became increasingly dependent on it. The last time he came in, he was in septic shock, looked bloated, was in kidney failure, and was in shunt failure again. Based on his CAT scan, I was confident in saying that this baby's brain was very badly damaged.

What we did for this baby epitomizes something that we sometimes do in the intensive care nursery that I hate. We aggressively treated his shock, gave him a lot of antibiotics, shored up his failing blood pressure, increased his urine production, and were more aggressive with his ventilation.

He improved marginally and there were still things we could fiddle with, but in my heart of hearts I knew it wasn't worth it. Even if he did survive, he wouldn't grow up to lead a productive life. It was doubtful that he would even recognize who his mother was or realize it was a sunny day.

It was pathetic to see this baby. It became a mechanical exercise to save him because we lost sight of him. There was nothing about him that resembled a baby anymore, in appearance or activity.

The baby's mother was single and hardly visited him. We had to go looking for her, and when we brought her in, the first thing she said was, "Do we have to continue to do this?" This was a very young, unsophisticated, withdrawn mother who saw everything we were doing, but she was able to ask whether we really had done everything we could for him. We had been agonizing with this baby, asking ourselves this question. But the answer was no, we hadn't done everything we possibly could have—but should we, under the circumstances?

I felt that to continue treatment in this case would be an abomination. The mother agreed to "no-code" him, which means we don't do anything heroic to keep him alive. I almost dislike no codes because of their ambiguity. Do they just mean you won't use traditional resuscitative measures to stimulate the baby's heart if he arrests? What if the baby develops an infection? Do you treat the infection or not? What if his endotracheal tube becomes plugged? Do you let him die for a purely mechanical reason? A no code basically says that the baby's chances of surviving are nil, but there are these gray areas that are very confusing. And one physician may interpret a no code differently from another.

We had the no code on for about forty-eight hours, and there were no changes. Then the mother agreed to take her baby off the ventilator. She stayed while I did it, but she didn't want to hold the baby. A nurse held the baby's hand while I removed the ventilator tube. Then the nurse held him in her arms while he died, with the mother watching.

The mother was not articulate and spoke very little anyway. She became very emotional. I could see that in her face.

I sometimes feel that I should be sadder when we discontinue treatment than I am. I think I'm not because by the time I've come to that point, I am comfortable in my belief that it's time to stop. I don't think I will ever be totally comfortable with having the ability to say, "Now it's time to die." That is very powerful; it's kind of scary. And I don't think there is ever a final answer as to whether it is or isn't the right decision. It may sound callous, but it's rare for me to lie awake at night agonizing over it. But then, no one comes around to say, "Look, you made a mistake here. You allowed a baby to die that could have survived." Maybe that's why I'm able to feel relatively comfortable.

*"A plausible estimate is that three percent of physicians, at some time in their career, are impaired as a result of drug or alcohol abuse. Other estimates place the figure at five percent or higher."*

"The Impaired Physician"
Harvard Medical School Health Letter
March 1987

*"Substance abuse is much more rampant among physicians than people in other professions."*

A doctor who treats addicted doctors
March 1987

# 9

# Impaired Healers

"When we first started our impaired physician program in our state in 1978, our average physician was in his early fifties, practiced in a rural area, and was primarily alcoholic," said a doctor who himself was a recovering alcoholic. "That has changed. The average physician we see today in our programs is in his late thirties, often is in a group practice or in a hospital, and his drug problem reflects society's—alcohol, marijuana, and cocaine, in that order."

At first glance, I found it difficult to believe that physicians—highly motivated people who often witness firsthand the terrible affects of substance abuse—would so easily fall victim to the same disease, but they do. In fact, in the opinion of the addiction experts I spoke with, doctors fall victim more often than the rest of the population. In addition, there is another, smaller group of physicians who become impaired through depression and other emotional problems.

What percentage of physicians become impaired? No one knows for certain, but some experts believe that as many as 15 or 20 percent of physicians, at some time in their lives, will have a problem that causes some impairment. A September 1986 article in *The New England Journal of Medicine* found that 78 percent of the students and 59 percent of the physicians they surveyed admitted to using psychoactive drugs in their lives, and 10 percent admitted to using them at the time of the survey.

Anesthesiologists seem to run the greatest risk of substance abuse, but obstetricians, and emergency-medicine specialists also have high rates of drug and alcohol abuse. Because obstetricians often get up at night for deliveries, they fall prey to a habit of using stimulants to wake up and depressants to get back to sleep again. Emergency-medicine specialists work regular shifts and aren't on call, so they have the time and money for abuse. Male physicians have more drug problems than females, but as women increasingly enter medicine, they are catching up.

Access to drugs is clearly an important factor in physician addiction. Anesthesiologists live in a world of drugs, and getting them for themselves is often as easy as reaching into the hospital drug cabinet. Like many cases of drug abuse, a doctor's can start innocently with taking a drug for a specific problem. One doctor I interviewed remembers a nurse who was herself an addict giving him a powerful narcotic when he complained of a headache. That was the beginning of his long history of drug abuse.

One addiction expert said that another factor is the enormous pressure put on physicians at a young age and the belief, inculcated into them during medical school, that they are special, highly select people. "This gives them a sense of invulnerability, a sense that bad things happen to other people, not to them," he contended. Moreover, doctors are taught to swallow their feelings, and to see death and dying as a failure on their part.

Easy access to drugs, the lack of adequate drug education among physicians, and these psychological factors make physicians especially susceptible to substance abuse.

The new drugs of abuse—both legal and illegal—create powerful dependencies much more quickly than alcohol ever did, and they cause more rapid deterioration in personal and professional lives.

"Cocaine and some of the new anesthetic drugs like

Fentanyl can do to you in two years what it takes alcohol twenty years to do," said one doctor who has treated many physician-addicts. In some ways this is beneficial because it gets some physicians into treatment more quickly.

Physicians and other health care workers are more willing to report doctors who have drug problems today than they used to be. But many doctors with serious drug and alcohol problems continue to go undetected or unreported. All fifty states now have an impaired-physicians program of some kind, usually under the auspices of the state medical society. However, in only fifteen to twenty states are these programs staffed and financed well enough to do the job that needs to be done, which is to get addicted doctors either treated or out of medicine.

The first person who confronted me about my drug use was a patient in the operating room. She was an addict herself and saw track marks on my arm that no one else had noticed, not even my wife. She said to me, "Oh, I see you do a little drugs yourself."

"Don't give me that," I said. "I just scratched myself."

You learn to think fast when you're an addict. I always knew what my comeback would have to be because I was so addicted to drugs that I didn't think I could live without them—even though they were killing me. But the pain of exposure, the shame to myself and my family and to my profession—that would be death to me.

The hospital had a very loose hold on its narcotics, so no one noticed any of the drugs I was stealing at first. But after a few months they began to think something was wrong, and I became one of the suspects. They tested me by asking me to rotate to intensive care for two months. I knew I wouldn't have access to drugs there, so I fought that very hard, and they figured out why I didn't want to leave the OR. Not long after that, one of my superiors caught me stealing drugs. I was scared as hell. I thought my medical career might end right there.

I confessed; they seemed understanding and told me to go into treatment. I saw a psychiatrist the next day and went through a detoxification program that did absolutely nothing to help me confront my drug problem. In three and a half weeks I was back at work. That was my "treatment."

*"My addiction got worse and worse. I was sometimes writing three prescriptions a day and filling them myself."*

I stayed clean for months, but the urge to use again became overwhelming. One afternoon I stole some drugs from the drug cabinet and slipped into the bathroom. I hadn't used since my "treatment" six months earlier, so when I took the same dose I had used before, I overdosed and fell to the floor unconscious. I stopped breathing. There is no question in my mind that I would have died had someone not found me and given me CPR. You'd think a doctor would know better, but I didn't.

When I came to, I asked what had happened, and one of the doctors who knew of my problem said, "The same thing that happened before." This time my superiors suspended me from my residency and told me to go to the psychiatric ward of another hospital. They really didn't know what else to do with me.

I was the only chemically dependent person at this hospital, and the psychiatrists had no idea how to treat me. They said I had a character disorder, that I was too tense, that I had to learn to take life easier. They talked about the underlying cause of my problem. Christ, my problem was that I was a drug addict!

I then entered an outpatient treatment program, where each week I gave witnessed urines. Someone would come to the bathroom and watch me pee into a cup every week. I remained clean and was allowed back into my residency, but I had to continue with the outpatient drug-treatment program.

When my residency ended, I chose to work at an urgent-care-center area because it was low pressure, which I thought I needed. Because I still gave witnessed urine samples every week, I remained clean for three entire years, but the compulsion to use drugs never left me. I guess there was some pain in my life that I could not face.

As soon as they stopped witnessing my urine samples, I began taking the prescription drugs I could get easily like Percodan, Percocet, and Valium. I convinced myself that I would just use drugs every now and then to help me along.

I still had to give unwitnessed urine samples, but being a clever physician, I knew how they did the urine tox screens. To confound them, I'd put vials of my contact lens solution into my shorts before I went down to give my urine. By the time I got there, the solution was warm. I would also take a lot of vitamins that morning, so my urine would be very bright yellow. I'd put three or four drops of urine into the vial, which would give the contact lens solution a pale yellow color that would look like urine to anybody. I pulled that trick once a week for nearly three years, and they never caught on.

I also monitored the medical consequences of my addiction by ordering liver tests on myself every two weeks. Doing that gave me a sense of control over my addiction. I told myself that I couldn't be in very much trouble because my liver was normal.

My addiction got worse and worse. I was sometimes writing three prescriptions a day and filling them myself. I lived forty miles from where I worked, and I had this long strip of drugstores along my commuting route. I hit forty different pharmacies. My partner at the urgent-care center suspected something was wrong. He knew about my history and offered to help me get treatment again. But I convinced him I had no drug problem. Here I was being offered an opportunity to come clean, and I denied it. My wife also wondered if I was taking drugs again. I lied to her, too. I had "clean" urines every week, so she believed me. She thought that everything that was wrong with our relationship was her fault.

Then one day the state drug enforcement agency called me.

"Would you please come down to the office?" they asked.

I said, "What if I don't?"

They said, "Then we'll come and get you."

They forced me to surrender my narcotics license. What had led up to this, of course, were the four hundred illegal prescriptions I'd written over an eighteen-month period. They were going to charge me with seventy-five felony counts of drug diversion.

A short time later, the state medical board suspended my license to practice medicine. I think that if the state had not intervened, it might have turned out worse for me because I had reached the point in my addiction where I was thinking about breaking into pharmacies and stealing large quantities of drugs so I wouldn't have to write phony prescriptions every day. I had also thought of ordering drugs through drug companies with other doctors' drug license numbers. Crazy stuff.

My medical career was almost over, and I finally came to the realization that I needed serious, long-term treatment. I needed confrontation. I needed someone to tell me I was full of shit.

I entered and completed treatment and remain drug free today. My medical license has been restored on a probationary basis, and I'm struggling to get back into medicine.

There is much to regret when you're an addict. I always had an image of myself as a caring human being and doctor. But when I was an addict, I know I wasn't the husband I should have been to my wife or the doctor I should have been to my patients. Those are the things that still pain me.

🖋  A few years ago, another physician and I were both reported to the state medical society for our alcohol problems. Word got back to my chief of medicine at the hospital. He refused to believe I had a problem and swore up and down that it had to be wrong. Well, if you think I would drink around my chief of medicine, then you don't understand the problem. There is a big misconception that if you have a drug or alcohol problem, you have no control whatsoever. It's only in the late stages of an addiction that you lose control. I mean, do you think a doctor would come to work drunk?

By the time I was reported, I had progressed into a fairly regular pattern of drinking about two six-packs a night at home. I never drank at my office, but my days at the hospital were becoming shorter and shorter because I came in later and left earlier. By the time I was reported, I suppose I was spending four hours a day at the hospital, from 10 A.M. to 2 P.M. Physicians are not monitored very closely in hospitals.

Toward the end, my memory became very poor. I had reached the point where if another doctor asked me to see a patient one day and I didn't write it down, I might very well forget by the next day. If they came back and asked me about the patient, I'd give them a strange look because I had absolutely no recollection of it. I had to be reintroduced to an anesthesiologist I already knew—that's how bad I got. I also developed a hand tremor. I was worried that someone might see it and that it would give me away, so I was careful to hide it. Even during my worst periods, I was always careful with patients. None of them ever complained about me.

Even though I had tried to deny it, I realized deep down that I had an alcohol problem. My father was an alcoholic. I remember when he drove me to my first medical school interview. I was so nervous, I was beside myself. He suggested that I go down the street and get a shot of whiskey to calm my nerves before the interview. Fortunately, I did not take his suggestion.

When I did go into serious treatment, it was successful, as it is for most doctors because we feel we have so much to lose if we don't recover. Our whole world collapses if we lose our medical license.

My marriage failed after I began my recovery. That's often the case because the relationship has learned to compensate for the alcoholism but often cannot adjust to sobriety. I've seen that a lot now that I'm involved in helping other doctors with drug or alcohol problems.

The second doctor who was turned in with me was a close personal friend. He was certain that we had been reported because we frequented the same bar, which is right across the street from our hospital. He tried to find out who reported us. He became very paranoid and would not ever go back to that bar. He refused treatment and denied that he had a drinking problem, although later he had to leave our hospital as a result of his drinking. He took what we call a geographic cure. He went to one state, then another; the last I knew, he was in West Virginia. He still hasn't stopped drinking, and I have personally reported him in two of the states where he's practiced because I want him to get help. I still see him, and when I do, I talk to him about his drinking problem, but his denial is so thick, he is very hard to reach.

I have some curiosity about who turned me in, but not a lot. Whoever it was, I consider him or her a friend.

After we determine that a physician has a drug or alcohol problem—usually by talking to other doctors and to family members—we take what we call the "velvet hammer" approach by offering the doctor treatment. Only if he stonewalls do we threaten to take his case before the state licensing board, which can suspend his license to practice medicine. If you take only a punitive approach, the doctor may commit suicide rather than lose his license. I also think doctors don't report problem doctors often because they don't want to destroy the other doctors' medical career.

Only twice have I had to go to the licensing commission as a final threat to force someone into treatment. One of those doctors did go into treatment and is doing well; the other, a woman, is married to a physician who is clearly an enabler. He's simply allowing her to continue her drinking.

She's in her forties, and from all I have learned about her, she is a well-trained, skilled, and well-liked ophthalmologist. She'd been in treatment programs before but refused to go again. So rather than practice medicine anymore, she has chosen not to renew her medical license and has dropped out of medicine. That's a real loss.

When I first went out into private practice after leaving academic medicine, I was seeing far too many patients—between fifteen and twenty a day, usually including five new patients who needed complete histories and physicals.

I'd see patients until six or seven, then dictate notes until eleven or midnight, then go home and take calls about patients I'd admitted to the hospital. After going to bed at midnight or one in the morning, I'd routinely get up at four in the morning to dictate charts and then get to the hospital early the next morning to make rounds. I was working like a madman at an absolutely backbreaking pace. Part of it was due to my worry that I had to build a large patient base to survive economically, and part of it was that I really loved what I did.

But during this time I began to drink more than I was comfortable with. Because my mother had had alcohol problems, I had always watched my own drinking carefully, but I'm not a moderate person by nature, and I did drink to celebrate, sometimes to excess. But now, as I was feeling burned out from my eighty- to ninety-hour work week, I started drinking the moment I got home. I didn't drink during the day, but I found I was drinking daily and on weekends and that I was beginning earlier in the day.

I became concerned enough to stop drinking at social occasions, but there were still times of enormous pressure when I'd go back to drinking. I knew that drinking could affect my career and my marriage, and I wanted to stop. Many times I did for weeks or months, but I'd slip after I had promised myself not to drink anymore. I was drunk for my young son's birthday party, and my wife got very angry with me and told me to leave and sleep it off. She made it clear that she would not put up with my drinking.

I attended some Alcoholics Anonymous meetings, ostensibly because I had referred some patients there and wanted to see what they were like. But in my heart of hearts I knew I could become a serious alcoholic if I continued drinking.

I never missed a day's work, never got a DWI, and don't know of any specific instance in which my drinking impaired my medical judgment, although it must have. I did have a blackout, which was very disquieting because I felt like I was losing control. I was also self-medicating, taking beta-blockers on a regular basis to ease tension and Valium and sleeping pills on occasion. I knew this was wrong, but I found a way to justify it to myself.

Many times I told myself that I had worked hard to establish myself in medicine but now I was blowing it by drinking, but that was not enough to get me to stop permanently. I monitored my liver enzymes, worried that they'd be too high, but they never were. But what worried me most was the uncertainty of it all, of what was going to happen and who would know.

One surgeon who I spoke with regularly would sometimes ask me, "Are you okay?" I'd say I was and seem puzzled by his question. But I could tell he was concerned about me, and I later learned that one of his associates had

had alcohol problems and that he had become acutely sensitive to this and had picked up on my drinking problem.

One Sunday afternoon I got a call from a resident in the emergency room, who asked about one of my patients. We talked about the case, and then the resident, whom I knew, asked me if I was having a party. This made it pretty obvious that she knew I was drinking at home at an inappropriate time.

This was one of the incidents that helped me reach a point where I knew I had to stop drinking altogether because I was jeopardizing my career. I continued to go to AA meetings and still do; I realized that there is no half way about it. I was able to stop altogether. I also cut back on the hours I put into my practice. I feel incredibly lucky to have stopped and to have my marriage and career intact.

✒ I went into an anesthesiology residency and began my love affair with Fentanyl, a narcotic-anesthetic that we use all the time. I saw how great it made patients feel. I tried it intravenously. With Fentanyl, if you use it once, you are hooked. It removed every trace of anxiety and tension I had felt. But I never became so high that I felt detached; I felt efficient and in control. My mistake was in thinking I would always feel this way.

Getting Fentanyl was ridiculously easy. All I had to do was open a cabinet and take as much as I wanted. I'd use a tourniquet and syringe to inject myself.

I got away with this for months, and all the time I was using more and more. When my addiction reached its height, I needed to shoot up every two hours. So if an open-heart case took four or five hours, I'd have to leave in the middle of the operation, go to the men's room in the OR suite, get my fix, and then go back to the operating room and continue surgery. I was so quick, I could inject myself faster than most people actually go to the bathroom.

I had the "M. Deity syndrome." You know—I'm

smart, I'm in control of this. And being an anesthesiologist, I told myself I would know when to stop to prevent any disasters.

During one twenty-hour neurosurgical operation, my relief came every two hours or so, and I went off for my Fentanyl fix. But later that night, my relief didn't show up for hours. I became edgy and distracted because I was experiencing withdrawal.

I was so distracted, I injected a blood product into the wrong port of an indwelling catheter. It caused a blood clot that went to the patient's lung, and the patient arrested. We gave him every drug imaginable—Adrenalin, calcium, bicarbonate—and we shocked him with the defibrillator pads a half-dozen times before his normal heart rhythm was restored. Luckily, he suffered no ill effects from the arrest.

People arrest during surgery for no apparent reason sometimes, so no one realized that my mistake had caused the arrest. At that time I was so deeply into my addiction that I even denied it to myself. Can you imagine? I had almost killed a patient, yet I convinced myself that I wasn't responsible.

*"I went into an anesthesiology residency and began my love affair with Fentanyl, a narcotic-anesthetic that we use all the time."*

Part of my recovery has been to admit my responsibility, which has been difficult, and to realize that I can no longer be an anesthesiologist. I have heard that about 85 percent of anesthesiologists and anesthesiology residents experiment with some of the drugs they give, especially Fentanyl, and I believe it. It's too tempting.

A doctor at my hospital was well known for being totally incompetent. He'd been trained in one of the best programs in the country, but he apparently developed some kind of psychiatric disorder. He was a very strange individual.

When I first met him, he was doing night call and was known among the nurses for prescribing vitamins and enemas no matter what the patient had. On one ward the nurses would bet whether he'd prescribe vitamin C or vitamin B that night. They considered him a joke.

This doctor had been in the public health service for more than ten years with these prescribing habits. Other doctors had raised questions in the past as to whether he was competent or not. I found memos in the file about him, but none of the higher-ups had done anything about him. He was still practicing medicine, despite being clearly disabled. One reason was that so few doctors are willing to work in public hospitals that if you're breathing, you can get hired. There's also the fact that doctors are unwilling to blow the whistle on other doctors. It's somehow bad manners or breaking the faith of the medical profession to report a bad doctor.

He was involved in two patient deaths that I became aware of. One patient, a very elderly woman, had a strangulating bowel, and he prescribed an enema. The enema caused a perforated bowel, which killed her. Another patient had a fever of 106 degrees, and he prescribed vitamins. This patient also died.

On the basis of this, I asked the medical licensing board to investigate the doctor. When they began the investigation, the doctor was told of it and resigned from the hospital. A few weeks later, he killed himself.

During my chief residency I started to snort cocaine. I had a friend who sold it, so it was always easy to get. I had about forty residents under me, and eight or ten of us snorted cocaine together regularly, sometimes at the hospital. We'd go into the physicians' lounge late at night and have a little cocaine party while we were on call. I'm a hyper, four-plus anal, type A personality anyhow. Cocaine very quickly made me paranoid, but I still had a compulsion to use it.

After my residency I was given a cardiology fellowship, an honor that can really help your medical career. But I resigned from it within a year because I had to be on call every third night for it and that meant I couldn't get high with alcohol or cocaine those nights.

I took a job in charge of an intensive care unit and a coronary care unit. I made $80,000 a year for a fifty-hour week. I could make up the schedules, so I could have weekends off and work four days a week.

I started having severe blackouts during this period. They would scare me. I'd wake up in my apartment and couldn't remember how I got there or where my car was. It was only by the grace of God that I didn't kill anyone or myself when I drove home from bars. I never even got stopped by a cop.

My drinking and drug-taking were definitely interfering with my ability to function as a doctor at that point. I lost my desire for it and some of my ability. I can't remember specific incidents where my medical judgment was impaired, but if I hadn't been hung over, I'm sure I would have been thinking more clearly.

I got into heroin next. I could get it pretty easily, but if I ran out, I would order a double dose of narcotics for a patient and give the patient half and myself half. I even had nurses I was dating get me prescriptions for Percocet, a narcotic. They would say it was for their grandmother and give it to me. No one ever confronted me about my drug or alcohol problem. You just don't go up to a doctor and accuse him of being a drug addict.

Each morning I'd carry about two dozen twenty-dollar bags into the hospital and take them into the bathroom or the on-call room. Here I was now making $100,000 a year, but I had to borrow money to get a flat tire fixed because I was spending $300 a day on heroin.

When I couldn't get high from heroin anymore, I took Quaaludes. I blacked out at the hospital once. At about the same time a nurse I knew told me she was worried about my behavior changes. My speech became slurred at times. I was really falling apart.

Also at this time I got a beep to come to the hospital administrator's office. When I arrived, he was standing there with the director of medicine, and he said, "A lot of people are concerned about you." I asked why. He said I wasn't acting myself. I said, "Yeah, I've been working too hard. I'm going to take some time off." I think they were hinting at drug problems, but they didn't come out and say it.

The next day was a Friday. I bought $600 worth of drugs to get me through the weekend. Within about three hours I had used them up. All the money I had in the bank was gone. I sat there looking at my TV set and tried to figure out how I could get it to the streets and sell it for my next fix. Then something came over me. I knew I couldn't live like this anymore. I knew I needed help. The next week, I went into treatment.

I'm recovering. I attend an Alcoholics or Narcotics Anonymous meeting every day of the week and will continue to go every day of my life. If I miss even one, my attitude changes. It's not that I want to use drugs again, because I think that God has lifted that compulsion from me. It's that I revert to that self-centered, alcoholic way of thinking. The meetings keep me sane.

🖋 I was getting ready to go to the OR when a woman brought her mother into the clinic with chest pain. I knew the mother had a history of angina, but I sent them over to my office to wait for me rather than take them right over to the hospital emergency room where I could examine her. This was in a rural area, and I was on alone to cover both the hospital and the clinic. Just as I was finishing in the OR, my nurse ran over, and I could see in her eyes that she was panicked. She said the woman had collapsed. I ran over, and the woman was unconscious in my office. We tried CPR, but we didn't have all the resuscitation equipment or the necessary drugs, and she died. She might have died even if she had been in the emergency room, but that's not the point.

I now know that I suffer from an organic predisposition to depression. The stress I was under in running my practice made my depression worse, and my depression made the stress worse. It kind of went around and around. The worse my depression got, the less energy I had to deal with everything that was happening, so that just created more stress.

My sending that woman and her daughter to my office to wait rather than to the emergency room was a result of my feeling kind of panicky about everything I had to do that day and not being able to cool it and just do the important things first. I wanted her to be in my office because that was more convenient, which is an example of my judgment being hampered by my stress. But there is a possibility that her death was caused by my decision. I made a decision to save a little time. It didn't make any sense.

Most of the reports of physicians with drug or alcohol problems that we get come to us on a confidential basis, usually from a fellow physician or sometimes from a spouse. Rarely if ever does a patient complain. That isn't surprising, because doctors go to great lengths to protect their careers.

But one time we did find out about a doctor from a patient. The doctor was a young guy, an internist, who worked at an urgent-care center, one of those "doc in a boxes." He was into all kinds of drugs—you name it. He turned out to be about as sick as they come. One of his patients caught him getting funny with some prescriptions he was writing and reported him to the state committee on medical discipline, which referred him to our impaired-physicians committee.

We had a lot of dealings with this guy. The first time two members of our committee went to his apartment to confront him about his drug problem. He excused himself, walked into his kitchen, and came back pointing a gun at them. He said, "Okay, guys. Get the hell out of here." They did.

We learned from that. You don't go into somebody's lair to confront them about something like that. You've got to find neutral ground, and that's the way we do it now. This doctor has been in and out of treatment programs. Recently we told him to go into another program. When he didn't show up, we decided to send the police to his apartment to find him. He's in another treatment program now, but I don't know if he'll ever recover.

One of my partners in my psychiatric group, a truly brilliant man, had suffered from chronic facial pain for eight years. He then found that a medication he used on depressed patients, an MAO inhibitor, miraculously relieved him of his facial pain. In fact, it was the only thing that did give him any relief.

But when he took it, he became manic and had wild mood swings. I saw it for the first time at a meeting. He became grandiose and began to take over the meeting, expounding on ideas that made no sense. This was really out of character for him. We talked to him and persuaded him to see a psychiatrist, who I don't think did a very good job. Either he was in pain and depressed, or he had no pain and was manic.

He abruptly left our group and went into practice for himself, which was just as well for us, but at that point he had no supervision. We did what we could for him, but his notes became more and more illegible, and he acted increas-

ingly strangely. He was denied hospital privileges one after
the other. He became more and more isolated.

He then came up with a theory that schizophrenia was
caused by scabies of the brain. Scabies is a skin disorder
caused by a mite and is contagious but is easily treatable.
His theory was that for centuries epidemics of scabies have
coincided with epidemics of schizophrenia. Of course, this is
nonsense. In the first place, there has never been an epidemic of schizophrenia. But he pursued his theory and began treating his schizophrenic patients by putting them in
lindane baths, which are used for scabies treatment.

He had a number of very loyal patients who became
worried about him, and many of them called me. He was
reported to the local medical society and was investigated by
the impaired-physicians committee. Finally, during one of
his depressive episodes he killed himself.

*✒* A patient came into the hospital with all the signs
and symptoms of subacute bacterial endocarditis. This is an
infection that is very treatable with antibiotics. But the doctor who saw her did not do the most basic of lab tests, such
as a blood culture, and completely missed the diagnosis. As
a result, the infection became virulent and the patient, a
woman in her thirties, died.

I reviewed the patient's chart and could not understand
how such a mistake had been made. But when I talked to
the nursing staff about it, I was told that this doctor came to
work many times with alcohol on his breath.

I became angry that something like this could happen,
and I spoke to my superiors about it. All of them readily
acknowledged that this doctor was an alcoholic, but it was
clear that none of them was going to do anything about it. I
took it upon myself to submit a report to the medical licensing board, requesting an investigation.

An investigator from the licensing commission called
and asked me if I was sure I wanted to submit the complaint

for investigation. "Do you realize the doctor may sue you and that you could lose your house and everything you own?" he said.

I asked him, "Are you telling me I should withdraw my request?"

He answered that he had a lot of work to do and that he'd be happy if I did withdraw it. Basically, he didn't want to do anything. I told him that I would not withdraw my request, so he went ahead with the investigation.

He interviewed the hospital supervisors—the same ones I had spoken to—and I later gained access to these interviews. I found out that these supervisors had denied any knowledge of this doctor's alcoholism to the investigator. They just didn't want to get involved. So on the basis of that the licensing commission dropped its investigation. To my knowledge this doctor is still practicing.

✎ I had stress. I had pressure. I had anxiety. I had all those things that doctors have and that they take drugs to relieve. But in my case all those reasons for using drugs were irrelevant. I used drugs because I loved them. I *loved* them! They were *wonderful*! I loved to get high.

I had always used drugs with other people, but in my fourth year of medical school I began to use them by myself. At the time I remember thinking, "Will I ever be able to stop this?" There was something obviously and inherently wrong about shooting up dope in the men's room of the hospital.

I used speed during my residency. I functioned better, was more alert. I was a star. I became chief resident. The delusion I had was that they would work forever and that I could control them. That's denial. You know what *M.D.* stands for? "Massive Denial." Physicians are very good at it.

When I began practicing, I took a job at a hospital where the whole goddamned place had cocaine. I was really

impressed. I tried snorting cocaine at first, and then one day
I mixed it up in solution and injected it. I jumped up and
down. It was spiritual-experience city, like a twenty-minute
orgasm.

I became deeply addicted very fast. That's what cocaine
does to you. I was willing to sell anything to get it—my car,
my house. I was making about eighty grand a year, but it
wasn't enough. I borrowed from banks. Being a doctor, they
loved to give me credit.

I totally disintegrated. Totally. I could shoot up twenty
to forty times a day, in my arms, my legs, my groin. I'd wear
long-sleeved shirts to the hospital, and when I shot up in my
hands, I'd put bandages around them and say I cut myself.

I realized that cocaine was ripping up my insides, so I
took other drugs to counteract the damage. I took Inderal to
slow my pulse and blood pressure and Valium so I wouldn't
hallucinate or get too frightened or have a seizure. It's all
part of the same cleverness that got you to be a doctor in the
first place.

When I didn't have cocaine, I'd use just about anything
I could get. I told my patients to bring all their medications
whenever they came to see me. And then I'd say, let me go
back into my office and check this, and if they had something I wanted, I'd take a handful and bring the rest back to
them. It may sound funny now, but I'm not proud of that.

I'd also make up medical procedures for patients and
order medications when they didn't need any. I'd just take it
myself. Fastest hands in the West. I also identified the patients who liked drugs, and unknown to them of course, I'd
split prescriptions with them. Someone at the hospital actually saw me stealing drugs once and did not report me, if
you can believe that.

The hospital administration suspected I had a drug
problem, but it was in a bind with me. Because although I
was a son of a bitch who everyone in the administration had
come to hate because of all my lies and cover-ups, I also had
patients in beds who were making money for the hospital.

So as long as I was upright and breathing and they could watch me to make sure nothing awful happened, they let me stay. There is nothing pure about all this.

Finally some people in the hospital administration had had enough of me. They made arrangements to replace me, and I was gone real quick. They changed the locks to my office and told me never to come back.

I went into a quick treatment program, but it didn't do squat. A thirty-day wonder program. When I came back, I surrounded myself with recovering people. I moved them into my house. I held AA meetings in my home and went to them doped up. What a role model!

There were multiple insane things going on in my life at that time, including my own personal insanity. And I mean frank insanity. Hallucinations. Total discomfort all the time. I was so paranoid, I bought guns. Once I thought people on television were coming to get me, so I shot out the television screen. Had a tête-à-tête with the law over that.

A group of the recovering doctors knew I'd gone back on drugs and came to my house one afternoon to get me. They found me on the roof shooting dope with my underwear on. They asked me if I had noticed that my life had become a bit unmanageable.

These doctors physically grabbed me, put me on a plane, and sent me to a long-term treatment center. I shot the last of my dope somewhere in the friendly skies. That was more than five years ago. Those guys are good friends of mine now. They saved my life.

I'm sure some of the patients I saw during this period of my life were compromised medically by me. That would have been hard to avoid. But there's a lot of mythology about how complex medicine is. There are many things where you don't need to know much. You tell me your throat is sore—I look at it, take a culture, and give you an antibiotic. It doesn't take any great brainpower to do that. It's like telling someone your street address. But there are other things where you do need to think, and I had stopped doing the more complex diagnostic maneuvers. I just got someone else to do them for me.

But I know I hurt one patient. He was a dying young man in pain. I stole drugs from him. I'll never forget that, and I don't want to.

*"I will prescribe regimen for the good of my patients according to my ability and my judgment and never do harm to anyone."*

From the oath of Hippocrates
Fifth century B.C.

*"I don't want to sound like a sentimental fool, but there is a sense of calling to the practice of medicine."*

Medical school dean
January 1988

# 10

# The Hippocratic Oath

"The embodiment of values that doctors live isn't just in the Hippocratic oath that you take when you graduate from medical school," a physician said. "They are slowly acquired during medical training and from what you have inside you. You can't codify this into a paragraph, but you can characterize them briefly: It's putting the patient first."

When I asked doctors what their biggest reward in medicine was, most said helping patients and doing some good for people. For many and perhaps most doctors, that transcends money and prestige. That is the Hippocratic ideal that doctors should live up to and that many do live up to. It means they stay up later at night, get up earlier in the morning, and put personal needs aside for the good of their patients. As one medical school teacher said, "I'm not all that impressed by doctors who got straight As in medical school. I'm impressed by the ones who get up in the middle of the night to take care of a patient."

The Hippocratic ideal may also involve serving the poor and disenfranchised, advancing medical knowledge, or being committed to day-to-day caring for and sensitivity toward troubled and frightened patients. In a word, to live by the spirit of the Hippocratic oath means giving of oneself for the good of patients and society.

It's not always as simple or as achievable as it sounds.

242       M.D.: DOCTORS TALK ABOUT THEMSELVES

Putting patients first can mean stepping on toes. It can lead
to turf wars and sharp conflicts with fellow doctors and
institutions. It can mean taking serious political, professional, and financial risks. In spite of this, an encouraging
number of doctors answer the call.

An eight-year-old boy was struck by a car and taken
to a nearby emergency room. He was conscious and alert
and had several superficial cuts that the doctors sutured. He
was kept in the ER for observation.

A short while later, the boy became sicker. He turned
pale and grew faint. Then he suddenly went into cardiac
arrest. They rushed him to the operating room, where everyone worked feverishly, but they couldn't bring him back. He
died on the table.

An autopsy revealed that the boy had a ruptured kidney—a completely repairable injury. He had simply bled to
death because no one had diagnosed him.

This happened at a hospital where I have privileges,
and I couldn't get that boy out of my mind. I knew he
should have walked out of the hospital alive and healthy
after a few days. I also realized that some of the responsibility for his death rested with me, because I had had training
in trauma care but I hadn't tried hard enough to change
what I knew was a poor trauma care system in my area. In
fact, it was no system at all. Injured people were taken to
whichever of the thirty-nine county hospitals was closest,
regardless of whether that hospital had the personnel or
equipment to handle a serious injury or not. And if an accident happened late at night, as most of them do, it could be
an hour or two before a doctor drove in from his home to
see a critically injured patient in the emergency room. That
young boy's death inspired me to try to change the way we
treated injured people.

In my spare time I collected data on a hundred motor-
vehicle accidents in my county. I used only death certificates

and autopsy and coroner's reports on people who had initially survived their accident but had died after arriving at the hospital. At the same time I asked a surgeon who ran a well-established urban trauma center in another part of the state to do the same thing. The results were so dramatic, they were hard to believe. In my county I found that 73 percent of the high-risk accidental deaths had been preventable! In the other surgeon's study of his trauma center, there had been no preventable deaths. Not one.

We published our study in a respected medical journal, and it caused a big stir. The local medical establishment attacked it and me. They insisted that my method was faulty, that basing my conclusions on the information I'd compiled from these documents was limited and had not given a true picture of what really happened to these patients in the hospital. I told them they were wrong.

The doctors and hospitals refused to act, so I took my study to the county board of supervisors and told them that people—most of them young—were dying unnecessarily from accidents and that I had proof of it. I was able to convince the supervisors that a problem existed, and they demanded that the local medical community examine what I had uncovered.

The county medical society and the office of emergency services then cosponsored a study of another hundred accident victims who had died in local hospitals. This time the study was done by four independent doctors. They came to an even more shocking conclusion than I had. They found that 85 percent of the in-hospital deaths of accident victims had been preventable. Later studies revealed that the local doctors who had said that my methods had given a false picture were right. We found that my method *underestimated* the number of preventable deaths.

Now the public became aware of the problem and so did the county leadership, and there was a demand to do something. Within a short time the county designated five strategically placed hospitals as regional trauma centers.

Each is now staffed and equipped according to guidelines established by the American College of Surgeons, and each can handle serious injury quickly and expertly. Because all major trauma goes to these centers, the doctors and support staff there develop real expertise in treating injuries.

A year after this regionalized trauma system went into operation, we did a follow-up study. We found that only a nine percent preventable trauma death rate and that the nine percent who died had been much more severely injured than those we had judged preventable in the earlier studies. Since then, the trauma system in our county has improved further. That means more and more lives have been saved. It took that young boy's death to do it.

I get compensated pretty reasonably; I make about $130,000 a year. That may sound like a lot to some people, but living in as expensive a part of the country as I do, it's a good living wage but I'm not getting rich off it. It's also less than half what I would get if I went into private practice, and I've had the opportunity to do so. I'd like to make a lot of money, but the fact is, I wouldn't get the satisfaction that I now get, and I wouldn't have the position of leadership that I now hold at my academic institution, especially one as highly regarded as this one.

In private practice I would have influence over my patients but not over a system of patient care that I have now. And my greatest satisfaction is training surgeons and building a team and a system that deliver the best medical care possible.

I also feel a deep commitment to my previous teachers. When you become a surgeon, you realize it is a privilege to be one. And to do it, somebody has to take you by the hand and show you how. I operated on hundreds of indigent patients in my training. It wouldn't make any sense to me to just translate my privilege into private practice where I would end up taking care only of patients with health insurance. It becomes an ethical problem for me.

I know that if I went into private practice, I wouldn't have all the hassles I get in an academic institution. I wouldn't have to go to the meetings I go to now. And I know that there are doctors out there who don't do half as much work as I do and make a lot more money than I do, and that grates on me a little bit because I also have to consider my responsibilities to my wife and children and to my parents who are not well off.

But I really think of surgery as deep in history, like the long gray line at West Point. There is a traditional way of teaching surgery and moving it forward by passing it down to younger people. I want to be part of that.

A fellow who is now a professor in a large medical school once told me that he realized that there is ultimately a limit to his scientific and intellectual interest in his specialty and that after a while a doctor's patients become more interesting to him or her than their diseases. I heard that when I was twenty-five. I understand it now that I'm forty.

Trauma is a nocturnal disease and a surgical disease. You have to be a psychopath to practice trauma surgery, especially given our attitude toward medical training, which is, you pay your dues and then you are expected to go out and earn big bucks.

So here I am at forty-five spending all night operating on patients who are often drunk, on drugs, abusive, and ungrateful and often not getting paid for what I do. Who else but a psychopath would get up at three in the morning to sew someone together who ran his car into a telephone pole or got stabbed by his girlfriend's husband?

And then during the day I fight the system to make sure I can provide care for these injured patients because so few people in our society—and I include doctors in this—really give a damn about people who get into accidents.

I could have been a plastic surgeon, and in fact I gave it some thought. I would have had regular hours and a big income, and the most I would have worried about was whether Mrs. So-and-so's scar was going to be eight-tenths or nine-tenths perfect. But I couldn't resist the challenge of trauma surgery. I do it because it's got to be done, and I gain great satisfaction from saving the lives of young people, because they are usually the victims of trauma.

I was uncertain about what I wanted to do after I finished my residency, so I volunteered for the Indian Health Service and was assigned to a tribe in the West. When I first arrived there, I had this naïve view that the Indians were a downtrodden people who would welcome any kind of medical care that came their way. Well, it wasn't like that at all. They look you over very carefully, and you have to win their respect.

Alcoholism was rampant there. It was the biggest medical problem. One Indian who worked with me at the health clinic told me that there wasn't one Indian family who didn't have an alcoholic in the immediate family. Alcoholism caused a lot of liver disease and upper gastrointestinal bleeding. I took care of seven or eight babies in my four years there who had fetal alcohol syndrome, which is a constellation of birth defects caused by drinking during pregnancy.

There was also a fair amount of spouse and child abuse and a lot of accidental deaths related to alcohol. A young couple died that way. They'd gone to a party and were walking home at three in the morning and had just passed out in a snow bank. They weren't found until the next morning.

I grew to like and admire the Indians enormously. Despite the alcoholism and the social oppression, many had very close families, and there was a great sense of community that at times was awe-inspiring. They'd hold big pow-wows and put on their ceremonial clothes—their buckskin and beads—and dance. It was wonderful to see. I ended up staying with the tribe for four years, which was a record at the time.

There was a small community hospital near the reservation. The Indians had always gone there to be hospitalized. This hospital was poorly equipped to handle things, and it was staffed by a group of local doctors who were of marginal competence. These doctors would overtreat and overhospitalize to get government reimbursements from the Indian patients. They just ran a lousy hospital.

The way Indians were treated there was probably a reflection of the way the whole town saw them. They regarded the Indians as subhuman and talked about them as if they were rodents.

An Indian went into the hospital with a shotgun wound in his chest. One of the surgeons there cut open the wrong side of the chest. Things like this happened all the time.

The thing that really set me off against this hospital happened late one night while I was covering in the emergency room. The charge nurse told me a patient had come to the ER in some distress, but she said, "I don't know if you should be seeing him because his name is on the list."

"What list?" I asked.

She said the hospital administrator had a list of people —some Indians and some poor whites—who would no longer be treated at the hospital because they had bad debts. I hit the roof when I heard that. Refusing medical treatment for any reason is unconscionable to me.

I vowed to accomplish one major goal before I left the Indian Health Service: to have the Indians in this tribe use a different hospital. There was a hospital in the next big town away that was excellent. It was probably the best hospital I've ever seen. On top of that it charged significantly less than the local hospital.

I thought that many Indians would resist traveling so

far to get to the new hospital, but when I recommended it, after some convincing and politicking the tribal council overwhelmingly agreed. They recognized that this change was in their best interests. The local hospital board complained and said they had a fine hospital, but I noticed that when the chairman of the hospital board's wife was ill, he took her to another hospital.

When I left the Indian Health Service, members of the tribe held a big party and presented me with a plaque that said in part, "The work you have done for our people will be forever remembered." They also gave me a handmade beaded buckskin jacket that I'll always treasure. After the presentation, one of the Indian nurses with whom I'd worked said to me, "We've never done anything like this before for anyone."

Once a year I go to a Third World country to do plastic surgery. It's all done for free—we pay our own way. When I went to the Philippines, I did four or five cleft-lip and -palate cases a day for a month.

The people we operate on mostly come out of the bush and know nothing about medicine. Many Third World children born with cleft-lip and -palate deformities are killed at birth, and if they're not killed they're ostracized. Almost all of the children I operated on were extremely self-conscious about their deformity—you could feel how much it pained them. Besides its abnormal appearance, the cleft palate controls speech; these children cannot speak normally. The thing about plastic surgery in this situation is that in one hour, under local anesthesia, you can do something for someone that will literally change their life. Besides making them look normal, they can learn to speak normally. There's nothing quite like it.

I did case after case where the child got up and walked back to the room where his or her mother was waiting, and the mother would collapse on the floor because she was so unbelieving and thankful.

In Haiti we did a series of cleft-lip and -palate operations under incredibly primitive conditions. No air conditioning, no postoperative care. It made the Philippines look like the Mayo Clinic.

One day while I was walking to the small hospital that we used, I noticed this thirty-year-old guy standing off to the side, sort of looking at us but not saying anything. His cleft lip was obvious. He had a huge gap. I kind of grabbed him and led him over to the hospital. I don't speak French and he didn't speak English, so there wasn't a lot of communication between us. Within an hour he was on the operating table.

We repaired his cleft lip under local anesthesia. After the surgery was over, we walked him down the hall to a mirror. He looked at it, and we could see he was studying his lip, but he didn't say anything. We kind of wondered what we had to do to make this guy happy. We even kidded among ourselves later, saying maybe he had had a hernia he wanted us to repair and he wasn't concerned about his cleft lip at all.

*"The thing about plastic surgery in this situation is that in one hour, under local anesthesia, you can do something for someone that will literally change their life."*

About two or three days later, one of our nurses who speaks French was talking to him about his surgery. She asked him how he liked his new appearance. He smiled and said, "Now I can go out and find a wife."

That's all I needed to hear.

There is nothing more floppy and awful-looking than a human heart taken out of a body for transplant. You are used to seeing a heart beating and full of life, and it is a magnificent sight—awe-inspiring. Then you take it out and it just collapses into this kind of small, ugly-looking muscle, and it doesn't even resemble a heart.

But then you transplant that heart into a recipient's body, and after you have sewn all the vessels together, you take the clamps off the arteries, and my God—it is magnificent! Bells and chimes! To see that lifeless-looking blob of muscle swell up and throb to life! Then you shock it, and it starts to beat. It is remarkable to see it toss in the chest. It seems to conjure up the source of all our spirit.

The excitement of that never goes away. It's like nothing else I have done. And after we do a transplant, I reflect on the extraordinary circumstances that made it possible, and I feel a connection with the donor who made it possible. Every time, I close my eyes and acknowledge the gift of the donor and the donor's family. It's always an emotional moment for me.

I'm worried about getting AIDS when I operate on AIDS patients, but I will do it. I don't like to do it and I'm not a saint, but I feel it is morally correct, and there is no basis in my mind for refusing to operate on an AIDS patient if he needs surgery. You can't eliminate a category of patients just because they have a contagious disease. I take precautions. I wear goggles and double gloves when I operate. Surgeons breach their gloves all the time during surgery, and sometimes I have a cut on my hand. But I think the chances of getting AIDS this way are minuscule. That doesn't mean that every time I come down with a cold, I don't wonder if I've got it, though.

I think it's much riskier for the residents than for the attendings because they have to draw bloods and there is always the risk of needle punctures. We had a resident drawing blood from a patient in the emergency room, and the resident's mouth was open at the time. The stopper popped out of the test tube, and he got a mouthful of blood. We later found out the patient was AIDS positive. The resident was crazy for six months until all his blood tests came back negative. It's no wonder that the people who draw blood are petrified.

 We give in-service seminars on AIDS to people all around our hospital because so many of them are worried. There is an atmosphere of fear. When we gave one to laboratory workers, we said, "There has never been a person in a laboratory who got infected with the AIDS virus from the workplace, but there is going to be one." And a week later there was. It was simply a matter of time.

I work with AIDS patients all the time. I take standard precautions, but I don't wear gloves when I round. I rarely wear gloves even when I see AIDS patients all day long. I don't think about my own possible infection all the time, but I do think about it. Somebody will sneeze, or I will handle a bloody rag and I will look at my hand. Everybody has got cuts and bruises of some kind. And I'll wonder if I'm going to be the one in the million—the first case in which it was transmitted that way.

I've never had a needle stick. If I ever have one, all of a sudden all these theoretical fears that I tell people are only theoretical will become very real to me.

 Another neurosurgeon once described a brain operation as four hours of hard work and thirty minutes of terror, and I agree with that. The hard work is the opening and closing, and the thirty minutes of terror are working on the tumor or the aneurysm or whatever else may be wrong.

I've had medical students ask me in the operating room what the structures are that I'm working around. What function do they serve? I tell them that if I thought about that, I couldn't do the operation. I'd fall to pieces because I'd become so nervous, I couldn't cut. I tell them, the thing you want to know is how to get into the brain and get out without causing harm.

Obviously you have to be technically adept to operate on someone's brain, but even in brain surgery I think the surgeon's technical skill is overrated. You know, you walk into a room and say you're a neurosurgeon, and everybody looks and says, "Oh, the golden hands." This is a crock of shit! You can teach almost anybody to operate—you really can. But I know some neurosurgeons who love the technical part of surgery. They love the macho, going in and cutting open somebody's head, holding life in their hands. That's their satisfaction. My satisfaction is getting something done to make someone better.

✐   I was recently offered a position as an oncologist in a private group practice in New England. They said, "We guarantee you $600,000 by the third year, and you can buy into the condominium and the art collection we own." That's close to ten times what I am making at my teaching hospital.

> *"My greatest concern for myself as a physician is that I'll grow callous with patients and think of medicine as only a way to make money."*

My wife wanted to go back to New England because we come from there, but I told her I could never live with myself if, one, I had to make $600,000 a year; two, if I ever owned condominiums; and three, if I ever owned an art collection.

My greatest concern for myself as a physician is that I'll grow callous with patients and think of medicine as only a way to make money. I'm pretty strong-willed and I try to guard against that, but medicine is becoming so competitive that you've got doctors stabbing other doctors in the back. It's not like Marcus Welby or driving to see a patient in a buggy or delivering a baby in a house. All that is gone from medicine.

The other problem with this practice was that it had many physician assistants who are the ones who actually see the patients. The doctors had little contact with the patients, but I need that one-on-one contact with my patients. That's also one of the problems I am having with academic medicine. As you rise in the hierarchy, you see patients less and less. It's a big part of why I'm leaving it and entering private practice. But I told my wife that if I come home at 3 or 4 A.M., it's not because I'm seeing a vast number of patients—one a minute—but because I may devote an hour to someone who needs my time. I know that is going to be hard, but I think it can be done even in this day and age. I think physicians can still practice medicine the way we were taught to practice.

I tried to commit euthanasia on one patient. He was in his seventies and had come in as an emergency. It was clear he was in end-stage respiratory failure.

He was already on the respirator when I first saw him because he couldn't breathe on his own. A breathing death is one of the worst ways of dying. You can't get air. You're gasping all the time.

His family came in. His son reminded me of myself, and the father reminded me of my father. He looked like him, and something about him struck a chord. I really put myself in that family's place.

After a couple of days, we decided to take him off the respirator to see if he could breathe on his own. I removed the breathing tube, and for the first time the man could talk. He looked right into my eyes, and his first words were,

"Why didn't you let me die?" That really reached me emotionally.

His family meanwhile wanted him transferred to the top guy at Columbia Presbyterian, or Mt. Sinai, or wherever he could get the best care. I told them, "It's no use. It's an impossible situation."

But this man continued to suffer, and it was pulling at me. So without telling anyone, I went to the drug cabinet at the nurses' station—which was wide open at this hospital—and took some morphine. I told myself that one way to deal with his suffering was to dull his senses with morphine, but I was aware that one of morphine's side effects for someone in his condition is to stop his breathing. I gave him a substantial dose, but certainly not a huge dose, and told whoever was on that night that I wanted to be called if there was any change with this patient.

I tossed and turned all night, knowing I might have become a participant in his death. I had real ambivalence about it. But I wasn't called, and the next morning I found out that he had spent his most comfortable night. I thought, this is out of my hands, so I decided not to try that again. In a short time we took him off the respirator, gave him an oxygen mask, and put him on a regular medical floor. In thirty-six hours he was dead.

I've never before or since felt a need to intervene like that, even though I intervened in an ineffectual way. I mean, my intent was there. It's a very slippery slope. I thought I was doing something completely ethical, and yet who am I to make those judgments? Do we want a society where doctors and nurses are going around making those judgments? Absolutely not! But in this specific case I did not feel—and still don't feel—that what I intended to do was morally wrong.

I operated on a young boy who had a brain tumor that had paralyzed him on one side and caused such intractable pain that he'd torn off part of one ear. It was painful just to look at him. It was the first tumor in this area of the brain that I had ever done—a very risky area in which to operate. I told his family that I didn't see any choice but to go after the tumor.

During surgery he became very unstable, and we nearly lost him on the operating table. I almost wanted to stop. But I kept telling myself, "You have to do this! You must do what you came to do!" I kept cutting away at the tumor because I knew that if I did not get all of it out, he would no have a chance of surviving. He recovered and is doing so well that all his pain is gone and he is now playing sports.

Very often, I think that the difference between truly talented neurosurgeons and those who are second rate is courage. I say that because it takes a lot of courage to operate on someone's brain, and I am not saying that in a self-flattering way.

Every neurosurgeon I know is scared when he operates on the brain. If you aren't scared, you shouldn't do it. You need courage to go in and persist and do what has to be done. There are neurosurgeons who go in and stop too soon when they're after a brain tumor. They'll never take the whole tumor out, never achieve what needs to be achieved, because they cannot overcome their fear. I understand that fear because I experience it, too.

DOCTORS RARELY LOSE LICENSES

*"The medical community has gotten more immunity than is healthy for society."*

# II

# Bad Medicine:
# Politics and Greed

In Maryland a gynecologist was convicted of forcible rape. He was given a suspended sentence, yet the Maryland Commission on Medical Discipline allowed him to continue to practice medicine, providing a chaperone was present during physical examinations.

In Rhode Island another physician is serving ten years in prison for extortion, conspiracy, and Medicare fraud for accepting kickbacks to implant unnecessary cardiac pacemakers in elderly heart patients.

These are but two dramatic examples of doctors gone wrong. There are many others. Some of them result in arrests or suspensions, but many, many others never see the light of day. The old axiom that doctors bury their mistakes is to a large extent still true.

Despite public demands that doctors clean up their profession, the medical establishment remains reluctant to discipline doctors. A 1984 New York State study found that only twenty-five of the state's more than forty thousand physicians had had their licenses revoked or suspended. Following this revelation, revocations and suspensions increased to eighty-three the next year, which is less than one-quarter of one percent. Even conceding that physicians are the best-trained professionals and that the vast majority want to do well both by their patients and by their profession, it is hard to accept that so few doctors in New York or anywhere else deserve to be disciplined. Utah, the state with the highest doctor-discipline rate, nonetheless revokes or suspends the licenses of less than three percent of its doctors.

Almost every physician I interviewed expressed anger at doctors who do badly by their patients. They feel that these doctors stain all of medicine, and they agreed that they should be thrown out of medicine. But although they want to see their profession cleaned up, they also feel intimidated by the legal climate, which they say not only makes it difficult to go after bad doctors but presents serious legal and financial risks for anyone who does. Many doctors also admit that they are restrained to some extent by an unspoken professional code.

There are different mechanisms for disciplining doctors who fall below the line. In the mildest cases, a well-intended doctor, such as an obstetrician who is performing too many Caesarean sections, can often be corrected by a suggestion from the hospital's physician peer-review committee. At a more troublesome level, a doctor who is negligent and harming patients can be stripped of his privileges by the hospital—a process, however, that is more easily said than done. In forty-seven states, such an action must be reported to the state board of medical examiners, which is the physician licensing commission. This information is then available to other doctors and hospitals.

The most serious action that can be brought against a doctor is an official complaint filed with the state board of medical examiners. The complaint can be made by another doctor, by a hospital, or even by a patient. A hearing is held; if the physician in question is found to practice below the standard of care, he or she can be reprimanded, and in more serious cases his or her license can be suspended or revoked. But as New York experience proves, this is seldom carried out.

Medical societies in many states have willingly accepted bigger staffs and greater enforcement powers for state licensing boards in exchange for tort reform to ease the malpractice crisis. But it is a fact that many if not most states still don't have enough manpower to police bad doctors.

But physicians injure patients in ways other than by gross negligence or incompetence. Patients can get caught in political cross fires of which they know nothing. They can end up at a lesser hospital or with a lesser surgeon because of jealousies, feuds, greed, or egos that don't permit doctors ever to admit they are over their head.

"I can forgive a doctor for making a mistake, even a serious mistake on a patient, as long as he was well-intended and competent," an academic physician said. "Unfortunately, mistakes are made in every walk of life, and medicine is no different. What I can't forgive is a doctor doing procedures on a patient for which he is not qualified, or a doctor who refers his patients to a certain specialist or refuses to refer to a specialist solely for political or economic reasons. I also can't forgive doctors who aren't caring with their patients, who don't give them comfort when the patient needs it. To me, that's bad medicine."

A doctor who applied for privileges at our hospital didn't meet our standards, didn't come within a mile of them. All our doctors are board certified, and he wasn't. Moreover, he had lots of gaps in his training and some creative explanations of how he had spent his time during those gaps. Yet he insisted that he deserved to be in the medicine department of our hospital.

After we had turned him down, he demanded a hearing. He argued before an ad hoc doctors' committee that he had a right to privileges at our hospital. The committee denied him privileges, and even though this case did not go to court, it cost the hospital more than $10,000 in legal fees just to answer the question of whether this guy met our standards when it would be obvious to just about anyone that he could not.

This is part of what is so disheartening about trying to do something about incompetent doctors. It's a long, draining, expensive exercise. I learned how time-consuming the legal process is, how you're at the total mercy of the court, and the emotional drain that you go through.

I operated on a young man with a work-related foot injury. He did very well, a good example of a spectacular success for this type of operation. A while later, he got a job involving heavy physical labor but found out that after a full day's work, his foot started to hurt.

He contacted a lawyer to look into workmen's compensation, and I was subsequently asked by an insurance carrier to examine him because I had done the original surgery. The young man's attorney had insisted that he see another orthopedic surgeon, who claimed the young man needed surgery. I examined him. From a medical point of view, I found that it was impossible that this other surgeon had either examined the patient or taken an X ray to have reached this conclusion. He did not need surgery!

> *"It's almost impossible to cull out the doctors who are not competent or principled because the lawyers take glee in charging by the hour to defend these doctors forever."*

I sent a copy of my notes to the insurance company, and that put a halt to the surgery. The young man came back to see me and said he was happy with the results of my surgery and delighted that he didn't need another operation. He thought the whole thing had gotten out of hand. I then received a letter from this other surgeon saying what a fine result the young man had had and how he had wanted to refer him back to me in the first place. But I had also seen the report this surgeon had originally sent to the insurance company, and you wouldn't believe he was talking about the same patient. Then I ran into this surgeon. He told me this young man was a real crybaby and that he had done everything he could to get him to come back to me, even threatening him with surgery. I guess he expected me to believe that.

This is a racket, a liability scam, and it goes on every day in every city in this country, like the movie *The Fortune Cookie*. The personal-injury attorneys send their patients to a small group of unprincipled doctors whose findings are always in excess of those that I might find and who give these patients expensive treatments and long periods of disability. This translates into larger settlements, because the bigger one's medical bills and the longer the length of one's disability, the bigger the settlement. So the attorney and the doctor both get more money. It's easy to see what's going on.

The doctors involved are usually orthopedic surgeons, and we're talking big dollars. A net income of a million dollars a year would be modest in a practice of that kind. The only saving grace is that the smartest physicians aren't in on it, although there are a few in it who are shrewd and have it down to a science. It sounds self-serving to say that the vast majority of physicians are competent and work hard at trying to do good, but it is true. The problem is that a few rotten apples really do spoil the barrel, and they are very busy rotten apples. And it's terrible that the economic rewards of being a physician are sometimes inversely related to the integrity of one's practice.

We can't do much to stop this because as a profession, we are due-processed to death. It's almost impossible to cull out the doctors who are not competent or principled because the lawyers take glee in charging by the hour to defend these doctors forever. That's the advocacy system!

Everyone is entitled to a defense! So our system doesn't give us a way to deal with a physician who is dishonest or incompetent.

Give me the opportunity and the backing, and I'd shut down three offices in my town that do this liability scam. But if I were to blow the whistle, I would be sued for defamation of character, and the doctors against whom I brought charges would beat me down with a legal onslaught. I would have to spend $400,000 or $500,000 in legal fees over a two- or three-year period to defend myself. And that would be out-of-pocket for the principle of trying to clean up my profession, whereas the doctor I was after could claim his legal fees as a legitimate business expense.

History has shown that neither the medical society nor the insurance carriers nor anybody else would help me. And although truth is a defense, there is no way to recover the costs. So I am not about to go on a crusade against any of these doctors. If the right time comes, I will try to do the best I can for society and for my profession; but unless you grant me some kind of guaranteed immunity, no thank you! My wife and family don't need it, and I don't need it!

✎ The nurses reported an obstetrician at my hospital who had put his foot against the delivery table and used that as leverage to extract a baby with forceps. You can rip a baby's head off if you pull too hard! The baby was damaged as a result of the unnecessary force he exerted in this delivery.

The hospital, which I think in general delivers excellent care, investigated and found that he had acted beyond the bounds of good care. This wasn't the first such incident we'd had with this doctor. Nurses had picked up on several horrendous episodes involving the same physician. One time he'd injured a child while doing a circumcision, giving the child less than nature intended. We suspended him for incompetence and went through the whole bylaws process and had a hearing, in which we were upheld. Then the physician sued. Every time you accuse a physician of incompetence or take away his privileges, you are going to be sued—one hundred percent of the time.

First this doctor sued us in federal court, contending that his rights had been denied and claiming restraint of trade. At the federal level, that's what you do. But we won the case. After going through several appeals processes, we were upheld, and the suit died a natural death after about two years.

He then sued us in the state courts after the federal case had ended. In the state courts he claimed that the hospital had acted in a malicious manner and hadn't given him his full rights under the hospital's bylaws. This case is still dragging on. I have little doubt that we'll win eventually in the state courts as well. However, the fact that this physician lost his privileges at our hospital did not keep other hospitals in our area from granting him privileges.

I think there is a mechanism that does work more efficiently than the legal process in many ways. I would liken it to the Amish shunning. I have witnessed it at the hospital with a couple of doctors. These doctors weren't blatantly incompetent, but they weren't up to speed, and all the other doctors stopped referring patients to them. It wasn't a boycott. It was just that these doctors were getting bad results, and referring doctors don't want their patients to get bad results. The shunned doctors picked up on the fact that they were not getting the referrals they once got and began talking about going into a different career or early retirement. Shunning moved them to a decision to leave the practice of medicine.

A young man in his late twenties who was fixing an awning at his home slipped and fell, and the awning landed on top of him. He didn't appear to be badly hurt. He experienced some chest pain for several minutes and then went to a nearby emergency room. He was checked out and was sent back home. About two hours later he became short of breath.

He returned to the same emergency room and remained there for about an hour and a half, during which time he became even more short of breath. During that whole time no diagnosis was made, and he was given no treatment. He began to gasp for air, and within a short time he died right there in the emergency room. The cause of death was a simple pneumothorax—a laceration of the lung that let air escape into his chest cavity. Because the air couldn't get out, the pressure buildup had caused his lungs to collapse. This young man died because he could not oxygenate his blood.

No one—I repeat, no one—should die from that kind of injury. It is a completely repairable, reversible condition if you know what you're doing. But this kind of thing goes on every day in this country with accidental injury.

In 1966 a National Academy of Sciences study called trauma "the neglected disease of American society." Well, it still is, and in my opinion it's a national disgrace.

About 50 percent of the approximately 160,000 people killed in accidents each year die immediately or very quickly after injury. Medical expertise or surgical help isn't going to help these people except in isolated instances. We've salvaged a few people who were brought into the hospital clinically dead, but not very many.

But as a society, we could prevent 40 percent of these deaths by doing things to cut down on injuries, by enacting mandatory seat-belt and motorcycle-helmet laws, by equipping cars with air bags, and by getting drunk drivers off the road. From a pure cost standpoint, these are the easiest ways to deal with the trauma problem, but they just won't happen.

*"In 1966 a National Academy of Sciences study called trauma 'the neglected disease of American society.'"*

In the San Francisco area recently they had a first-time trial of randomly pulling drivers off the side of the road and giving them breathalyzer tests. The goddamned American Civil Liberties Union challenged that in court. And then you get some disc jockey in Massachusetts leading a movement to repeal the seat-belt law. I mean, this is the kind of bullshit Americans have to put up with. It just pisses me off so much! I'd like these people to spend a Saturday night in a trauma center and see the carnage, the deaths, and the injuries that we have to face, then look me in the eye and tell me about their principles.

My license to drive says I can only drive a car. It even goes so far as to say I can't drive a truck. But my medical license says I can do any damned thing I want, under any guise. The one restriction is that the hospital I do it in grants me only certain privileges.

My field is obstetrics and gynecology. In my area about 40 percent of the doctors have given up obstetrics because of malpractice insurance. Well, if a guy gives up obstetrics, he has to find something to do. He's in a medical marketplace where competition has become the name of the game. So all of a sudden he will be a self-declared expert on fertility or gynecological cancer. Doctors have opened up centers based on this kind of thing.

I mean, I know of cases where doctors have treated a childless woman for an ovulation problem without ever checking to see if the husband produces sperm. That's like fixing the car's engine before you have wheels. Now, it isn't a life-threatening problem, but it is emotionally charged because people want to have children and have only a certain amount of time—especially if they are older, as many couples are nowadays. But by virture of this doctor's supposed "expertise," he has really done damage to both their present well-being and their future happiness.

I have seen other people come into my office for second opinions and be told that they must have surgery immediately, if not sooner. I tell them, "I can't argue with the surgery, but could you tell me what it's for? Because I can't find anything wrong."

There are some doctors practicing medicine—and I believe it is a significant number—whose work would be classified at best as mediocre. Some are totally incompetent and should not be allowed to practice. They are not always dangerous and are not without some success or good patient rapport, but if you look at what they are doing, it is absolutely meaningless trash. They have no scruples, morals, or ability. I wonder how they can shave in the morning.

A young Puerto Rican girl was in labor. I don't know if what she was enduring was the most excruciating pain known to man or not, but she was expressing a lot of pain. A resident was standing in the room with her. Instead of going to her aid, he was yelling back at her, laughing at her. I don't think he realized that anybody else was there, but I was. I pulled him out by his shirt, turned him around, and slammed him against wall. I told him that one, he was off the service. Two, if I saw his face again anytime that night, I would probably break it in two. He was subsequently thrown out of the program, and I'm not sure where he went. I've looked in physicians' registries but have never found his name. So I hope he never became a doctor.

A general surgeon was on the staff of my hospital who is one of those guys who thinks he can perform any kind of general surgery because his license allows him to. He had a record of operating on patients that he had no business operating on.

A newborn once came to our hospital with an imperforate anus. That means there is no opening to the anal-rectal canal on the buttocks. It can be surgically corrected, but it is a difficult reconstructive operation. It's been said, and I agree with this, that the only surgeon who has a chance to correct this problem is the first one, because if it is done wrong, so much scar tissue is created that it becomes extremely difficult to ever line things up properly again.

This surgeon was not trained in pediatric surgery and most especially not in this kind of exacting neonatal surgery. Even though it was suggested to him that there were others who knew how to do that operation much better than he did, he went ahead and operated on this little child. The result was that her anus never functioned, and she ended up with a permanent colostomy.

It might seem very straightforward to be able to identify and discipline doctors like this who aren't doing well by their patients, but there are a lot of problems. When a surgeon is operating, it is not the custom for a peer monitor to walk into the operating room and say, "Let me see what you're doing." That kind of system is not in place. Now, when a young surgeon begins in any hospital, you have the right to inspect his work. That's all part of the probation process. But over the years, when a surgeon begins to fail physically or no longer does the job well for reasons of age or alcoholism or behavior changes, we don't have a good way of monitoring his behavior unless we take a major action against him.

Also, anybody can occasionally miss a diagnosis, or have a bad result, or have a patient who becomes infected. So a clear-cut demonstration of failure becomes very difficult—it's a lot more complicated than the lay public thinks. I am not copping out on the issue by saying that, because I am as concerned about quality as anyone. It's just very hard to document that a doctor is below the line. A lot of patients get well in spite of terrible medicine or in spite of mistakes. A lot of patients get well even though the wrong operation was done. So it becomes hard to build a smoking-gun kind of case against a doctor.

Think about it! We give doctors an examination in the American Board of Surgery, and they have to get 75 percent to qualify for the oral examination. That grade of 75 is pretty scary. What happens to patients' lives with a grade of 75? And then some hospitals permit surgeons who have never passed their boards to operate.

The surgeon who performed the anus operation on the little baby was finally brought before a medical review board at our hospital. He mounted all sorts of defenses and made suggestions that professional jealousies were involved and that the other surgeons were just trying to get more cases. But we had documented enough cases that we were able to restrict the type of surgery he could do at our hospital. He then went to another hospital.

A seventeen-year-old girl who had been injured in a minor car accident was taken to a hospital. There she was operated on by a surgeon who is one of these guys who is congenitally irresponsible. He's evil.

He repaired a small liver laceration and put her on the floor. Nobody saw her for a couple of days. But she had a small, completely repairable lung contusion that had been missed completely. She began to have difficulty breathing because of lack of oxygen, all due to this minor lung bruise. They put her on a ventilator and kept her on it for six weeks. Six weeks! Her surgeon finally called me, and they sent her to our hospital, but it was way too late. By that time her lungs had fibrosed from so much scar tissue that she was beyond saving. She died within a couple of weeks.

This is a perfect example of medical mismanagement. This surgeon never follows his patients closely enough, so he never picked up on the lung problem. And he wouldn't dream of saying, "I've got a real sick patient, and I've got to find the best system of care I can." All he does is call in a consultant to cover himself, not caring if this consultant is competent or not. And of course this consultant is someone who will refer him back patients. The result is that a seventeen-year-old girl who should have walked out of the hospital five days after she was admitted died.

I was chief of surgery at a big children's hospital, and we had a number of surgeons who had no business operating on the young patients. A lot of the patients got well because people endure, but they were not necessarily given good care.

I went to the board of directors and told them that I wanted to get rid of this group of surgeons, and they agreed. We demonstrated to these surgeons that they did not have the necessary training that we demanded, and we just dismissed them. There was a big hue and cry, but they were gone, and the surgical service got straightened out.

This all happened twenty years ago, and I can tell you it's different now. Very different. One surgeon at my hospital is very obstreperous and upsetting to the nurses and the patients. He's thrown nurses out of the operating room and screamed and sworn at them. He's gone out and told patients, "This hospital is so terrible that I can't be responsible for what happens to your child." He couldn't control his behavior, and we brought charges to dismiss him from the hospital. He sued back, charging restraint of trade and damage to his reputation. A legal battle developed, but he was able to continue operating at our hospital.

I agree that a dictatorship, where the chief of surgery could just say, "You won't operate here," would have serious dangers, and capricious decisions would be made for the wrong reasons. So I'm not decrying the loss of autonomy of some chiefs of surgery. But the medical critics say, if the doctors don't get rid of the bad apples, who will? Well, it's very difficult to get rid of them in this legal climate.

This one doctor was given a temporary suspension and finally, after nine years of legal fighting, a full suspension. But what we got him on was not keeping complete records! We couldn't get him on his behavior. It was sort of like getting Al Capone on income-tax evasion.

We have surgeons at my hospital who we know are grossly incompetent. They make terrible errors! Kill people! Our last chief of surgery left here because he was absolutely mentally debilitated by trying to get rid of one of them, and he couldn't.

Their patients love these doctors. They sit and hold the patient's hand, act very concerned; they talk to the family members. I bet they are not sued much for malpractice.

This one surgeon's judgment is way off. He's closed up patients who were bleeding inside and left patients with peritonitis without reoperating. He made a series of bad judgments, and we tried to get him off the hospital staff.

They had an investigation of this guy. They called in the state, and they had many cases reviewed by good people, and the review demonstrated a series of consistent, persistent, recurrent wrong judgments leading to harm to patients.

And do you know what happened? This doctor, who was on the part-time faculty, organized the support of the other part-timers and dragged us into a town-gown controversy because the part-time faculty supported him. They said that he had been there for more than twenty years, and they accused us of trying to deprive him of his income. If we got rid of him, they threatened not to admit their patients to our hospital anymore, which is a real threat in this time of declining patient days and surgical cases in the hospital.

The part-time doctors knew he was incompetent, but

they viewed this as a political issue. As a result, the hospital administrators kept him.

There's another one. He does his own form of human experimentation on patients. One time he decided he would do a new kind of colostomy. We often put a little rod on to keep a colostomy from falling back in. He decided he didn't want to put the rod on. It was like reinventing the wheel; this operation has been done for a hundred years, and we know how to do it and what the problems are. So he did this operation and put in this crazy chest tube instead of the rod. Well, the patient developed a horrible wound infection because of this chest tube.

Another time he had a cancer patient. The case was presented in surgical conference, and he was told that the patient was too old and the tumor too large to operate. He went ahead anyway and ended up cutting a major abdominal vein, and the patient died on the table—just bled out. And I want to tell you that with anesthesia what it is today and with acute-care physiology what it is, it's rare that patients die on the table anymore. Very rare. But he's lost two patients this way, and nobody stops him.

> *"We have surgeons at my hospital who we know are grossly incompetent. They make terrible errors! Kill people!"*

One time he screwed up so badly, the chief of surgery came to the operating room to bail him out. The patient came off the table alive, thanks to the chief. Later this surgeon had the nerve to say to the patient, "You're very lucky you came to me, because I saved your life."

Another time he left a tumor in a patient because he hadn't done enough surgery. He did a routine hernia operation and cut a big hole in the duodenum, which is not easy to do.

It's horrible the way he does harm to patients. The

students and residents here come and talk to us about him. They say, "You won't believe what he did today. He put a stitch through the bowel when we were closing the abdomen." Or he did this or he did that. They ask us, how can we let this go on? They are very upset. The chief residents don't want to scrub with him.

We all agree that this doctor should not be practicing medicine, but the actual mechanism of getting rid of a doctor is very difficult. We just kicked a kid out of his fourth year of medical school. He was crazy, didn't carry out his responsibilities, and lied, and we had documentation a foot thick. We won finally, but it was very time-consuming.

It's even more difficult with an attending. On a case-by-case basis an attending can defend a lot—not everything, but a lot. So it becomes hard to prove incompetence. And if you try to remove a doctor, you end up getting harassed, tortured, and unable to practice surgery yourself, and the reputation of the institution is ruined. Is that a good reason not to go forward and get rid of a doctor like this? I don't know. Maybe we should just do it and take the flak. But the chief of surgery knows what the last chief went through, and I don't think he wants any part of it. So when the public says we're not getting rid of our bad apples, they're right.

We had a surgeon at our hospital who was so bad that as he was ripping up one patient, an operating-room nurse called her nursing supervisors from the OR and said, "You've got to call in another surgeon because this one doesn't know what he's doing." Can you imagine what it took for a nurse to do that?

Among other things, this surgeon suffers from being dishonest. You can tell from talking to him that he lies. The hospital wanted him to leave, and it told him that he would no longer be salaried, but it didn't revoke his operating privileges. I guess the administrators didn't want to face a lawsuit from this guy. They told him he would have to earn his own salary from his surgery. So what he did was to operate on people who didn't need surgery.

He has a relative who is a psychiatrist, and the psychiatrist dragged in these demented patients for him. All these patients got *something* done surgically. A patient would come in for a breast exam, and he'd do a biopsy. He'd biopsy everyone who walked into his office.

He's now working for an HMO that's advertised on television. The unsuspecting HMO patients are victimized. When they need a surgeon, they'll get him because they don't have a choice, and he still does unnecessary surgery. It's very distressing.

When the federal government agreed to reimburse for kidney dialysis, it created a huge growth industry of private dialysis clinics all over the country.

I practice in a pediatric dialysis unit at a teaching hospital. Kidney dialysis for children is much more complex than it is for adults. Whereas the private dialysis centers in your local shopping centers have one nurse for every six patients, I have to have almost two nurses for every three patients because there is so much more that needs to be done.

For that reason, private dialysis clinics have no interest in our patients. Kids are too care-intensive, so they can't make enough money. They want to keep only the kidney patients who are teenagers or older at their places and dump all the children on us. And that's pretty much what happens.

There's a lot of town-gown politics in medicine, and it's getting worse because of the growing economic pressures. Nowadays, full-time academic doctors have to pay for a lot of their income and research costs by seeing patients, so they've come into direct competition with private doctors. I know that in one teaching hospital the chairman of

medicine told the full-time faculty docs that a patient who
needed a consultation had to be referred to another member
of the medical school faculty. He made it very clear that
full-time doctors were not to send patients outside the hospital, even though a private doctor might be better than anyone on the faculty. So now in many areas of the country full-
time faculty doctors rarely refer to private doctors. I've even
had some academic docs privately tell me they shudder
when they send patients to some of the departments in their
hospital.

Private doctors play the same game. They know that if
they send a patient to an academic doctor, that doctor won't
refer anyone back to them. So their business interests aren't
served by referring to academic doctors. There's no tit for
tat. And of course, the patient's best interests aren't served
when this goes on.

There's a lot of resentment over this. Academic doctors
think they're better than private doctors, and private doctors have the strong impression that the academics look
down on them as dumb or else they wouldn't be in private
practice. The private doctors are angry because they think
the full-time academics are competing unfairly, so a lot of
them send their patients to other private doctors, and you're
getting a brotherhood forming in both camps.

I'm a private doctor with an academic position, and I
think that the full-time academics are more guilty of playing
this game than the private docs. But both play it. And given
the way things are going in medicine, it's going to get worse.


        I think hospitals, and medicine in general, deserve a
lot of the blame for our failure to effectively treat injured
people in this country, but they are not the only ones at
fault. The public thinks trauma only happens to poor people, and a lot of them say they deserve it. Obviously, this
isn't true, but this attitude is out there. I've experienced it,
and it helps make trauma a low priority. And for some

reason I don't understand, people are more accepting of automobile accidents than they are of cancer. Accidental death seems to be an act of God. It has always boggled my mind that the American public would accept forty or fifty thousand people being killed annually on our highways. But when fifty thousand Americans got killed in Vietnam over a period of more than ten years, we were all aghast.

The care of injured people in this country is a political football. It always has been. Look what happened in Pennsylvania a couple of years ago. The state health administration designated certain hospitals as regional trauma centers. Two hospitals that didn't get selected as trauma centers sued to block the trauma system. They argued restraint of trade. Absolute crap! Pennsylvania has a good system now, but as far as I'm concerned, if any of those hospital lawyers and adminstrators who sued are ever in an accident, they should be taken to the nontrauma centers.

Hospitals wage these wars because many of them are now running at only a 50 percent occupancy rate. They fear they will lose valuable patients to the designated trauma centers, especially after they do the wallet biopsy and know a patient can pay. Many hospitals look on their emergency rooms and their trauma patients as filling some of their empty beds.

This competition has led to an absolutely ludicrous situation in some parts of the country. A bunch of hospitals all designate themselves as trauma centers but neglect the most important element, which is developing the staff, the twenty-four-hour coverage, and the institutional commitment to deliver definitive care the moment an injured patient rolls through the door.

And you've also got urban hospitals all wanting to buy helicopters so they can fly out to the suburbs to pick up accident victims, who are usually Blue Cross–positive. This has created what I call the Strategic Arms Race among hos-

pitals. They are all competing for the patient dollar, and
who pays for it? You and I do, because not only does medical treatment become expensive in these circumstances, but
the quality of care suffers because no one center gets enough
cases to become proficient in trauma treatment. I'm not exaggerating when I say that there are no more than fifty bona
fide trauma centers in the entire country.

What is so tragic is that we know how to treat trauma
effectively. But our failure is that we don't have a system
that gets injured people to the right place in the shortest
amount of time because medical politics gets in the way of
saving lives.

My state has a law that empowers a state agency to
designate certain hospitals as regional trauma centers. It's
an understatement to say that a lot of hospitals really covet
this designation for reasons of prestige and money.

One small hospital in my state requested an inspection
in order to gain trauma center designation. I was part of an
inspection team that went to this hospital for an announced
visit.

We were really surprised to find that this hospital's
emergency room was outfitted with the latest and most expensive resuscitation equipment. The respirators, broncho-
scopes, and all the other equipment gleamed. When one of
the inspectors asked the hospital administrator about it, he
told us that his hospital was committed to good trauma
care. We were impressed.

The next day, we returned to the hospital for an *unan-
nounced* visit, and we couldn't believe what we saw. All the
new resuscitation equipment was being loaded onto trucks.
It turned out that the hospital had rented it to pass our
inspection. Needless to say, that hospital did not become a
trauma center.

*"Estimates show that there are going to be 145,000 excess doctors by the year 2000. Yet, at the same time, we take fifty percent of Pakistan's medical school graduates. That is crazy. They need the doctors, we do not."*

"Infinite Needs: Finite Resources"
*Journal of Neurosurgery*
October 1986

*"The revolution in the American way of health care will be as profound and turbulent as any economic or social upheaval our nation has experienced."*

"A Revolution Looms in American Health"
By Joseph Califano, Jr.
*The New York Times* op-ed page
March 25, 1986

## 12

# The Future

The pace of change in medicine is bewildering. The new frontiers of biomedical research are uncovering the most basic secrets of the human cell and unlocking the keys to cancer and other diseases. Gene-replacement therapy may one day end genetically transmitted diseases. Techniques for organ transplantation continue to advance, making replaceable hearts, livers, kidneys, pancreases, skin, bones, and corneas an everyday reality. Brain implants to cure Parkinson's disease have already been attempted in humans. Lasers are burning away atherosclerotic plaque inside human coronary arteries, and nuclear magnetic resonance imaging can examine the brain and nervous system with spectacular precision and detail.

At the same time there are insistent demands to cut health care costs and to find ways of trimming the national health bill, which will grow to 15 percent of the gross national product by the year 2000. Everywhere there are new possibilities, competing demands, and unprecedented changes that are forcing us to examine a number of questions.

How will the available health care money be spent? Will we not be able to use existing technologies—or technologies still to be developed—because they're too costly? Will we ration medical care? Will only the well-to-do get first-class medicine, and will the rest travel tourist? Will doctors simply become another layer of management, taking orders from the federal government and corporate health care directors?

Doctors admit that they are caught in a whirlwind of change that they themselves helped create, and they also know that they are powerless to control it. As one said, "I suspect every generation of physicians has thought that his profession was changing, but in the final analysis, the changes were not significant and practicing medicine remained essentially unchanged. I think we're the first generation that actually is seeing our profession become radically different."

The future is guesswork, of course, and different people make different guesses. The one common factor I found is that virtually all doctors are worried about the future, and all expect their profession to suffer in the coming years. They're about to enter a brave new world of exploding knowledge and new technologies, but along with it will come less power, less money, too many physicians, too much competition, too many temptations, and thorny—if not unresolvable—ethical questions. All this is already having a profound effect on doctors, and it appears it will grow more profound. Doctors all realize that the American way of medicine and the way they've practiced it will never be the same.

Most observers believe there's a doctor glut in the country today. I'm one of them, although it is almost impossible to prove. The doctor surplus we see today began in the late 1960s, when the federal government began bribing—that's the word for it—medical schools to increase their class size. They said, "We'll give you money, if you'll increase class size." In effect, they gave medical schools a per-capita payment for every additional student.

At my medical school, we increased our class size by 50

percent, and so did medical schools all over the place. We went from a class size of about 130 students to over 200. We increased our faculty and built new buildings. Also, for the first time in decades people built new medical schools. More than thirty new ones went up. This was actually done unwillingly, in response to federal spurring.

I think the federal government did this to drive down medical costs. Their push was based on a widespread belief that the medical establishment had previously limited the number of physicians in the country so that it could eliminate competition and set fees as high as it wanted. In effect, the doctors were said to be guilty of antitrust. I think this belief was held by everyone. I know I'd heard it all my life, and I think almost everybody else did, too.

My guess is that some bright young planner in what was then the Department of Health, Education, and Welfare knew a lot about economics but nothing about medicine. He thought the medical profession was a classic Adam Smith economic model and if you increased the number of physicians, you'd decrease medical fees because the competition would drive the price down. This is the only explanation I have for why the federal government flooded the market with physicians.

If this planner had asked any physician, he'd have learned that medicine doesn't work that way. Very well-known studies in Pennsylvania and California prove that the federal government policy actually produced exactly the opposite of what it had intended. These studies show that the number of surgical procedures varies directly with the number of surgeons. If you have twice as many surgeons in a state, you'll have twice as many operations. I think we've come to realize, in a way that isn't as sleazy as it sounds, that physicians make business.

So the federal government, which enacted policies in the 1960s and 1970s that drove up the number of procedures and the overall health care cost, is now doing everything it can to drive these costs down. I find some irony in that.

Even when these federal incentives ended after about fifteen years, medical schools still had the new buildings and the increased faculties, so we didn't decrease class size. The costs were passed on to the students, which is one of the reasons why medical school tuition is so high today. We're now producing between fifteen and sixteen thousand doctors a year, which is far more than the number of old physicians dropping out of practice. My institution is committed to slowly cutting down the size of our medical school classes, but it is difficult economically to do this. You have tenured faculty and a big institution to run, so you have to look very hard for ways to reduce your budget to replace the money you will lose from the decreased tuitions.

A number of other medical schools are also cutting down their class size, but even if every medical school in the country by some miracle cut down drastically on the number of medical students, the glut wouldn't end because the tail of the pipeline hasn't yet gone through. So into the next century we're going to have a doctor glut in this country. I think you'll see doctors' incomes drop and increased competition among doctors, and I fear a decline in the overall dignity that we associate with medicine.

✒  My hospital is being sued for nearly $50 million over AIDS issues. It's not patients but the health care workers who are suing. One doctor claims he got the disease at the hospital, and he is mad. He wants to go at somebody, and he is coming at us. A nurse who got a needle stick and turned up AIDS positive is also suing the hospital.

A hospital with AIDS patients is not a safe place to work. Nobody ever said it was. In the old days doctors got TB left and right and there is a long list of people who got hepatitis from working in the hospital, and some died. But it was never an issue before. But now in this climate it is a big issue, and all of a sudden there are a bunch of lawsuits. And there is a whole new cadre of lawyers called AIDS lawyers.

I don't see how we can defend ourselves because there is no way on God's earth that we can prevent these accidents from happening. No way! And I don't know what's going to happen to hospitals, which assume huge losses by taking care of most AIDS patients in the first place, if they get swallowed up in these lawsuits.

Then we have the problem of patient confidentiality. We had a woman who had been accidentally shot. A policeman tried to resuscitate her and brought her to the hospital and left. The policeman found out later that the woman tested positive for the AIDS virus, and he was furious that we hadn't notified him. But we didn't know if we even could notify him because of patient confidentiality. Should we violate patient confidentiality? Because I tell you when a case like this happens, it ends up on the front page of the newspaper.

I am really worried about these legal issues because I don't see how hospitals can win in this no-win situation. Somebody's got to spend some time thinking about this.

✒  At our hospital we have had more admissions last year and this year than we've ever had before but less revenue because we have fewer patient days. The cost-cutting techniques mandated by the federal government and followed by many private health insurers are working. Patients are simply not staying in the hospital as long as they used to.

Hospitals all over the country have less revenue coming in. When this crunch began, the first thing each hospital thought was that they were so good, they'd survive, and it would be the other guy who'll fall to his knees and go out. This thought has been quickly followed by the realization that maybe they're not all that well-perceived by the public, so many hospitals have had to go out and advertise, including ours. It's not just private hospitals; you have prestigious university hospitals advertising on television and in newspapers. They do it to attract patients. I think there's so much

advertising that the public is beginning to see it the same
way they see a tobacco company advertising Lucky Strikes.

## "I can imagine hospitals offering weekend bargains or other come-ons to bring in patients."

But hospitals all over the country are facing the problem of shrinking income and increased costs, so it's kind of a
situation of survival of the fittest. Many hospitals are going
to close—they're just going to go under. Some already have.

I don't think the fighting for survival among hospitals
will ever resemble the used-car business. But it will get
worse than it is now. I can imagine hospitals offering week-
end bargains or other come-ons to bring in patients. I'm
afraid we're going to see some sleaze in this.

I don't think there will be any significant change in
malpractice in this country until the health care system collapses, and I think that is going to happen. A few years ago
I thought it would probably collapse in 1988, but it looks
like it's going to take a little longer than that.

It will collapse when doctors stop working because they
aren't able to function. So people will not have the access to
medical care, and this will cause a crisis. There have already
been small pockets of this in Florida and Maryland. In
Miami in 1987 a small group of trauma surgeons resigned
from emergency rooms, and there was a crisis. This happened with just a very few doctors refusing to work, so you
can imagine what will happen if this spreads out to more
and more doctors. In many parts of the country it's already
becoming difficult to find an obstetrician because so many
doctors are leaving the practice of obstetrics.

I think this kind of thing will accelerate as the malpractice situation continues to deteriorate, and I see nothing in

any of the approaches to the problem that convince me that they are anything more than Band-Aid solutions.

When the breakdown comes, it's going to be a real mess because nobody is politically ready to put in the kinds of changes we need. There has to be a system that compensates patients who are injured through negligence, but it has to get out of the adversarial system and move to something like workmen's compensation. It will be fought tooth and nail by trial attorneys, who tell everybody they must have the right to sue, which is a lot of crap. You can't sue in workmen's compensation, and that system, despite its problems, works pretty well.

But it's going to take a near-catastrophe to reach this point because it cannot be solved by logic or intelligence. Public pressure is the only thing that will solve it, and that won't come until people realize that they can't get a doctor when they need one or can't get the doctor they want.

I think this has to happen, because what is going on now can't continue.

Until just a few years ago, the great majority of the best medical students—the ones in the honorary societies like AOA, the medical school equivalent of Phi Beta Kappa —went into internal medicine. It's the field most allied with science, the most complex, and the most intellectually challenging. It's really the hub of any good hospital. The internal medicine departments all around the country could just sit back and pluck off 80 percent of the AOA students.

It's different now. Many internal medicine departments are having a hard time filling their residency slots. They're starting to scramble. But ophthalmology, and orthopedics are very hard to get into now, as are other specialties such as radiology and anesthesiology. There are complex reasons for this, but as a medical school dean, knowing what I know about the high cost of medical education, I believe that students are going into these procedure fields because they're more lucrative. You'd have to be deliberately obtuse not to realize that students want to get into these high-paying fields to pay off their huge medical school loans and to get out of debt.

Medical students aren't saints, but they're good people. I think only a small fraction go into medicine because of the prospect of making a high income. My real concern is that by burdening our young doctors with so much debt, we are making their work as physicians harder and making it that much more difficult for them to keep their ideals in mind. I am concerned about the impact of this on medicine's future.

In the next five to ten years we will have the capacity for gene-replacement therapy, the ability to change the genetic information of people and fundamentally alter their lives.

I think this raises a number of important moral and ethical questions about whether we should do all we can to alter the genetic information in our bodies and thereby alter the role of natural selection. Even more worrisome is the overwhelming likelihood that this technology will be used for undesirable ends by some group somewhere. There's ample history for this. The military at one time used a very common bacterium to trace air-flow patterns over California. It was thought that this organism was innocuous, but now there is a high rate of infection in hospital patients whose immune systems have been compromised; some infectious disease experts trace this to the military's promiscuous release of the organism into the air. I fear that the same kind of thing could happen if we begin to tamper with the human genome.

I don't know if we have any moral license to alter people's inheritance by altering their genes, even if the purpose is to cure disease. Clearly, we should not make people taller or smarter or simply make life more convenient for people through genetic engineering. But if a person comes down with multiple sclerosis at the age of twenty and we know that by altering that person's genome we can improve his or her disease, or if we can prevent a disease like Huntington's chorea by inserting a gene into a fetus very early after conception, the question becomes murkier. I think we do have an obligation to ameliorate that patient's suffering and that child's future suffering. But there are still serious ethical questions even when the ends are desirable.

I think we should wrestle with these questions, but I'm not sure that we will. In our society there seems to be an obligation to apply everything we can do. There seems to be an imperative to do everything that's possible. We're not very good at deciding not to apply a technique. I'm a great believer in the law of unintended consequences, and I worry about the unforeseen consequences for future generations if we run headlong into gene-replacement technology.

One of the biggest threats to medicine is what's happening to nurses. The hospital where I practice has a long tradition of high-quality nursing care. It's been the high point of this institution. Our nursing staff has had extraordinarily high morale, low turnover, high satisfaction, and no trouble recruiting new nurses.

The nurses must derive a strong sense of satisfaction from their work because they don't make much money. They take care of the dregs of society, as well as people who are not the dregs but who are at their most vulnerable and the least appealing. Nurses do this not because it's the only thing they can do but out of a sense that what they do means something.

During the last snowstorm, the nurses figured out by themselves through their network which of them had four-wheel-drive vehicles and therefore could make it to work, and which of them couldn't. The ones who couldn't slept over. You don't see that kind of dedication in any other profession.

But in the past eighteen months, our nurses have seen a doubling of their patient load. Moreover, patients who used to stay in the hospital for twelve or fourteen days now stay in for six to eight days because of reimbursement pressures. So the nurses are seeing more patients in a week's time than they ever saw before. They are being told that their job performance is based not on how well they get a patient through an illness but on how many patients they get through.

The nurses are run ragged. They cannot make commitments to their patients because they don't get to know them well enough to feel the importance of what they're doing. So they're being denied the prime source of their motivation and morale. It's like a football team. If it doesn't have good morale, it isn't going to win. If we continue taking this away from nurses because of economic constraints or because we're told to do it by the government, it will be the coup de grace for medicine.

A recent report from the federal Office of Science and Technology said that if Medicare were to pay for annual mammographies, this would result in a saving of 5,200 lives a year because of early diagnosis of breast cancer. But the report also said this did not appear to be "cost effective."

This is the issue we have to face in medicine and that we will continue to face in the future—how to allocate our resources. Most major medical schools now offer courses in which the students are made aware of the cost of tests. This means we're teaching doctors very early to be sensitive to this issue. In my view, as both a teacher and a practicing physician, this is going to lead to bad medicine, because no longer will a medical decision be based on what is appropriate; instead, doctors will ask what it costs.

I think this kind of potential intrusion is where doctors have to take a hard stand. They should not let outside agencies dictate what is right for an individual patient. What is a doctor if not an advocate for patients?

Whenever there is a discussion of the high cost of medicine, doctors make easy targets. We're visible, and we have high incomes. And because we're the decision makers, we are perceived as generating the costs. Other cost issues, like expensive medical technology and patient demand for services that may not be medically indicated, seem to be overlooked.

I have no problem with the idea that physicians' incomes are going to have to come down as part of the overall reduction of medical costs. As an internist, I've always thought that specialists like orthopedic surgeons and cardiac surgeons make too much money. But we as a society also have to bite the bullet on things like cigarette smoking, which is responsible for a huge portion of our national health bill.

I fear that the economic constraints on the medical care system will cause the system to become more and more chaotic. We're already heading down that road. We have more government regulations that are aimed at cutting costs; yet at the same time we're encouraging more and more the profit motive in medicine.

I worry that as the medical care system becomes more fragmented, it will undo the great accomplishment of the 1960s, which was the integration of the elderly and the indigent into full-service hospitals, in effect allowing them into the medical mainstream, through the Medicare and Medicaid programs. In the future, as bits and pieces of the system fly everywhere, I think we'll see market forces having a greater and greater impact, and we'll end up with two-tiered medical care. We'll have medical boutiques for the well off, and everybody else will go to K mart. Because when you allow the profit motive to become so important in medical care, there is no incentive for taking care of people who have no money. I'm against that happening to any aspect of our society. It's not healthy.

Right now there is no national group that is looking at this problem and trying to figure out how to allocate our medical resources. That's why we need a bipartisan, in-depth commission to look at this and say, let's all pull together and try to come up with a reasonable and equitable medical care system. If we don't, I foresee nothing but greater polarization.

I've received more than twenty contracts from private health care plans, such as health maintenance organizations and preferred provider organizations, in recent months. I haven't signed any of them, but it's clear that they are the wave of the future in medicine.

In the next few years we'll see health plans taking over health care more and more, and private practice doctors will become rarer and rarer. Because malpractice premiums will become so high, doctors won't be able to afford them, so they'll become the salaried employees of health plans.

Doctors will also be hired and salaried by private hospitals. They'll practice in private offices, but a hospital will demand that a doctor bring all his hospital patients to that hospital and do all surgeries there. Because hospitals are in a competitive situation, too, this gives them a guarantee that they will fill their beds. They'll oversee to make sure that doctors bring all their patients to that hospital and do not overutilize services like laboratories and X rays. Doctors will be treated like any other employees.

The income a hospital makes off the patients these doctors bring them will be used to pay the doctors' salaries. Things like this are going on right now. When I entered private practice in 1982, this was unheard of. It's changing that fast. I'm not angry about it. It's just the way it is.

The rewards in medicine are personal—doing good for a patient—and the economic rewards are obvious. But medical practice is changing for the worse, in my opinion. I do complicated orthopedic surgery, and it's very stressful. It's hard to do what I do again and again and perform up to my own standards, which are much higher than the legal or ethical standards that anyone else might have. And the increasing load of paper work and malpractice problems only makes that more stressful.

Despite the fact that surgeons are the captains of the ship, more and more we are at the mercy of vast, inefficient organizations like hospitals and operating rooms that hire subsistence-wage people to do jobs without which we cannot go foward.

There is also an increasing limitation of freedom of action that is very frustrating, and it is getting more frustating. The ability of the physician to practice as we envisioned it twenty years ago, when I was in medical school, is disappearing. Serious inroads are being made in different areas. There is a calculated attempt on the part of hospitals and hospital administrators to run the show rather than allow the doctors to run it. The medibusiness is becoming like agribusiness and the military-industrial complex. It's getting bigger and bigger, and hospitals are becoming parts of chains. Everything is becoming more standardized and more mechanical, and the physician is becoming more of an employee, more of a mid-level person filling a slot rather than an independent agent who is the center of the medical care delivery system. You've also got insurance carriers, as well as the government, trying to shift power and compensation away from physicians. The problem is that there is not a whole hell of a lot of public support for physicians, and the physicians are too busy being physicians to fight effectively.

I look at the track record for curing infectious disease and see that that is where the major progress in medicine has been in the last fifty years. First in public health, then in antibiotics, and then in vaccines. It's been the greatest curative revolution in the history of medicine. As soon as anyone got an infection that we knew anything about, we quickly figured out a way to attack it with an antibiotic or prevent it with a vaccine. Look at Legionnaires' disease. What a beautiful scenario! They found the bacterium that causes it, they did the epidemiology, they studied the clinical spectrum of the disease—and they found a cure for it. Now they are working on a vaccine. Curing infectious disease is a litany of progress that's unparalled in medicine.

Then along came AIDS, the worst disease of the twentieth century, and we can't stop it. We can't get on top of it. I mean, that curve just keeps going up and up. This is a real bad disease, and it's going to get worse. It's going to get a whole lot worse!

AIDS is frustrating not so much because we haven't been able to conquer it but because I can't see any light at the end of the tunnel. I can't see that we are ever going to be able to cure this thing. AZT will only temporize, not cure. We've never stopped a persistent, slow virus before. So we resort to vaccines. But when I examine that, I realize that we are dealing with a virus that constantly changes. It may change even in the body itself. It's like influenza, for which you need a new vaccine every year because the virus changes. How can you make a vaccine against a virus that is constantly changing?

Plus, every AIDS patient I see has antibodies that obviously don't stop the disease, but the production of protective antibodies is the way vaccines have traditionally worked. So somebody is going to have to be real damned creative. A lot of people are saying we need education, but I'm not sure that education has ever stopped a sexually transmitted disease.

I think a lot of us have incredible faith in the system. Most of us believe that when the country decides to marshal its efforts, when it really decides to put a lot of money into something, an answer will be found. But when I look at the AIDS virus, I see an incredible challenge but no precedent to allow me to believe that it will be successfully met. It makes me depressed. Very depressed.

     In the modern era the most damaging thing to good science and to really moving medical research forward is the number of committees you have to deal with to do new work. It is absolutely the most counterproductive thing we have to do. There are too many committees, too many discussions, and too many people that get in the way of original, creative research. You get pecked to death by the bureaucracy.

And they all blame one another. That's what's beautiful. They all tell you that the FDA requires this or another agency requires that, and what happens is that you end up spending a full day a week just on meeting these requirements alone. I am not exaggerating. I spend a fourth to a fifth of my time on the phone or doing paperwork to satisfy all the committees, and I am a well-established researcher with—I like to think—a good reputation in the scientific community. When some things heat up, I can spend two weeks on paperwork alone. It's the single thing that most discourages me about doing research. There are too many people to answer to. It's endless. It goes beyond rationality.

I guarantee you that if I started out today asking the same research questions that I asked in the 1970s when I began, I wouldn't bother. It's just too much hassle. Life can be simpler than that. One of the best researchers I ever had in my lab looked at what I had to go through, and he quit and went into private practice. He said, "It just isn't worth it." So what you're going to get is a lot of researchers in gray suits who will do A and B versus C and D, or ABC versus DEF, but you're not going to get the guy who comes in and says, "Look, Z is a brand-new idea we want to try." You're going to discourage these kind of people, and it's going to be destructive to our society.

Not long ago, only about one out of every six medical school applicants was accepted, and virutally every applicant came from the very top of his or her undergraduate college. In my opinion, medical school students were the most academically qualified of all professional school students in our society. Medicine got the best.

But now this has changed dramatically. Medical school applications are way, way down, and now more than one out of every two applicants is accepted. And the academic achievement of these applicants is demonstrably lower than it was a few years ago. I think today's students are finding medicine less attractive because of the way it is being reorganized and regulated, and they realize that that will only increase in the future. There's a lot of uncertainty in medicine right now.

What this means for the future is that we're going to get lower-quality medicine because we're going to get lower-quality doctors.

In the past five to ten years we have witnessed, and in the next five to ten years I hope we will continue to witness, the greatest biological revolution that has ever occurred and is ever likely to occur. The human cell is running out of places to hide. We are on the verge of knowing every nucleic acid in the human genome. We have identified many of the specific genes responsible for causing cancer, and I think we are getting close to developing strategies for introducing genes into cells to repair or suppress these cancer-causing genes.

But paradoxically, we also have an effect going in the opposite direction. We are witnessing an extraordinary decline of physicians going into research. They just can't afford it. Many of our brightest people find research either unattractive or financially impossible. Researchers are disappearing. So we're on the verge, in my opinion, of overcoming a disease like cancer, really coming to understand in the most fundamental way how this disease originates, yet we're losing the research minds to carry on the work.

The high cost of going to medical school means that students are getting out of there owing $80,000 or $100,000, and this makes them very money-hungry. Not only are they in debt, but they are working their asses off as house officers, and they want to know, when is it going to be my turn?

Take a standard case. By the time a doctor finishes his training, he's about thirty and has a couple of kids, and he's deeply in debt and worried. He's not going to want to go into research and make a fraction of what he can make in private practice. I've trained dozens of people who have gone into academic life or private practice. I write letters for them, and I know all about the jobs they're getting, so I know there is a substantial and consistent decline in the kind of offers these people get. And these are outstanding people.

Doctors fear that medicine is losing its magic. They fear that it's going to become like plumbing or auto mechanics, that it will be just another trade. The feeling that what doctors do is magic has sustained most of them through their training and has kept them in medicine. It is extremely powerful.

The magic comes from the fact that most doctors feel that what they do in medicine is special. Not just doctors, but nurses talk about this, too. We feel what we do means something, that we can make a difference in patients' lives or in the quality of life for the patient's family.

Doctors like me, who are sustained by this sense of magic, fear it is becoming trivialized. We fear that what we do will no longer be valued or seen as special. We fear that we'll no longer strive for excellence. Instead of striving to become the best restaurant in town with the best French chef, we're all going to become McDonald's.

A number of forces acting together today are causing this, and I think they pose a serious threat to the future of

American medicine. Malpractice is one, but it gets more attention than it merits. Financial insecurity is another. Even physicians who don't have a great deal of debt fear that there is going to be a tremendous economic shakedown that will cause significant financial repercussions for doctors. You hear doctors saying, "I'd better see a lot of patients this year because next year we may have cutbacks."

Another force is the insecurity that comes from the doctors' loss of freedom and autonomy caused by a burgeoning government and a private bureaucracy that is exerting more and more control over medicine. This isn't an economic issue. In fact, many physicians would choose to be paid less if they could continue to have responsibility for their patients' welfare. This bureaucratization of medicine in many ways is a more powerful threat than economics or the malpractice climate. By the time the present generation of young doctors is senior, I think we'll see the real demoralization of medicine.

A lot of people choose to see this as beneficial. They think doctors are too exalted anyway, that we think we are special because what we do is special. Unfortunately, many doctors do think this way and are guilty of conspicuous consumption. I think that's deplorable. But that's only one segment of our profession. The doctors I fear for are the ones who truly care about their patients and their profession. These doctors are not sustained by money or consumption, not even by the feeding of their egos. They are sustained by a feeling that they are doing something that is intrinsically important for patients and society, and there is genuine fear that this sense of magic is being taken away from them.

It's natural during periods of revolutionary change for people who live and work in the midst of it to feel disrupted, disheartened, and even depressed. It's something we've seen all through human history, and it's happening right now to doctors. It is caused by what psychiatrists call adjustment disorders.

In the past twenty years, which is not that long, there has been a revolution in medicine so breathtaking that many doctors now feel medicine is not what they thought it would or should be. They are very upset by this, and I think it has prevented many of them from seeing the possibilities the future holds for them and for medicine.

But first consider what has happened in the past few years. Doctors have been buffeted by an explosive growth in medical knowledge. Fields like pharmacology, biochemistry, microbiology, virology, and molecular biology—a field that didn't exist twenty years ago—have altered our entire concept of human disease. We are learning about things like neurotransmitters in the brain, which were not even discovered when most doctors in practice today were in medical school. We now have technologies like magnetic resonance imaging that are absolutely revolutionizing medical diagnosis.

Another force for change is the educated patient. Newspapers now have regular health sections, and a number of magazines are devoted entirely to health and medical issues. This is all very new, and I think it has created a profoundly different relationship between patients and physicians. Years ago if I asked a patient to take notes about what I was going to say, they'd fall off the chair with surprise. Today when I ask them, they tell me they've brought their pad and pencil.

There also has been a major emphasis on quality of care and accountability that is simultaneous with a revolution in the economics of care. That has meant more paperwork, more peer review, more forms to be completed to justify what you do for a patient. And along with this has been a tremendous upsurge of corporate medicine. There didn't used to be a medical company on the New York Stock Exchange, but there they are now, and many doctors find this very threatening.

When you take all these changes together, it's clear there have been several revolutions going on at the same time in medicine. But physician training is essentially the same as it was since the end of World War II, so doctors have not been prepared to deal with these changes. As a result, they see the crisis but not the opportunities. I think doctors who express their despair—and there are many today—are only seeing a piece of the elephant.

The whole elephant will show the real promise in medicine. Things that were science fiction when I was in medical school are happening now. We're seeing an opening up of knowledge in behavioral sciences and mind-body interactions which is extraordinary. Knowledge in virtually every field—plastic surgery, rehabilitation medicine, cardiology, you name it—is expanding dramatically. It's opening up the possibility for us to prevent and treat illness much more effectively than is possible now. And I don't think cost will be a major problem. You needed connections and a lot of money to get penicillin right after World War II. Now you can get it anywhere and it's as cheap as dirt. I think the same will happen with these new technologies.

I also think the revolution in patient health information will prove a boon. I realize there are doctors who become defensive when patients question them, but within a decade most doctors will see this for the benefit it is. Educated patients make my work more interesting and help make the patient more responsible for his or her own care, so I see it as a positive force. In the end it will make medical practice a lot more interesting.

In another two decades we'll work out the issue of prolonging life that so many physicians get caught up in. I think we will find ways to integrate the advances in medical technology with issue of life and death and reconcile the tremendous human and financial costs this life-support technology demands. This will be an exciting and rewarding area.

As for all the added paperwork and the legal concerns

involved in the practice of medicine today, I think it does no good to bitch and moan about it. We doctors simply have to accommodate ourselves to these changes and see them as a cost of doing business. I'm in private practice and I have a lot of paperwork. I hate it, so I hire someone to do it so I can do what I do best, which is taking care of patients.

I know what worries doctors the most is the loss of autonomy and the fear that they will be made into mid-level functionaries who carry out the orders of the government or their health-care corporations. But I don't think this will go to the extremes many doctors envision. I don't think we'll will end up with a cold, alienating, mechanistic health care system. I'm optimistic enough to believe it will not reach this point because I think most patients still want a good and trusting relationship with a doctor, and I think they are too well informed about medicine today to allow this to be taken away.

# Special Offer
# Buy a Dell Book
# For only 50¢.

Now you can have Dell's Home Library Catalog filled with hundreds of titles. Plus, take advantage of our unique and exciting bonus book offer which gives you the opportunity to purchase a Dell book for *only 50¢*. Here's how!

Just order any five books from the catalog at the regular price. Then choose any other single book listed (up to $5.95 value) for just 50¢. Use the coupon below to send for Dell's Home Library Catalog today!

**DELL HOME LIBRARY CATALOG**
**P.O. Box 1045, South Holland, IL. 60473**

Ms./Mrs./Mr. _____

Address _____

City/State _____ Zip _____